# Benefits Realization Management

Strategic Value from Portfolios,
Programs, and Projects

# Best Practices and Advances in Program Management Series

Series Editor
**Ginger Levin**

# Benefits Realization Management

### Strategic Value from Portfolios, Programs, and Projects

Carlos Eduardo Martins Serra

CRC Press
Taylor & Francis Group
Boca Raton   London   New York

CRC Press is an imprint of the
Taylor & Francis Group, an **informa** business
AN AUERBACH BOOK

CRC Press
Taylor & Francis Group
6000 Broken Sound Parkway NW, Suite 300
Boca Raton, FL 33487-2742

© 2017 by Taylor & Francis Group, LLC
CRC Press is an imprint of Taylor & Francis Group, an Informa business

No claim to original U.S. Government works

Printed on acid-free paper
Version Date: 20160815

International Standard Book Number-13: 978-1-4987-3925-2 (Hardback)

---

### Library of Congress Cataloging-in-Publication Data

---

Names: Serra, Carlos Eduardo Martins, author.
Title: Benefits realization management : strategic value from portfolios, programs, and projects / Carlos Eduardo Martins Serra.
Description: Boca Raton : Taylor & Francis Group, 2016. | Series: Best practices and advances in program management ; 29 | Includes bibliographical references and index.
Identifiers: LCCN 2016036015 | ISBN 9781498739252 (alk. paper)
Subjects: LCSH: Project management. | Strategic planning. | Portfolio management. | Organizational change.
Classification: LCC HD69.P75 S427 2016 | DDC 658.4/04--dc23
LC record available at https://lccn.loc.gov/2016036015

---

**Visit the Taylor & Francis Web site at**
**http://www.taylorandfrancis.com**

**and the CRC Press Web site at**
**http://www.crcpress.com**

Printed and bound in the United States of America by
Edwards Brothers Malloy on sustainably sourced paper

# Contents

# Preface

Since 1999, when my career in project management began, I have been gradually developing interest and expertise in the areas of management of multiple projects, project portfolio management, and project governance. In 2008, my first post-graduate dissertation analyzed case studies of four portfolio management offices within large Brazilian organizations. By analyzing such case studies, I identified some common hurdles for project success that could be found even in high-maturity project management environments. Later, I exchanged views with other project portfolio management professionals and learned that similar issues were happening in many organizations.

In 2011, I was leading a large project management office and overseeing a multimillion dollar portfolio when I made a decision that would change my life entirely. Motivated by the questions I had nurtured across the previous 12 years, I decided to investigate the extent to which effective governance could influence project success. To do so, I left my job, family, and friends in Brazil to embark upon a one-year full-time master's degree program at the University of Warwick, in the United Kingdom. I had in mind that a full immersion in an academic environment would be the best way for me to seek and find the answers that I sought.

From the time I started my research, it was clear to me that Benefits Realization Management is a key part of governance, since it supports the strategic creation of value and provides the correct level of prioritization and executive support to the correct initiatives. Therefore, because of its relevance in the governance process, Benefits Realization Management (BRM) has a strong influence over project success. After some additional research, I realized that BRM could be the missing building block to fill the gap between strategic planning and strategy execution. Could it be true? I had to find the answer.

To investigate my assumption, I developed a research proposal that was reviewed and supported by the British Association for Project Management (APM) and the Project Management Institute (PMI®), and that took part in the PMI® Survey Program. The research assessed the experiences of more than 330 professionals, which gave me the data input to identify a strong influence of BRM practices necessary for project success.

Because of the relevance of my findings, I received the Postgraduate Student Award 2012 from the APM Benefits Management Specific Interest Group. I also published an academic peer-reviewed journal article in partnership with Dr. Martin Kunc, my supervisor in Warwick, in *The International Journal of Project Management (IJPM)*. I presented a session in the PMI Global Congress EMEA, and I co-authored another *IJPM* article with Richard Breese, Steve Jenner, and John Thorp about the development and current acceptance levels of benefits realization practices. All this has been very rewarding and motivating.

However, although I love researching methods to improve the way we do things, I love even more applying research findings in practice to make people's lives more efficient and effective. I found I was unable to live for a too long a time far from a busy and complex organizational environment. As a result, I left the University of Warwick and am once again working on implementing, performing, and enhancing portfolio governance—always learning, applying, developing, testing, learning, improving, sharing, exchanging practices with others, and then learning more. Learning comes at the beginning, middle, and end of my list because, as my Dad used to tell me when I was a child, "we only stop learning when we die."

This book is about what I have learned and experienced so far, and what I want to share with you. As I usually say at the end of my lectures: "I hope you find the contents very informative and relevant. And I hope this book, that we can consider as a deliverable (or a product), can help you to enable changes that will create some desired outcomes and that they are ones to help you to realize the expected benefits."

Carlos Eduardo Martins Serra, MSc, PMP®

# Overview

In the past decades, the strategic alignment of any investment and the increase in project success rates have been two of the most relevant concerns that organizations have been facing. Over the same period, project, program, and portfolio management practices have been gradually enhanced by academics, professional associations, and organizations to better support the management of increasingly more effective and more strategy-focused portfolios of change initiatives. Nevertheless, despite this effort, high project failure rates and a strong need for improvement in the alignment between project outputs and the achievement of strategic objectives have still been found by several surveys that have been performed by organizations and academics all across the planet in the last years.

In this scenario, after the global financial crisis of 2007–2008, organizations in general developed an increasingly stronger need for more efficient project portfolios. To a great extent, this need has motivated organizations and professionals to become increasingly interested in Benefits Realization Management, a management discipline developed and employed precisely to guide the strategically aligned conception and the successful management of projects as well as to support effective project governance. Such a set of practices provides an effective link between strategic alignment and project success, driving organizations toward the management of more effective project portfolios while also ensuring that project portfolios are creating strategic value to the business.

This book discusses ways to perform effective strategy execution by understanding project success as a fundamental enabler for successful strategic change. To support organizations and professionals in successfully achieving the business goals, this book presents Benefits Realization Management as a key set of practices for strategy execution that are instrumental in enabling effective project portfolio governance and strategic project success.

# Acknowledgments

First of all, I thank Ginger Levin and John Wyzalek for the invitation to write this book and for their effort and commitment to get it carefully edited to high-quality standards.

In second place, and equally important, I would like to thank all my friends, former and current colleagues, managers, clients and other professionals I had never met who supported my research on Benefits Realization Management. It would be impossible for me to analyze such practices without so many people giving me their support and dedicating their precious time without getting anything in return for it.

I am also very glad and thankful for all the support provided to me in these last years by several authors, professors, and representatives of professional associations such as APM, APMG, IPMA, and PMI. They were fundamental for me in obtaining the information that I needed in order to reach my objectives. Special thanks are due to Peter Glynne, Nick Wensley, Carlos Augusto Freitas, and Paulo de Buzin.

Special thanks to the extremely experienced professionals, academics, and "Benefits Realization Management gurus" who have inspired me, guided me, and in many cases supported me. I need to express my gratitude to Richard Breese, Steve Jenner, John Thorp, Ben Ganney, Sarah Harries, David Waller and Claire Dellar.

My very special gratitude goes to Dr. Martin Kunc, professor of the Warwick Business School, for the partnership, motivation and frequent assistance—even after the conclusion of my master's coursework—and to the University of Warwick, more specifically to the Warwick Manufacturing Group (WMG), an outstanding institution of which I am so proud to be an alumnus.

Finally, I owe much to Sue and to my parents. Although for a number of years my hectic work and study schedule have taken me away from them, they have always been close to me when I most need them.

—C.E.S.

# About the Author

Carlos Serra is an enthusiastic project management professional, researcher, and entrepreneur with more than 16 years' experience in portfolio, program, and project management in sectors such as oil and gas, energy supply, retail, information technology, and business management consulting. He started his career working on program planning and controlling and moved into several other roles, working with small, medium, and large companies.

He holds a master's degree with merit in program and project management from the University of Warwick (United Kingdom), a postgraduate specialization certificate in project management from the Federal University of Rio de Janeiro (UFRJ) (Brazil), and a bachelor's degree in engineering from the Federal Center of Technological Education (CEFET-RJ) (Brazil).

For the past few years, Carlos has been living and working in London, England. Previously, he worked for several years in Rio de Janeiro, Brazil, where he was born. In a short break during his university studies, he spent about five months in a "work abroad" program in Virginia, in the United States. These international experiences, in conjunction with having worked in both local and global projects, programs, and portfolios, gave him a broad view of a variety of organizational cultures, structures, and management practices, which has been instrumental to his academic work.

He is an active member of the Association for Project Management (APM) and the Project Management Institute (PMI®), serves as a volunteer reviewer for the *International Journal of Project Management,* and actively participates in and supports professional forums and research programs and projects aimed at developing the project management profession.

# PART I

## Benefits Realization Management and the Creation of Strategic Value to the Business

# Chapter 1

# Introduction

Organizations succeed by mastering the management of their strategic changes, with project, program, and portfolio management as the recognized set of processes and tools to manage such changes. However, projects still fail on a large scale. In parallel, it is suggested that organizations are not managing their projects in the way they should in order to ensure the achievement of their strategic objectives. This book aims, then, to present Benefits Realization Management* as a set of practices that has been shown to increase project success rates from a strategic perspective (Serra and Kunc 2015). These practices prioritize investments as required by business strategy and support effective delivery by focusing on creating strategic value for businesses. They also ensure business operations realize expected benefits, even after the end of program and project lifecycles.

This introduction begins with some background information that explains the relevance of this book in the present context. Then it provides a brief overview of the following chapters.

At the end of this chapter are a case study to illustrate the theory and end-of-chapter review questions to provide means for a self-assessment of the

---

* "'Benefits Realization Management' (Bradley 2010), 'Project Benefits Management' (Melton, Iles-Smith and Yates, 2008), and 'Benefits Management' (Jenner, 2010; Ward and Daniel, 2012; Jenner, 2012) are terms regarding the management of a set of processes needed to ensure programs, projects and portfolios delivering and embedding into the current day-to-day business all requirements of business strategies, in order to perform a meaningful and sustainable creation of value" (Serra 2013).

understanding. The answers to all questions can be found at the end of the book in *Appendix A*.

## 1.1 Making the Case: Relevance of Project Benefits for Business

The following background presents how high rates of project failure are currently challenging businesses success, and then it introduces Benefits Realization Management as an essential set of processes to ensure effective governance, project success, benefits and business success.

| Subsection | Subject |
|---|---|
| 1.1.1 | High Rates of Project Failure |
| 1.1.2 | Business Success Depends on Project Success |
| 1.1.3 | Effective Project Governance Enabling Strategic Success |
| 1.1.4 | Benefits Realization Management for Succeeding in the Most Relevant Projects |

### 1.1.1 High Rates of Project Failure

Many surveys performed in the last 20 years have found that between 60 percent and 80 percent of all organizations fail in executing their strategies by failing to deliver the expected outcomes of the changing process (Kaplan and Norton 2008). Project failure leads to the failure of business strategies. An overview of the market perspective on project success is provided in Table 1-1, which presents some relevant findings from six surveys performed from 2008 to 2015.

Their arguments indicated high levels of project failure. Although the majority of these figures clearly indicate the high incidence of project failure and consequent huge financial losses they cause, these figures clearly vary greatly by sector, market, and report. Furthermore, some sources of failure rates available in the market have been questioned regarding their reliability. An example is the reports issued yearly by the Standish Group, which may have presented exaggerated conclusions about failure rates (Alter 2006; Emam and Koru 2008; Eveleens and Verhoef 2010; Glass 2006). Nevertheless, although there are variations in the results presented by the various sources of data, and questions are being raised about the reliability of some of these sources, the scenario provided by the analysis of most sources unveils a clear dissatisfaction with project success and also exposes a clear need for the improvement of project success rates.

## 1.1.2 Business Success Depends on Project Success

The current economic environment is composed by organizations continuously changing to improve their processes in order to develop competitive advantage (Porter 1998). This concept, introduced by Michael Porter, an authority on competitive strategy and the competitiveness and economic development of nations, states, and regions, is widely recognized all across the globe. It is fundamental for understanding the relevance of Benefits Realization Management

**Table 1-1  Project Failure Reports**

| Survey | Relevant Findings |
|---|---|
| CHAOS Report (The Standish Group 2015) | 19% of the software projects failed to deliver on time, on budget, with a satisfactory result. 50% are completed but late, over budget, and with unsatisfactory results. |
|  | 16% of the software projects failed to deliver on time, on budget, and on scope. 38% are completed but late, over budget, and did not meet the target specifications. |
| Pulse of the Profession (PMI® 2015) | On average, 64% of the projects are successful in meeting their goals. |
| Industrial Megaprojects (Merrow 2011) | "65% of all industrial megaprojects failed to meet business objectives." |
| KPMG New Zealand Project Management Survey 2010 (KPMG 2010a) | "...70% of New Zealand companies have experienced at least one project failure in the past 12 months." |
|  | "...projects undertaken by New Zealand companies often perform poorly in at least one of the following areas—lack of timely delivery, cost (project runs over budget), or inability to achieve the stated deliverables." |
|  | "Over 50% of respondents stated that they do not consistently achieve stated project deliverables." |
|  | "Only 36% of organizations reported that their projects were consistently delivered on time." |
|  | "Less than half of respondents reported that projects were consistently delivered on budget." |
|  | "22% of organizations reported that less than half of their projects were delivered on budget." |

*(Continued on next page)*

Table 1-1  Project Failure Reports *(Continued)*

| Survey | Relevant Findings |
|---|---|
| 2010 Project Management Survey Results (First Line Projects LLP 2010) | "Confidence in project delivery is down. Only 24% of respondents could confidently tell a client that a project would be delivered on time. (2009: 28%)" |
| PMI®-KPMG Study on Drivers for Success in Infrastructure Projects 2010 (KPMG 2010b) | "While modest strides have been made in enhancing project delivery, projects are still burdened by serious time and cost overruns, misconduct, wastage, all within an inflationary environment. Of the 1,035 infrastructure sector projects completed during April 1992-March 2009, 41% faced cost over-runs and 82% witnessed time over-runs."<br><br>"60% of our respondents comprising contractors feel that delays in completion of assigned tasks and damages claimed thereof is the main reason for disputes." |
| Adapting to complexity—Global Major Project Owners Survey 2008 (KPMG 2008) | "…less than a third of projects are completed on time and under two-fifths come in on budget." |
| Review of the Australian government's use of information and communication technology (Australian Government Information Office 2008) | 23% (45) were delivered over budget.<br><br>33% (64) were delivered over time.<br><br>44% (86) reported achievement of benefits but did not provide evidence of measurement.<br><br>Only 5% (10) reported actual measurement of benefits and compared anticipated benefits with actual benefits realized.<br><br>45% (86) reported outcomes that were not measurable. |

in supporting the successful execution of business strategies. It happens because in such a competitive environment, organizations need to have a structured way to manage change in order to achieve their business vision (Turner 2009). The management of all changes that are required to the achievement of the business vision can be called by the term *strategy execution*.

The management of regular operations and the execution of strategy are processes that need alignment, and although both are fundamental to business success, they are performed in different ways (Kaplan and Norton

2008). Within this context, business strategies are similar to maps to guide the changing process (Turner 2009), and project management has increasingly been recognized by organizations as the preferred way to manage work in order to implement these business changes (APM 2012; Buttrick 1997). Project management is the application of "knowledge, skills, tools, and techniques" (PMI® 2013) or "processes, methods, knowledge, skills and experience" (APM 2015) that are the best ways to cope with changing processes, merely because the traditional organizational structure and management processes have not been conceived to manage changes, while project management, on the other hand, has been incrementally developed precisely to cope with them (Kerzner 2013b).

Projects are widely recognized by professionals and organizations across all industries and geographies as the structured way to manage the implementation of business changes (Dworatschek and Oekonom 2006; German Project Management Association 2010; PIPC 2005; PricewaterhouseCoopers 2007; *The Economist* Intelligence Unit 2009). Because project management is widely recognized as important in managing changes, it is easily conceivable that between 20 percent (PMI® 2009) and 30 percent (Turner 2009) of the global economy is project based. These values can be more significant in developing economies, reaching 41 percent in China and 35 percent in India (McKinsey 2010), countries where the employment of project managers tend to increase respectively by 33 percent and 60 percent between 2010 and 2020 (PMI® 2013b). An increasing pattern is perceivable, for example, in the increasing quantity, complexity and total budget of information technology (IT) projects (KPMG 2005).

Because of its recognition as the best way to manage changes and because of the clear dependency between performing changes and successfully executing business strategies, project success is widely recognized by organizations as a vital component of business success (PIPC 2005; PricewaterhouseCoopers 2007). Therefore, organizations clearly need to ensure the success of their projects in order to succeed in executing their strategy and in turning their vision into reality.

### 1.1.3 Effective Project Governance Enabling Strategic Success

Project governance is a management framework that takes place within wider frameworks of an organization's governance processes. It ensures that a project is conceived and executed in accordance with the organization's standards and policies and also with best project management practice. It defines the way decisions are made all across a project's life cycle, which includes all relevant aspects of the decision-making process, such as the objectives of the decision-making process (why), the type of decisions to be made (what), the periodic or ad hoc events when the decision making happens (when), the place where the decision making happens (where), the roles and responsibilities involved in the decision-making process (who), and the ways decisions are made, recorded, and communicated (how). Project selection, authorization, prioritization and cancellation are all parts of project portfolio governance (PMI® 2013c).

The effective governance ensures that important and relevant decisions are made at the correct time by the appropriate group of people according to a standard set of rules and that these decisions are appropriately recorded, communicated, and implemented. It enables a project to progress smoothly throughout its life cycle, by having its key decision points happening in a standard, tested, controlled, well-rehearsed, and well-executed way. Therefore, effective project governance is expected to increase the chances of project success.

Project governance becomes project portfolio governance when it is expanded in the organizational context. No longer does the governance cover only on a single project; now it covers the entire project portfolio. In such a context, a project portfolio is a group of projects, programs, and operational work that is funded and managed together. Such a portfolio is conceived and implemented as a way to execute the organization's business strategy and then to enable the achievement of the organization's strategic goals. Therefore, on an organizational level, effective project governance contributes to the effectiveness of wider organizational governance processes by improving the performance of the strategy execution process and then enabling strategic success.

Effective project governance enables strategic business success, because in order to execute their business strategy successfully, organizations need to succeed at least in a set of these programs and projects most relevant to their strategies. It is nearly inconceivable that an organization could succeed in every single program and project because several risky ventures will often fail (McGrath 2011). To be successful, then, organizations should make the most of their portfolio, implementing changes to programs and projects or even canceling them whenever necessary and learning from the failures whenever they fail. The relevance, the scope, and the desirable outcomes of each program and project can frequently change, driven by changes in business strategy. It happens because the variables that affect business strategies are constantly changing (Morgan et al. 2007). Governance processes are needed to enable strategic success by providing means to managing programs and projects in constant alignment with the frequently changing business strategies.

In a governance model, some individuals are defined as being responsible for managing the alignment between regular operations, business strategies and the execution of changes (Gardiner 2005). These are individuals who, depending on different governance frameworks, are charged with a set of responsibilities that can include selecting, authorizing, prioritizing, requesting, and approving changes, or even canceling programs and projects. Such decisions are taken to ensure the delivery of benefits required by the business strategies (Gardiner 2005).

The effectiveness of such governance models depends on the clear understanding of some important premises. First, the organization's Portfolio Governance Board, which is sometimes also called Portfolio Review Board, is able to *select* the projects that will be performed based on defined business cases. Based on how well each project meets the selection criteria, a number of projects are selected to become part of the organization's project portfolio. Second, organizations expect all of their projects (which means their project portfolio) to succeed and implement governance to help ensure this success. This means that organizations prioritize their efforts, so that meaningful investment is made towards the achievement of strategic objectives. On another perspective, no investment is wasted on efforts that are not strategically aligned or prioritized.

In this context, priority—that is due to strategic relevance—makes projects happen and also makes governance bodies make sure people dedicate enough effort to achieve project success. Such priority is achieved by a combination of prioritization models and the judgment of senior managers. Therefore, in a process driven not only by numbers but also by judgment, the support of the most relevant project stakeholders is fundamental to the success of a project. The project stakeholders are able to provide the adequate level of prioritization that is a fundamental driver for project success. Because of that, the engagement of the most significant stakeholders and the level of support provided by them to the project are recognized as two of the most relevant critical factors of success for any project (Bryde 2006; ESI 2009a). Therefore, since governance of project management provides processes and methods for prioritization and also for effective communication and alignment between the stakeholders (APM 2004), it is probably the business process with most responsibility in driving programs and projects to success or failure.

Effective governance happens when project stakeholders are aware of the business value that a project aims to deliver to the organization as well as other important factors, such as the project management performance and the risks that are associated to the project delivery process. Their awareness is extremely important to ensure their continuous and adequate level of support to the project. Effective communication between the project management team and the project stakeholders is fundamental to the development of the necessary level of buy-in from the relevant stakeholders (Moore 2010). The appropriate levels of buy-in ensure the provision of the required level of support to the project from the stakeholders.

In addition, project managers need to know exactly what the relevant stakeholders within—and perhaps also outside—the organization expect from the project (ADB 2011). Again, effective communication between project managers and stakeholders increases the chances of project success, since it enables project managers to establish a clear understanding about available funding, project rationale, and expected outcomes (ADB 2011; Allport et al. 2008). By being aware of the value of the project for their customers, project managers can more proactively manage change and adapt the project to external issues. Because of that, communication and project management experience are the skills most needed in project managers, as well as the capacity to evaluate a project financially (FMI 2006). In turn, effective communication supports other soft skills that are perhaps even more important for a project manager, such as leadership and influencing skills (Fisher 2011). These required skill sets, which were identified by research among practitioners (Fisher 2011; FMI 2006), reflect how well the organizations and professionals recognize the importance of communication to support an effective relationship between project managers, sponsors, and customers. It becomes clear that project management teams should be able to recognize outcomes and benefits expected from their project; then they need to make sure the relevant stakeholders are aware of these outcomes and benefits, as well as of the value of the project to the business. Therefore, skills and good practices related to benefits valuation, as well as to communications and stakeholder engagement, are strongly required to ensure effective governance.

By performing governance, organizations can focus on the programs and projects that can deliver more value. It is a way "to get more by spending less," which is a real priority in difficult times. Since project governance is a significant part of project portfolio management (PMI® 2013c), project portfolio management became even more necessary after the 2008 global economic crisis and to the consequent increased complexity of funding decisions (ESI 2009b; *The Economist* Intelligence Unit 2009). To reduce cost and support a more effective delivery, it is vital to perform intensive control of each project (ESI 2009a). Even the public sector faces an increased exigency for efficiency in delivering change (Sowden 2011). Because of the shortage of funding and the consequent global need for efficiency and effectiveness, more than ever business managers are looking to obtain the most relevant outcomes and have their project portfolios and their strategies aligned and optimized (Wheatley 2009). Therefore, organizations need to ensure the success of their relevant programs and projects, and they can do so mainly by performing effective governance.

### 1.1.4 Benefits Realization Management for Success

*Benefits Realization Management* is a set of practices that positively influences project success on the creation of value to the business and therefore positively influences the successful execution of business strategies (Serra and Kunc 2015). This journey toward success starts from identifying what success looks like for a specific project: the so-called *success criteria*. The success criteria are about identifying what exactly a project is expected to deliver and to enable. Projects have clearly defined outputs, which should be delivered in a specific time frame (Chittenden and Bon 2006). These outputs are products, results, or services (PMI® 2013a) expected to enable positive changes and to achieve business objectives (APM 2012; PMI® 2013d). The improvement caused in the business by these changes is called a *benefit* (Chittenden and Bon 2006), which is an increment in the business value from the shareholders' perspective (Zwikael and Smyrk 2011).

> *Benefits are measurable and quantifiable improvements, which are normally expressed in financial terms, so they can justify any investment that may be required from the business.*

Furthermore, benefits can also flow to other beneficiaries of projects, such as customers, suppliers, or even the society (Zwikael and Smyrk 2011). The process behind all this is called *benefits realization*.

> *Benefits Realization is a process to make benefits happen and also to make people fully aware of them throughout the entire process.*

These benefits realized as a result of the successful changes fill the value gap, which is the difference between the current situation and the target future situation expected in the strategic plan (Kaplan and Norton 2008; see Figure 1-1).

The value of project benefits is that they provide a strong argument to obtain the buy-in required from project stakeholders to enable effective governance. Buy-in happens because benefits translate the value of a project to measurable terms—preferably, financial terms. Determining the value of benefits enables organizations to identify, prioritize, and support their most relevant initiatives, as well as to evaluate whether they are successful or not. The company with the most mature processes of benefits estimation and realization is the one that most often has concluded promising projects and rarely undertaken less promising projects (Gartner 2011a). Organizations with mature processes of benefit realization have significantly better project outcomes (PMI® 2015). In such high-benefits-realization maturity organizations, the Portfolio Governance Board or the Portfolio Review Board prioritizes and supports those programs

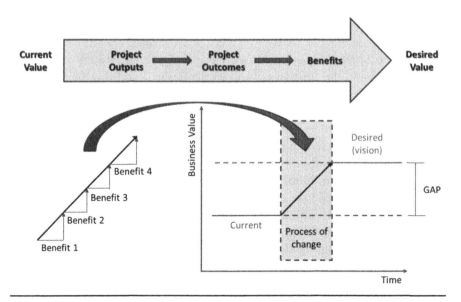

**Figure 1-1**   Filling the value gap. [*Source:* Serra, C. E. and M. Kunc. *Benefits Reali-zation Management and Its Influence on Project Success, Project Governance, and Execution of Business Strategy: Analysis of Brazil, the United Kingdom, and the United States of America.* Project Management Institute (2013). Used with permission of Project Management Institute.]

and projects that can deliver the most relevant benefits (HM Treasury 2011). Valuable for the business are the initiatives that cost less than the benefits delivered. Project costs need to be paid by project benefits in order to perform a sustainable process of change, creating value for the organization (HM Treasury 2011; Turner 2009). When an organization knows the value of each project and realizes that a project will not deliver the expected benefits, it often is better to cancel the project than to keep spending resources aimlessly (KPMG 2005; McGrath 2011). However, decision makers are often affected by a psychological bias that makes them optimistic to keep investing in a project even when it seems to be no longer going to provide the expected return on the investment (Meyer 2013). Therefore, periodic review and update of each and every project's business case is required to confirm the justification for the investment in each project. Each project's project business case should provide a tangible and measurable input for any further decision making about and reprioritization of investments on project, program, and portfolio levels. Stakeholders are more likely to provide support to the programs and projects with the highest priority. Clear appraisal and communication of the value of each project have been seen as effective ways to ensure the support and prioritization each project needs in order to be successful (ESI 2009a). On portfolio level, the application by senior managers of a structured process for the early termination of projects that are no longer aligned to the business strategies is a highly effective practice to ensure the strategic fit of the project portfolio (Unger et al. 2012).

Perhaps, because of its importance in these processes, benefits realization is gradually being seen by organizations as the most relevant way to evaluate project success. In recent surveys, most companies and professionals agree that the assessment of project success should be performed based mostly on the benefits provided to the business, not only on such measures as timeliness and budgetary performance (PIPC 2005; *The Economist* Intelligence Unit 2009). The increasing performance of strategic governance leads organizations to work at aiming the delivery of planned benefits (Gardiner 2005). Then, in order to be able to perform governance effectively, the Portfolio Governance Board or the Portfolio Review Board needs to know the exact value each project has for the organization.

Therefore, any organization can perform the most valuable set of programs and projects by managing project benefits. However, by not performing a well-structured process, organizations can have some programs and projects with less value still performed and successful, while other relevant ones fail or are not even started.

## 1.2 Guide to the Subsequent Chapters

This short section summarizes the contents of the next six chapters of this book as well as its appendices both to provide the reader with a guide on how to read this book and to enable a better understanding on how each chapter provides the basis to support the discussion that will take place in the following ones.

*Chapter 2—Strategy Execution: Translating Corporate Strategy into Program and Project Strategy* provides an overview on the evolution of the connections between strategy, change, and operations in the last century. This chapter is a reflection on the reasons and causes that drove organizations to develop and adopt some of the practices that are currently applied by most organizations. It also discusses business strategies and project strategies, including differences, similarities and interdependencies between them.

*Chapter 3—Project Success and Creation of Value to the Business* discusses the different dimensions of project success and the relevance and complexity of dimensions related to the creation of value for business. It also discusses why and how programs and projects are expected to enable the creation of value to business and it identifies the relevance of Benefits Realization Management supporting this process.

*Chapter 4—Establishing the Environment for Benefits Realization* presents an approach for strategy execution which embeds Benefits Realization Management practices in each stage of the process in order to effectively link business strategies, strategic management, senior business management, project governance, portfolio management, program management, and project management. It identifies key organizational roles involved in these practices and their responsibilities. To provide a simple reference that can be mapped against any organizational structure, it divides the roles into three key groups: strategy execution governance roles; strategy execution implementation roles; and benefits ownership roles.

At the end of Chapter 4, a case study illustrates the utilization of the Benefits Realization Management practices discussed in the chapter. The case study continues at the end of each of the three following chapters to illustrate the application of the theory discussed in each chapter. The examples described are all based on real-life situations observed within several different organizations, which were recreated using fictional parameters and nomenclatures. The case study happens within ProjectEng civil engineering services, a fictional organization created to ensure the anonymity of the examples provided.

*Chapter 5—Planning Benefits* presents practices, tools, and techniques that are applicable to translating business strategy drivers into expected benefits, and then to the subsequent composition of a program and project portfolio that can realize expected benefits.

*Chapter 6—Realizing Benefits* presents practices, tools, and techniques that are applicable to the planning benefits realization that is expected from programs and projects. These tools and techniques are used to execute program and project delivery with the focus on realizing expected benefits and making these benefits happen.

*Chapter 7—Reviewing and Evaluating Benefits* presents practices, tools and techniques to keep programs and projects on track, as well as to review and evaluate the benefits achieved or expected against the original baselines and the current expectations.

At the end of each chapter, a set of end-of-chapter review questions is provided to enable a self assessment of the understanding. The answers to all questions can be found at the end of the book in *Appendix A*.

At the end of the book, *Appendix D—Enterprise Benefits Realization Management Toolkit—Blank Templates* provides a set of generic templates, and *Appendix E— Enterprise Benefits Realization Management Toolkit—How to Use Guidance* provides clear and detailed instructions for the utilization of the templates provided across the book. The templates are useful tools to support most steps of the Benefits Realization Management processes. All the templates can be applied as presented or they can be easily tailored as appropriate in order to fulfill any specific organizational needs.

The *Appendixes* also provide recommended further reading, a set of extracts from project failure reports that are discussed in this chapter, a list of figures, a list of tables, and a list of the references made throughout the book.

## 1.3 End-of-Chapter Review Questions—Chapter 1

In this section, a set of end-of-chapter review questions are provided to enable a self-assessment of understanding the chapter. The answers to all questions can be found at the end of the book, in *Appendix A*.

1. What does Benefits Realization Management mean?
2. How can Benefits Realization Management support project success?
3. Are organizations in general comfortable with their project success rates? Explain your answer.
4. Can we affirm that business success depends on project success? Explain your answer.
5. How relevant is project management in the global economy?
6. How can effective project governance contribute to business success?
7. Can we say that Benefits Realization Management has an association with project governance? To what extent?

# Chapter 2

# Strategy Execution: Translating Corporate Strategy into Program and Project Strategy

Program and project management were introduced in the previous chapter as being widely recognized as structured ways to execute business strategies. To do so, program and project strategies should be connected to the business strategies as well as to business operations. To discuss how Benefits Realization Management supports the journey from the corporate strategy through program and project strategies to the final achievement of business objectives, a previous understanding of some strategy execution best practices is required.

Therefore, this chapter* starts by providing a brief overview on some ways that the link between strategy, change, and operations has evolved during the last century, taking us then to a broader understanding about the reasons that led organizations to develop and to adopt the current practices. After that, it briefly discusses the meaning of business strategy, and then it introduces some of the

---

* Most of this chapter is composed of adapted excerpts from a manuscript that was produced and submitted by Carlos Serra (2012) as a post module work for the Programme and Project Strategy module of the Masters in Programme and Project Management at the University of Warwick. This work was awarded with distinction by the academic reviewers.

differences between business strategy and program and project strategies to make it clear how much they are different but at the same time dependent on each other.

At the end of this chapter, review questions are available to provide means for a self-assessment of the concepts presented. The answers to all questions can be found at the end of the book in *Appendix A*.

## 2.1 Increasing Effectiveness in Strategy Execution

The majority of organizations affirm that they plan their business strategies, although most of them recognize that their strategy execution still needs improvement (Kaplan and Norton 2008). Interestingly, research suggests that students and managers too often view strategy execution as less meaningful or something lower in the organization than strategy planning (Amason 2011). However, there is evidence that formal processes to execute business strategies support organizations in outperforming those that do not have such processes in place (Kaplan and Norton 2008). This happens because, although it is important to plan the strategy, the plan becomes meaningless if the strategy is not successfully implemented (Amason 2011). Because of the relevance of strategy execution for business success, this section provides a brief overview on the evolution of some methods, models, and tools for the execution of business strategies. These aim to clarify some of the key concepts, such as business objectives and goals, business performance management, and business change,

| Subsection | Subject |
|---|---|
| 2.1.1 | Management by Objectives: Setting the Targets |
| 2.1.2 | Total Quality Control (TQC) and Hoshin Management: Committing the Organization to Deliver Strategies |
| 2.1.3 | Balanced Scorecard (BSC): Measures that Drive Performance |
| 2.1.4 | Project Management: A Structured Way to Implement Business Strategies; or, "Doing the Things Right" |
| 2.1.5 | Program Management: Implementing Business Strategies in a Coordinated Way; or, "Doing Things Right, and Then Achieving the Benefits" |
| 2.1.6 | Project Portfolio Management: Delivering What Business Needs; or, "Doing the Right Things" |
| 2.1.7 | Benefits Realization Management: Closing the Value Gap |
| 2.1.8 | Strategy Execution: A Conglomerate of Processes and Techniques |

among others, that are important to understanding the reasons why Benefits Realization Management has emerged as a key element that is instrumental for successful strategy execution.

## 2.1.1 Management by Objectives: Setting the Targets

Strategy execution is a journey from a current situation to a future desired situation or vision, and then as any journey it requires a starting point as well as a desired future place. Setting objectives is the starting point of any journey, because only by knowing where the person or organization currently is and the desired future state that one is then able to plan what route to take in order to get there. Around 150 years ago, in 1865, Lewis Carroll brilliantly immortalized that need in his masterpiece, *Alice's Adventures in Wonderland*, when Alice asked the Cheshire Cat, who was sitting in a tree, for directions:

> *"Would you tell me, please, which way I ought to go from here?"*
> *"That depends a good deal on where you want to get to,"*—said the Cat.
> *"—so long as I get somewhere,"* Alice added as an explanation.
> *"Oh, you're sure to do that,"* said the Cat, *"if you only walk long enough."*
>
> (Carroll 1965, 55)

Nevertheless, setting objectives for an organization may not be as simple as deciding the destination for a person's journey. Therefore, organizational leaders, management professionals, and academics have been increasingly developing methods to provide structured processes for objective setting, enabling the organizational leaders to plan their strategies in order to achieve such objectives.

In 1954, Peter Drucker introduced the process of participative setting of objectives throughout the organization and their subsequent control (Namaki 2012; Vohra and Mukul 2009) by publishing *The Practice of Management* (Drucker 2007), which launched the concept of Management by Objectives (MBO). Drucker also suggested strategic planning as a three-step process composed of strategy formulation, tactical planning and budgeting, which is the basis for the performance of further management processes (*The New Corporate University Review* 2001). The strategic dialogue inside the organization is strengthened by the utilization of performance management systems, which leads to questions such as "what to achieve?" and "how to achieve?" being asked, and then provide the basic ideas for the inception of the Japanese tool called *Hoshin Kanri*, or policy deployment (De Hass and Kleingeld 1999). The MBO model recommends the following a five-step management process: (1) Set corporate objectives; (2) cascade the objectives; (3) monitor execution; (4) evaluate performance; and (5) reward performance (see Figure 2-1).

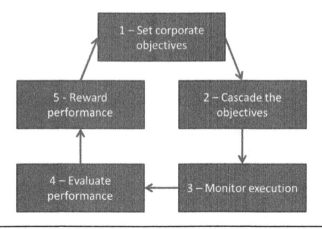

**Figure 2-1**    Management by Objectives (MBO), Five-Step Process.

Although MBO may not be applied as often as in the past (Namaki 2012), it can be considered as a starting point for subsequent strategy implementation models and tools, such as the Balanced Score Card (*The New Corporate University Review* 2001), which will be discussed in a further topic.

## 2.1.2 Total Quality Control (TQC) and Hoshin Management: Committing the Organization to Deliver Strategies

Following Drucker's ideas, organizational leaders looked for a practical way to ensure the achievement of their strategic objectives and also for ways to motivate their workforce to improve performance. Quality control emerged then as an effective way to manage business processes. First used in 1957 in the United States, the term Total Quality Control (TQC) suggests a system where all departments should participate in Quality Control (QC), being led by QC specialists (Monden 2012). In a slightly different approach, in the Japanese system, called Company-Wide Quality Control (CWQC), QC or quality assurance is the responsibility of all employees, being implemented primarily by the *QC circles* but supported by several other control processes such as profit planning, pricing, scheduling and production, and inventory control (Monden 2012). The Japanese method emphasizes the active participation of the entire workforce in developing the processes, not just leaving the responsibility to a few specialists, which is a very important aspect.

Representatives of various organizational departments make cross-functional decisions in *functional meetings*, which receive input from the QC activities that happen inside each department (Monden 2012). These decisions are later communicated inside the various departments through policies, and then are developed and implemented further in specific plans. Decisions about the implementation are made in *departmental meetings*. The decisions made in both departmental and functional meetings typically are subject of approval by *management meetings*, which are the highest level of the decision board inside the organization. This model called *functional management* (*Kinohbetsu Kanri*) establishes specific roles for each participant in functional meetings, related to their specialties (Monden 2012).

*Hoshin Kanri* is employed as a planning tool to capture long- and short-term policies and goals that are usually established through an annual planning process called *Hoshin* Management (Morgan and Liker 2006). Through quality policies, departmental objectives, cross-functional objectives, business plan objectives, and objectives with a purpose, a "vital few objectives" are cascaded and disseminated throughout the organization during this process (Witcher and Butterworth 1997). According to Morgan and Liker (2006), at Toyota, *Hoshin* comprises the four stages presented in Table 2-1.

The enhancement of human relations and communication between departments, the quick and clear negotiation between managers, the effective communication where any employee can reach the functional meeting through their departmental managers, and the high speed of implementing policies are all advantages of functional management (Mondon, 2012).

TQC and Hoshin Kanri are still employed in several organizations around the world. Nevertheless, since the inception of such management techniques, organizations have been increasingly seeking higher levels of productivity

**Table 2-1  Hoshin Phases**

| Stage | Summary of Procedures |
|-------|----------------------|
| Strategic Planning | Identification of problems and opportunities, analyzing internal performance and environmental data. |
| | Short-term steps (objectives or policies) are developed to achieve long-term vision. |
| Hoshin Deployment | Corporate policies are translated (cascaded) to departmental and functional policies. |
| | Operational plans are developed to implement the policies. |
| Controlling through Metrics | Means and results are periodically measured and reviewed, following the Plan Do Check Act (PDCA) methodology. |
| Check and Act | Managers check the progress against the objectives and then make necessary adjustments. |

*Source:* Adapted from Morgan, J. M., and J. K. Liker. The Toyota Product Development System: *Integrating People, Process, and Technology.* New York, NY, USA: Productivity Press, 2006.

and effectiveness in order to develop and sustain their competitive advantage. Internal processes have to be increasingly more flexible, cost efficient, and strategically driven to cope with the fierce competition. As a result, organizational leaders have had an increasing interest in process management as well as in its integration with strategic and operational planning, with a set of process management waves emerging since the mid-1980s such as total quality management, business process reengineering, process-oriented organizational design, and process-based competition (Smith 2007).

### 2.1.3 Balanced Scorecard (BSC): Measures That Drive Performance

The Total Quality Management tools discussed in the previous topic are focused on processes and performance, but they lack of a clear relationship between the business objectives and the financial measures. The Balanced Scorecard was later introduced as a tool to manage performance and support the execution of the business strategy. It drives the organizational strategy execution process to clearly reach a final financial objective by establishing a logical link between a number of objectives that are distributed throughout four different perspectives. Drucker's MBO concepts were expanded, updated, and amplified by Kaplan and Norton in *The Strategic Focused Organization* (2000), providing a business model clearly understandable by the workforce that is an operational and realistic translation of the organizational strategic plan (*The New Corporate University Review* 2001).

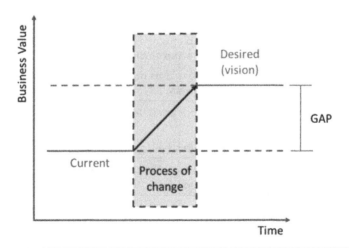

**Figure 2-2**   The value gap.

Basically the Balanced Scorecard is a map to guide the organization in fulfilling the value gap proposed by the business strategy. If we assume the value of a firm as being a financial measure of its assets and expected costs considering other factors such as cost of capital (Amason 2011), the value gap is the difference between this financial measure in the present moment and in a given point of the future. In such context, the business strategy establishes objectives aiming to move the organization from the current situation to a desired future situation, which increases the organization's value and then fulfills the value gap, the difference between the current value of the organization and the desired future value of the organization (Kaplan and Norton 2008). To turn the current situation into the future situation (also called vision) by achieving strategic objectives and the fulfillment of the value gap, a portfolio of changes is required (see Figure 2-2). Therefore, the successful management of the journey from the present to the future value of the firm requires a reliable set of tools and processes.

More than a simple strategy map, the Balanced Scorecard is a strategy planning and management system, which provides a set of processes to guide the strategy execution journey. The Balanced Scorecard splits an organization's business objectives into four complementary perspectives: Financial, Customer, Internal Business Process and Learning and Growth; then it provides a comprehensive set of measures that guide the organization through the execution of its business strategy (Kaplan and Norton 1996).

The Balanced Scorecard works on a long-term and high-level basis, rather than focusing on cascading procedures and operational activities as the previously presented Hoshin Kanri does; even though Balanced Scorecard assigns owners to the achievement of the business objectives as in Hoshin Kanri, it is done in a slightly different way. The Balanced Scorecard recommends the identification of theme owners and theme teams for each strategic perspective suggested by the model such that these theme teams are composed by representatives from different business areas, in order to ensure clear accountability for linking the theme's strategic objectives to the required operational tasks (Kaplan and Norton 2008).

## 2.1.4 Project Management: A Structured Way for the Implementation of Business Strategies; or, "Doing the Things Right"

As discussed in the previous topics, business objectives are achieved by organizations' successful implementation of strategic business changes. This is when project management comes into place as a fundamental element to support successful strategy execution. Project management is widely recognized by professionals and organizations (Dworatschek and Oekonom 2006, German Project Management Association 2010; PIPC 2005; PricewaterhouseCoopers 2007; *The Economist* Intelligence Unit 2009) as the best set of knowledge, tools, and techniques to manage the execution of changes (APM 2012; Buttrick 1997).

Although there are several definitions for a project, most of them are quite similar, as we can exemplify with the following examples. The Project Management Institute (PMI®), a USA-based professional organization that has local chapters all around the world, defines *project* as:

> ... *a temporary endeavor undertaken to create a unique product, service, or result* (PMI® 2013a, 2).

Very similarly, the International Project Management Association (IPMA), another professional organization that has stronger reach in Europe, defines *project* as:

> ... *a time and cost constrained operation to realise a set of defined deliverables (the scope to fulfil the project's objectives) up to quality standards and requirements* (IPMA 2006, 13).

To illustrate the complexity that exists behind multiple professional organizations in different countries adopting different definitions and terminologies, the British Association for Project Management (APM), a member of the IPMA, defines *project* as:

> *A unique, transient endeavour undertaken to achieve planned objectives* (APM 2012, 241).

Another U.K.-based organization—this time a governmental one, the Office for Government Commerce (OGC)—introduces the business case into the scope of a project:

> *A temporary organization that is created for the purpose of delivering one or more business outputs according to a specific business case.* (OGC 2011b, 286).

In addition, an Australian author who has work published within the Benefits Realization Management arena, Trish Melton, adds benefits to the description, finally attributing to projects some responsibility for the realization of benefits:

> *A project is a distinct package of scope which when delivered will enable the organization to realize a distinct package of benefits. Once the benefits are being realized substantially the project has been integrated in to organizational processes—it has enabled some change in "the way we do things round here"* (Melton 2007, 7).

Nevertheless, although the utilization of project management is widely recognized as the best way to manage changes, the expectations related to the responsibility of the project manager to contribute to the successful execution of business strategies are quite controversial. This situation is clearly noticeable in the definitions presented above. As the next section of this chapter will discuss, the concept of project strategy is currently under discussion, and many organizations are making significant efforts to increase the alignment between their projects and their business strategy. Then, this alignment between the objectives of project management and the business objectives is gradually taking place as a fundamental step for the successful execution of the business strategy.

The project rationale is based on the concept that projects are managed to satisfy objectives related to goals and commitments as well as objectives related to project management performance (Levine 2005). Because of that, the project manager needs to define the objectives and establish how the project intends to achieve them (Melton et al. 2008). Starting from the principle that a project intends to satisfy needs, the first and an important step when defining project objectives is to clearly identify what specific need or even what set of needs the project comes to fulfill. These needs will guide the definition of project objectives. To do so, an agreement between the project manager and the key business stakeholders is essential to define the rationale of the project, on the same way that is important having business sponsors responsible for linking project objectives to the business strategy (Melton et al. 2008).

Nonetheless, although there is increasing interest in aligning projects to business strategy, the synergy between project management and successful strategy execution seems to be still in its early steps. During the last two decades, several surveys identified the failure of 60 to 80 percent of all organizations in implementing their strategies by failing in delivering the expected outcomes (Kaplan and Norton 2008). A large number of organizations have been still evaluating projects only by project management performance (cost, time, and scope) and not by the benefits delivered to the business (PIPC 2005; *The Economist* Intelligence Unit 2009), which may contribute to the high levels of failure experienced by organizations in executing business strategies. Therefore, such results make clear that a large number of projects may still fail to deliver the organization's needs.

Therefore, although several processes, tools, and techniques are required for effective project management, we understand most these as an element of project management success, which will be discussed in Chapter 3. This book focuses on the correct identification of the required strategic objectives and requisites for a project, and then in ways to deliver what has been planned in the business case.

## 2.1.5 Program Management: Implementing Business Strategies in a Coordinated Way; or, "Doing Things Right, Then Achieving the Benefits"

We have now just reached a point that seems to be getting close to the end of our quest. We have looked into ways to ensure the achievement of business objectives and then we identified a powerful method to develop commitment within the organization towards the achievement of such objectives. After that, we realized how important it is for the effective communication of these objectives to identify the way objectives connect to each other to support the achievement of a desired vision. Objectives become much more powerful if translated into value, preferably economic value. Then, an adequate way must be found to manage the changes required to the achievement of such objectives. However, we have also realized that our means of managing change might be as not as committed to embedding all these individual changes on the regular business operations as we would expect in order to create value for the business. What would we need now? Perhaps we need something to put all this together and finally close that value gap: to do things right and then realize the benefits required by the business strategy.

Program management comes into place as another set of processes, tools, and techniques to support the management of a group of projects and related non-project work, which are directly related to the achievement of a same set of strategic objectives. The organization is provided with better means for managing complex networks of benefits enabled by various projects and by managing these projects together, maximizes the benefits realized by individual projects and increases the chance of achieving the end benefit required by the business strategy. Differently from projects, rather than delivering only products or services, successful programs are considered complete after the expected benefits are delivered to the organization (Maylor et al. 2006) or after making sure the required capabilities have been put in place, the benefits realization lifecycle has been successfully initiated, and the business operations are prepared to realize any further expected benefits.

Some definitions of program management are provided below to illustrate the common understanding about what a program is expected to be. PMI® defines a program as:

> *A group of related projects managed in a coordinated way to obtain benefits not available from managing them individually. All projects within programs are related through a common goal, often of strategic important to the sponsoring organization. If the projects have separate goals, are not characterized by synergistic benefit delivery, and are only related by common funding, technology, or stakeholders, then these efforts are better managed as a portfolio rather than as a program* (PMI® 2013c, 2).

The IPMA defines a program as:

> *. . . a set of related projects and required organisational changes to reach a strategic goal and to achieve the defined business benefits* (IPMA 2006, 13).

The British APM defines it as:

> *A group of related projects and change management activities that together achieve beneficial change for an organization* (APM 2012, 241).

The also-British OGC offers this:

> *In MSP [Managing Successful Programmes], a program is defined as a temporary, flexible organization created to coordinate, direct and oversee the implementation of a set of related projects and activities in order to deliver outcomes and benefits related to the organization's strategic objectives. A program is likely to have a life that spans several years* (OGC 2011b, 5).

Williams and Parr, authors of *Enterprise Programme Management: Delivering Value* (2006), a reference in terms of providing an enterprise-wide program management framework, state:

> *We define enterprise program management as the capability to lead and manage resources, knowledge and skills in the effective deployment of multiple projects designed collectively to deliver enhanced value* (Williams and Parr 2006, 11).

Different from project management, all definitions of program management have the delivery of benefits or value clearly explicit as a key goal of a program. Conversely, as with project and portfolio management, program management has different approaches and models to be implemented. This book is not going to get into details of all existent approaches but will cite two to illustrate the discussion.

In *Managing Successful Programs*, OGC (2011b) has provided a detailed approach, which is backed and to same extent enforced by the United Kingdom's government. Enterprise Program Management is an approach proposed by Williams and Parr (2006), which aims to ensure successful implementation of strategic initiatives through strategic, portfolio, program and project management processes. This approach is supported by two organizational streams, which are called change architectures and program architectures. The effective program architecture is supported by executive leadership, high-performing program and project teams, effective communication mechanisms, appropriate infrastructure, and a process of cross-functional resourcing (Williams and Parr 2006). According to Williams and Parr (2006), in parallel to the program architecture, an appropriate change architecture is required; it is deployed by developing change strategies, planning change journeys, and then embedding and reviewing changes.

Program management is therefore proposed to be an effective tool to link project management to the achievement of strategic objectives, which is the final goal of any organization.

### 2.1.6 Project Portfolio Management: Delivering What the Business Needs; or, "Doing the Right Things"

Now, we can say that we have reached the last step of our journey across strategy execution, which discusses one of the first required steps for successful strategy execution. Organizations will not succeed in implementing their business strategies by merely planning their strategies and then executing their program and project management processes well, aiming to deliver project outputs, outcomes, and benefits. As presented previously in this book, organizations need to ensure the delivery of the outputs, outcomes, and benefits that are actually needed by the business. Therefore, it seems that along with effective strategic planning and management processes and systems and along with project management methods, organizations also need effective ways to select, prioritize, and manage the execution of their collection of programs and projects as a whole (see Figure 2-3).

Project portfolio management has been designed exactly to fulfill that need. It is composed by a set of processes that can be employed to ensure the successful selection and then execution of the projects needed by the organization. It includes activities associated to the definition, prioritization and periodic review

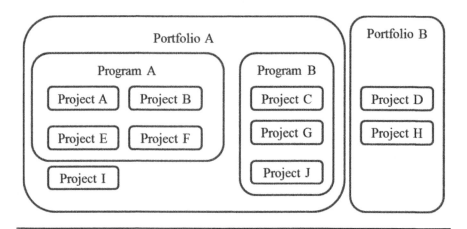

**Figure 2-3**   Program and project portfolio.

of change initiatives, ensuring strategic alignment and the appropriate balance of business change and business as usual (OGC 2011a).

Three of the several definitions of project portfolio and project portfolio management that can be found in the literature are presented here. As our first example, in a couple of sentences PMI® emphasizes the possible independence of individual programs and projects and the quantifiable characteristic inherent to all the components of a portfolio:

> *A portfolio is a collection of projects or programs and/or other work that are adopted and grouped together to facilitate the effective management of that work to meet strategic business objectives* (PMI® 2013c, 39).

In its turn, the IPMA also emphasizes the possibility of independent initiatives inside the same portfolio and adds in a further paragraph the possibility of having several portfolios in the same organization:

> *A portfolio is a set of projects and/or programmes, which are not necessarily related, brought together for the sake of control, coordination and optimisation of the portfolio in its totality* (IPMA 2006, 13).

While the APM summarizes it as:

> *A grouping of an organisation's projects and programmes. Portfolios can be managed at an organisational or functional level* (APM 2012, 240).

Although the definitions are slightly different, all the references mentioned above recommend Project Portfolio Management as a set of processes that are instrumental to support organizations in ensuring the successful execution of the projects that are required by their business strategies (APM 2012; IPMA 2006; PMI® 2013c). There is no common consensus on a unique list of processes. Nevertheless, in order to enable an agnostic analysis of good practices, this books splits project portfolio management activities compiled from a variety of books, practitioners' guides, and methodologies into the following four groups of processes.

First, there are processes that aim to structure the organization to apply project portfolio management by *aligning strategies* across the organization. Some examples of processes suggested by Meredith and Mantel (2010) and Jenner (2010), which could take part in this group, could be the establishment of a project council, the identification of project categories and criteria, and the implementation of the process (Meredith and Mantel 2014),or developing governance, control, culture, and behaviors; establishing the scope of the portfolio; implementing standardized processes, templates, and guidance; determining investment criteria; and defining portfolio segmentation (Jenner 2010).

A second group is composed by processes related to the *composition of the portfolio of initiatives*, which includes practices such as identifying components (APM 2012; Meredith and Mantel 2014, Levine 2005; PMI® 2013), evaluating components (APM 2012; Jenner 2010; PMI® 2013) and selecting components (APM 2012; Meredith and Mantel 2014; Levine 2005; PMI® 2013c). The third group is associated with *concluding initiatives and embedding changes to realize benefits*. It has practices related to the management and delivery of value and benefits to the business (Jenner 2010; Levine 2005; OGC 2011).

The last but not least important group is focused on *managing the ongoing portfolio of initiatives*, which has practices such as keeping the portfolio balanced and prioritized (APM 2012; Jenner 2010; Levine 2005; Meredith and Mantel 2014; OGC 2011a; PMI® 2013c), monitoring and controlling the portfolio (APM 2012; Jenner 2010; Levine 2005; OGC 2011a; PMI® 2013c), managing changes (APM 2012; Levine 2005; Meredith and Mantel 2014; PMI® 2013c), managing risks (Levine 2005; OGC 2011a; PMI® 2013c), managing resource allocation (Jenner 2010; Meredith and Mantel 2014; OGC 2011a), managing stakeholders (OGC 2011a) and managing expenditures and revenue (Levine 2005; OGC 2011a). Therefore, a set of processes that are suggested by most references cited above would cover most activities that are required for the successful management of project portfolios including: preparing the organization for the management of a project portfolio, identifying portfolio components, evaluating portfolio components, selecting portfolio components, keeping the portfolio balanced and prioritized, monitoring and controlling the portfolio, managing risks, managing changes, managing resource allocation and managing value and benefits.

### 2.1.7 Benefits Realization Management: Closing the Value Gap

Benefits Realization Management now comes into place as a considerably new set of processes, tools, and techniques, in comparison to most of the others previously discussed in this section. It provides an organization with the means to establish the link between projects and business objectives in a dynamic and practical way. It also supports the organization to walk through the several steps required for the transformation of project outputs into value for business, to ensure then the fulfillment of the value gap. It does not replace any of the sets of ideas currently in place, but comes to build a solid link between all the elements discussed in the previous topics. Since Benefits Realization Management is the main subject of this book, it will not be discussed in this topic, but all across the following chapters in much more detail.

Table 2-2 Theory and Key Points of Strategy Execution:
A Conglomerate of Processes and Techniques

| Theory | Key Point |
|---|---|
| MBO (Management by Objectives) | Efforts pointed towards the achievement of a set of clearly defined business objectives which are shared within the organization |
| TQC (Total Quality Control) | Tactical implementation process focused on effective control and communication |
| BSC (Balanced Scorecard) | Clear and tangible high level map for strategy execution and measurement of performance |
| Project management | Way to successfully manage changes |
| Program management | Way to manage changes in coordination to maximize the realization of benefits |
| Portfolio management | Way to successfully manage the right set of changes |
| Benefits Realization Management | A clear and easily manageable route linking business strategy, project outputs, business changes, and business objectives |

Data derived from Serra, C. E. *Post-Module Assignment for the Module Programme and Project Strategy of the Masters in Programme and Project Management.* Coventry, UK: University of Warwick. 2012.

## 2.1.8 Strategy Execution: A Conglomerate of Processes and Techniques

In summary, strategy execution is a long journey that is supported by several sets of theories, processes, methods, tools, and techniques that can be employed in different combinations (see Table 2-2), although all aim to support the successful journey from the strategic planning to the achievement of business objectives and the consequent materialization of the business vision.

## 2.2 Strategy Execution: A Journey from Business Strategy to Project Strategy

Many times when people talk about strategy inside an organization, it sounds as though it were something important to the organization, but most times, it is thought of as something related to senior managers who understand it and are able to manage it. It might sound as though it were developed by the Senior Executive Boards and beyond the scope of work of regular employees.

However, although this is not the main objective of this book, it is important to highlight the existence of several different strategies inside an organization. There are marketing strategies, operations strategies, information technology strategies, human resource management strategies, research and development strategies, program and project management strategies, program and project strategies, and several others. The last ones on our list are the ones specially designed to drive business changes and then to ensure the successful delivery of business objectives.

The key success factor in the design of all these strategies is the integration between all these strategies, like an umbrella with what could be called the *business strategy* as its a central point. The business strategy sets the business objectives and drives the way all the others are designed. Since this book's main objective is related to the successful execution of business strategies, the next two topics will quickly establish a high-level understanding about the difference between business strategies and project strategies.

| Subsection | Subject |
|---|---|
| 2.2.1 | What Does Business Strategy Mean? |
| 2.2.2 | From Project Management Strategy to Project Strategy: A Much-Needed Evolution |
| 2.2.3 | Different Strategies, Same Final Goals |

## 2.2.1 What Does Business Strategy Mean?

From the middle of the 19th century, business strategies and strategic business management have been increasingly studied and discussed. Recently, Mintzberg (2009) researched the various streams of thought in this area of knowledge and suggested 10 different schools of business strategy, each one having specific approaches and definitions. However, although there are a variety of approaches, by analyzing some well-recognized definitions we can identify similarities between some of them and then establish a common understanding that enable us to make our judgment about this subject and the way it connects to Benefits Realization Management and to project, program, and portfolio management in general terms.

By analyzing some definitions provided by Johnson and Scholes (2002) and Lynch (2006), this book summarizes business strategies as long term and sustainable orientations for organizations, usually working toward the development of competitive advantage. To do so, the business strategy guides the scope of an organization's processes and activities, which very often requires resource changes and affects operational process and decisions. To provide competitive advantage or to yield new opportunities, it may require the organization to stretch resources and organizational competences. However, it is important to note that a business strategy is heavily affected by resource availability and by the values and expectations of the organization's stakeholders. Finally, it defines and exploits the relationship with the environment, although it is also heavily affected by environmental forces.

It is important to highlight that inside an organization, the corporate strategy is often cascaded into a number of sublevels, such as a corporate-level strategy, business unit strategy, strategic business unit strategy and operational strategies (Johnson and Scholes 2002; Lynch 2006).

To illustrate how different perspectives present quite similar definitions, some of these well-recognized definitions of *corporate strategy* are presented below. Andrews (1971) defines that:

> *Corporate strategy is the pattern of major objectives, purposes or goals and essential policies or plans for achieving those goals, stated in such a way as to define what business the company is in or is to be in and the kind of company it is to be.*

According to Kay (1993),

> *The strategy of the firm is the match between its internal capabilities and its external relationships. It describes how it responds to its suppliers, its customers, its competitors and the social and economic environment within which it operates.*

Johnson and Scholes (2002) stated that

> *It is the direction and scope of an organization over the long term, which achieves advantage for the organization through its configuration of resources within a changing environment and to fulfill stakeholder expectations.*

According to Lynch (2006),

> *Corporate strategy can be described as the identification of the purpose of the organization and the plans and actions to achieve that purpose. ... Corporate strategy can be described as finding market opportunities, experimenting and developing competitive advantage over time.*

Then, for Mintzberg, Ahlstrand and Lampel (2009),

> *Strategy is a plan ... Strategy is a pattern ... Strategy is a position ... Strategy is a perspective ... Strategy is a ploy ... Strategy sets direction ... Strategy focuses effort ... Strategy defines the organization ... Strategy provides consistency ..."*

## 2.2.2 From Project Management Strategy to Project Strategy: A Much Needed Evolution

While business strategies are plans, project management has been much more associated with the execution of such organizational strategies, most times aiming to deliver something straightforward and tangible. It has been understood as a set of knowledge, practices and tools available to deliver unique outputs under specific requirements, where most of them are related to time, cost and scope (Artto et al. 2008). However, the perspective of projects as merely tools obeying the organizations' directions is increasingly discussed, and a "project strategy" has been discussed during the last decade as a new perspective in order to provide better support to business strategies and sustainability (Patanakul and Shenhar 2012).At each project's inception, an important decision should be made to determine whether the project is going to deliver predefined objectives, or if the project team is going to define the project objectives (Anderson and Merna 2003). To maximize performance and value creation at this early point in the beginning of a project's life cycle, a project strategy should be developed as a static or dynamic high-level plan that should be specific and original for the project (Artto et al. 2008). Such project strategy should guide all the further steps of the project life cycle, starting from the understanding of business needs, passing through the productions of the outputs, the incorporation of the outputs into the business routine, and then finally reaching the decommissioning processes (Anderson and Merna 2003). Different from the business operations, projects are recognized as temporary organizations, and then, as for any organization, their strategy is developed based on the analysis of external and internal factors, such as needs of different stakeholders (Artto et al. 2008). Therefore, at the stage when a project strategy is defined, there is an opportunity window to enable the creation of value, although if a poor alignment strategic is established as well, there is actually a risk of compromising further performance (Anderson and Merna 2003).

Since the distinction between project management strategy and project strategy as well as the connection between business strategy and project strategy are quite recent discussions, there are not many formal definitions available for the term project strategy. Artto, Kujala, Dietrich and Martinsuo (2008) defined project strategy as ". . . a direction in a project that contributes to success of the project in its environment." Later, Patanakul and Shenhar (2012) defined project strategy as "the project perspective, position, and guidelines for what to do and how to do it, to achieve the highest competitive advantage and the best value from the project." Both definitions suggest project strategy as a way to be successful in contributing to the organization, rather than being successful in delivering scope in the agreed-upon schedule and budget—this links more to project management strategy. Both definitions are moving away from old-fashioned project management strategy and seeking better strategic alignment and perhaps a stronger perception of projects to be an essential part of the businesses.

### 2.2.3 Different Strategies, Same Final Goals

Since projects are understood as temporary organizations inside their parent organizations, it seems pretty obvious that projects and businesses have to share the same objectives or at least complementary ones. However, this understanding increases the responsibility of project managers in enabling the realization of benefits and consequent creation of value to the organization, rather than focusing only on the delivery products or services.

Having the same final goals, projects and organizations should share the same strategies, although in different levels as discussed previously. Business strategies should be cascaded in a way that each project's strategy will have partial responsibility for the execution of the overall business strategy. In this scenario, business success strongly depends on project success as well as on operational performance, since the two are complementary. Therefore, after this chapter has made clear the needed connection between business strategies and project strategies, the next chapter will discuss how to evaluate the success of a project, and then how successful project projects contribute in creating strategic value to the business.

## 2.3 Chapter Summary: Strategy Execution: Translating Corporate Strategy into Program and Project Strategy

Business success depends directly on the way organizations are managed. Poor management dramatically reduces any chance of success, while effective management certainly increases probability of success. When thinking about management we should not associate it with bureaucracy only—although some bureaucracy is always needed. Management should be efficient and effective. The application of widely tested and utilized methods and frameworks enables organizations to make decision faster and with better support. Behind the achievement of business success in a highly competitive world, there is a lot of science involved; the effort is not limited to the application of common sense by highly motivated people, as some might suggest.

The first required step required for successful management of a business is obviously understanding where the business has to go. This is about objective setting. Objectives are a needed set of inputs for every plan. To achieve the objectives, the business needs to have business processes in place—and under control. These sets of processes transform inputs into output to generate value. However, technology evolves, market changes, competition increases. To succeed, business must sustain their competitiveness. Therefore, these business processes are likely to be subject to continuous improvement initiatives, which require frequent investment in change. To effectively manage the entire set of change initiatives, the organization has to ensure that the overall business strategy and all change initiatives are identified, mapped, and communicated. Then, it is finally time to start the implementation of such set of strategic initiatives, which we call strategy execution.

To execute business strategies, organizations need effective, failproof methods to manage changes. That is where project management comes into place, as a widely recognized set of practices to manage changes. In sequence, program management is also responsible for managing together a set of project and other non-project work in order to maximize the benefits realized from the investment made. Progressing even further, there is portfolio management to provide means for the selection, prioritization, and overall governance of the entire set of projects and programs.

This entire journey toward success requires a route map, which is called business strategy. However, given the complexity of the strategy execution, one map would not be enough to drive the organizations from one extreme to the other. That is why a set of strategies are needed. To meet that need, business strategies, project and/or program strategies, and project and/or program management strategies are applied. These are probably the three main types of strategies involved in this process, but not the only ones. A variety of other strategies are also employed; for example, benefits realization strategies.

The following chapter will discuss different ways to evaluate how the successful strategic journey towards business success is effectively managed, and how the desired strategic objectives are finally achieved.

## 2.4 End-of-Chapter Review Questions—Chapter 2

In this section, a set of end-of-chapter review questions are provided to enable a self-assessment of the understanding of the Chapter 2. The answers to all questions are at the end of this book in *Appendix A*.

1. What is Management by Objectives (MBO)? Why is it relevant for other practices?
2. What are Total Quality Control (TQC) and Hoshin management? Why are they relevant for other management practices?
3. What is the Balanced Scorecard? Why is it relevant for other practices?
4. What is project management?
5. What is project portfolio management?

6. What is program management?
7. What is strategy execution?
8. What is business strategy?
9. What is the difference between project management strategy and project strategy?

# Chapter 3

# Project Success and Creation of Value to the Business

This chapter reviews the literature, identifying ways to describe project success as well as discussing the different dimensions of success. It highlights the relevance and complexity of achieving success from a strategic perspective. Then it provides an overview on how organizations can achieve strategic project success and then deliver value for business. As a result, it identifies criteria to define project success considering the contribution to business strategy. In addition, it provides an understanding about how Benefits Realization Management practices support project success.

Therefore, the first section of this chapter discusses the different dimensions of project success and the relevance and complexity of dimensions related to the creation of value for business. The second section discusses how projects should deliver value for business and how Benefits Realization Management is relevant in supporting this process.

At the end of this chapter, end-of-chapter review questions are available to provide means for a self-assessment of the understanding. The answers to all questions can be found at the end of the book in *Appendix A*.

## 3.1 Multiple Dimensions of Project Success

This section discusses what project success means and the different dimensions by which it can be assessed. The first subsection begins by defining project success, and then the following two subsections discuss how to assess project success using two different approaches already introduced in the previous chapters, which are project management performance and creation of value to the business. Then, the fourth subsection discusses how complex it is to evaluate project success because of the various different variables that may affect a consolidated evaluation of success. Finally, the fifth subsection suggests a list of seven criteria that support the evaluation of project success from a strategic perspective.

| Subsection | Subject |
|---|---|
| 3.1.1 | Defining Project Success |
| 3.1.2 | Success on Project Management Performance |
| 3.1.3 | Success in Creating Value for the Business |
| 3.1.4 | Different Approaches, Criteria, and Perceptions of Success |
| 3.1.5 | Project Success Criteria from the Strategic Perspective |

### 3.1.1 Defining Project Success

As introduced in Chapter 1, both program and project successes are achieved by meeting success criteria defined among their stakeholders. Simplifying a general set of criteria into a single phrase: Projects are usually perceived as successful by their stakeholders when they keep an acceptable cost-benefit ratio, deliver outputs in a timely fashion, achieve target benefits, and then satisfy the stakeholders' needs (Kerzner 2013a). Consequently, projects are complete when their stakeholders' needs are satisfied, when their needs are unachievable, or even when the needs no longer exist (PMI® 2013a). In the last two cases, projects can be inevitably terminated (PMI® 2013a). Therefore, projects must be frequently reviewed to keep tracking relatively unstable success criteria based on stakeholders' needs, and their final success depends on the effectiveness of this process.

Project success is assessed in two steps, usually called appraisal and evaluation. The appraisal, also called *ex-ante assessment,* occurs before the beginning of each project in order to support the approval of the business case (Zwikael and Smyrk 2011; Jenner 2010). It is an input to assess project success, and Chapter 4 will explain it in more depth. The evaluation, also called *ex-post assessment,* occurs at project closeout in order to support the judgment of success or failure

(Zwikael and Smyrk 2011; Jenner 2010). The first measures the relevance of each project and defines expectations, and the last generate inputs to define whether projects were successful.

The next sub-subsections discuss the evaluation of project success from the approaches of project management performance and benefits delivered to the organization.

## 3.1.2 Success Based on Project Management Performance

The first approach the literature employs to evaluate project success assesses three dimensions of success related to how the project's results fit into the expected budget, schedule and output requirements (Ika 2009). From the 1960s until the 1980s, this approach was considered by organizations as the only reference when assessing project success (Ika 2009). Currently, even though other aspects are considered, it remains important. In 2007, PricewaterhouseCoopers (2007) found that missed deadlines, changes in requirements, and insufficient budget represented 50 percent of the causes for perceptions of project failure. Five years later, PricewaterhouseCoopers (2012) found quality, scope and cost management were still the three main areas where organizations have processes in place to manage performance, with poor planning estimates still being the largest contributor to project failures. As another example, when selecting contractors for infrastructure projects, 75 percent of the organizations assessed by KPMG (2010b) responded that they consider commitment to timeliness and budget as the most relevant success criteria.

Different tools and techniques are employed to control these three dimensions of project management performance (PMI® 2013; APM 2012) and generate inputs for the judgment of success. However, all techniques generate input, and this judgment generates a final perception if the fulfillment of the expectations for each dimension was satisfactory. This book will not go into detail on specific measures, but it will focus on the final perceptions of how projects are successful in each dimension.

Therefore, it is conceivable that, according to the perspective of project management performance, a successfully managed project is the one that delivers the expected outputs, on time, and on budget. In other words, a successful project is one that:

1. Satisfactorily delivers the required outputs (i.e., it fulfills its requisites)
2. Satisfactorily meets the schedule goals
3. Satisfactorily meets the budget goals

These three dimensions of project success are called the *iron triangle* or *golden triangle* (Zwikael and Smyrk 2011) or the *triple constraint* (Levine 2005; Kerzner 2013a). However, it is important to keep in mind that project management performance evaluates how well a project has been managed, but it does not evaluate how much value the same project has delivered to the business. Because of that, project success should be assessed also by a value component (Kerzner 2013a), which is discussed in the next sub-subsection.

### 3.1.3 Success in Creating Value for the Business

In the past, projects were evaluated mostly based on the triple constraint, which is composed of targets related to outcome, cost, and schedule (Levine 2005). These three factors are strongly related to the evaluation of project management performance, as discussed in the previous subsection. However, this behavior is increasingly changing to another focused on the project contribution to the business strategy as well as on the consequent creation of shareholder value (Levine 2005). In the 21st century, the literature increased its focus on the strategic alignment and support of business success when discussing project success criteria (Ika 2009).

Here we summarize the success criteria recently proposed or identified by four authors. These four references provide an idea about the current views that academics, researchers and organizational leaders support for the evaluation of project success by different perspectives. Of these, three recognize the importance in linking success criteria and benefits for business, but this summary makes it clear that there is no commonly accepted set of criteria in the recent literature.

First, *Linking Project Management to Business Strategy* (Shenhar et al. 2007), suggests four approaches for project success. The first, *project efficiency,* assesses success based on the achievement of schedule and budget goals. The second, *impact on the customer,* assesses the effective delivery of functional performance and technical specifications as well as how well the project fulfills customer needs and solves customer problems. It also assesses usefulness of the outputs delivered and the satisfaction associated with these outputs. The third, *business success,* basically assesses how well the project contributes to the success of the business, such as by increasing sales and market share. The fourth and last, *preparing for the future,* assesses how well it prepares the organizational and technological infrastructure for the future.

Second, *Project Success as Topic in Project Management Journals* (Ika 2009) performs an extensive review of the literature about project success and suggests four approaches for project success. The first, *project management success,* is based on the triple constraint. It basically assesses project success by analyzing how effectively cost, time and scope measures are managed against pre-agreed baselines. The second, *project/product success,* assesses the satisfaction of end users as well as the benefits to stakeholders and to project staff. The third, *strategic project management,* assesses project success by its contribution to business success and to achieving the client's strategic objectives. The fourth and last criterion, *symbolic or rhetoric evaluations,* takes into consideration subjective evaluations of success, which are not based on objective criteria but are instead context-specific and associated to each person's process of judgment, driven by personal and individual ways of thinking, understanding, learning, and remembering.

Third, *Project Success: Critical Factors and Behaviors* (Camilleri 2011) is another reference that suggests four approaches to project success. The first approach, *project management success,* assesses success against the performance in managing budget, time, and specifications, which is similar to project efficiency and project management success suggested by the previous two references. The second, *repeatable project management success,* assesses the employment of a consistent project management methodology. The third, *project success,* assesses how well project outputs produce expected outcomes and benefits. The fourth and last approach, *project corporate success,* assesses how well project outcomes support the achievement of strategic objectives.

Fourth, *Project Management for the Creation of Organizational Value* (Zwikael and Smyrk 2011) suggests three different approaches for project success. The first approach, *management success,* is similar to project management success and project efficiency suggested by the previous three references, and assesses how successfully the project has met scope/quality, schedule, and cost targets. The second, *investment success,* assesses the financial return each project brings to the organization. The third, *ownership success,* analyzes the worth of a project, which, as suggested by the authors (Zwikael and Smyrk 2011), can be calculated by measuring the benefits provided by project outcomes, less the disbenefits* produced and the costs associated.

Therefore, lacking a common definition, this book summarizes the criteria suggested by these authors for an assessment of how successful a project is in creating value to the business in the following four criteria:

1. Delivery of expected outcomes (supporting the achievement of needed benefits)
2. Management of disbenefits
3. Adherence to the business case (ensuring the strategic alignment)
4. Return on investment

---

* Disbenefits are by definition something disadvantageous (Merriam-Webster 2015; Collins 2015). A disbenefit is something perceived as a negative consequence of a project by at least one stakeholder. Example 1: The financial loss associated to the environmental impact caused by the construction of a nuclear power plant. Example 2: Negative impacts of people redundancies due to the implementation of new software. Impact on the brand image, judicial proceedings, and impact on motivation/productivity can all be translated to financial terms so that they can be assessed in a financial analysis.

In other words, these suggested criteria assess whether the project outputs enabled the business to produce expected outcomes, avoid undesired benefits, realize the expected benefits needed for the achievement of strategic objectives, and then provide the expected return on investment.

### 3.1.4 Different Approaches, Criteria, and Perceptions of Success

Although there are several criteria available to evaluate project success, the judgment of success or failure can be based on a more situational or subjective basis (Ika 2009). Different perspectives can evaluate the same project as a success and as a failure. Project management success, ownership success, and investment success are assessed by different criteria (Zwikael and Smyrk 2011). When a project only partially meets the perspectives of success, or when it meets only one perspective, success cannot be judged by following clear rules. As an example to illustrate such complexity, Melton, Iles-Smith, and Yates (2008) suggest a matrix that combines the achievement of project objectives and strategic objectives. The matrix suggests that:

- A project with good project management performance and delivering expected business benefits is considered a star, because both the strategic and project management objectives were met.

- A project with ineffective project management might be considered a question mark, even if delivering the expected business benefits.

- A project not delivering business benefits might be considered a white elephant, even if with effective project management.

- A project with bad project management and not delivering business benefits can be clearly considered as a failure, since it has not met neither strategic nor project objectives.

To be able to succeed, project managers should ensure the alignment of expectations among stakeholders (Kerzner 2013a). Project managers, who have been kept apart from the rationale for project selection and prioritization, need to understand the relevance of their projects in order to deliver the expected benefits to the business (Melton et al. 2008). Variables employed in project appraisal should take part in project success criteria in order to ensure the fulfillment of the strategic needs that generated the project. Therefore, project managers have to be aware of the relevance of their projects as well as the criteria for evaluating their success by the different stakeholders.

### 3.1.5 Project Success Criteria from a Strategic Perspective

Based on the theoretical background presented in the previous subsections of this section, the complete assessment of strategic success should apply two different but complementary approaches:

1. Success on project management performance
2. Success on the creation of value to the business

By combining the two approaches, organizational leaders make sure their projects are managed in effective and efficient ways, at the same time they create or enable the creation of strategic value to the business.

The analysis of project success criteria identified by four authors and briefly presented in a previous section led us to identify seven generic project success criteria that can be applied to the assessment of project success from a strategic perspective. These seven criteria can be split into two different groups depending on their approach:

**Table 3-1  Seven Generic Project Success Criteria**

| Type of Assessment | Criteria | Description |
|---|---|---|
| Project management performance | Budget goals | Project satisfactorily meets the budget goals. |
| | Schedule goals | Project satisfactorily meets the schedule goals. |
| | Required outputs | Project satisfactorily delivers the required outputs (i.e., fulfilled its requisites). |
| Value for business | Expected outcomes | Project's outputs support the business to produce the expected outcomes (planned in the business case), and then to realize the expected benefits. |
| | Undesired outcomes | Undesired outcomes are managed and avoided. |
| | Return on investment | Project provides the expected return on investment. |
| | Business case | Project's outcomes adhered to the outcomes needed by the business strategy and planned in the business case. |

Data derived from Serra, C. E. *Benefits Realisation Management and Its Influence on Project Success, Project Governance, and Execution of Business Strategy: Analysis of Brazil, the United Kingdom, and the United States of America. Dissertation submitted in partial fulfillment for the degree of Master of Science in Programme and Project Management. Coventry, UK: University of Warwick. 2012. (Description of table on following page.)*

1. The first set of criteria assesses project management performance. It has been increasingly employed since the 1960s and is now used by most organizations.
2. The second set of criteria assesses the creation of value for the business (or organization). It has been developed more recently and, although important, it is not yet widely employed.

The two complementary sets of criteria can be used to assess project success from a strategic perspective (see Table 3-1).

## 3.2 Delivering Value through Project Management

This section links business strategic success and project success. Since Benefits Realization Management practices were previously introduced as a way to ensure this link, this section reinforces the fact that delivering benefits is a key part of project success. It discusses why the right set of projects should succeed in order to support strategic success, what kind of value is needed for strategic success, and then how to link business strategy and the right set of projects.

| Subsection | Subject |
|:---:|---|
| 3.2.1 | Execution of Business Strategies through the Most Valuable Projects |
| 3.2.2 | What Value Do Businesses Need? |
| 3.2.3 | Project Benefits Deliver the Value That Businesses Need |
| 3.2.4 | How Benefits Realization Management Can Support Project Success |

### 3.2.1 Execution of Business Strategies through the Most Valuable Projects

After organizational leaders set their visions and create their strategy, creative people can suggest many different ways to move from one point to the other while achieving the desired objectives (Gray and Larson 2010). These approaches are organized by the management team in individual projects or in programs, where programs are a group of projects and other work, managed together in order to deliver an expected business change (APM 2012; PMI® 2013c).

However, organizations do not have infinite resources to invest (Amason 2011). Therefore, they should perform those projects that deliver the value needed by the business strategy (Gray and Larson 2010; Amason 2011). The project portfolio is the set of programs and projects that organizations' Portfolio

Governance Boards select to execute their business strategy and then achieve their objectives (APM 2012; PMI® 2013c). When composing their portfolio, managers need to be selective and choose the most effective and efficient projects (Gray and Larson 2010). Therefore, project portfolio management is exactly about selecting and prioritizing the best set of projects (Jenner 2010).

To understand the relevance of Benefits Realization Management for project success, an initial required step is to identify what is relevant and valuable for business, and then the types of projects the organizations need to succeed.

## 3.2.2 What Value Do Businesses Need?

Effective business strategies are those that increase shareholder value, which is the organization's long-term cash generation capability (Johnson and Scholes 2002). Financially speaking, the value of a firm is the financial measure of its tangible and intangible assets, plus the expected profits, discounted by a risk-adjusted opportunity cost of capital (Amason 2011). Organizational leaders define objectives in order to increase this value by increasing assets, profits or reducing the cost of capital.

According to Serra and Kunc (2015), business strategies are plans for the achievement of an organization's vision in terms of achieving its target value at a future point in time. Strategic objectives are defined to build a structured pathway from the present value to the desired future value (vision). Organizations execute their business strategies to achieve their strategic objectives and then gradually achieve their target vision. To enable a controlled journey from the current present value to the desired future value, such strategic objectives should be measurable, and when combined they usually result in the achievement of a financially measurable end-target.

That final target usually represents the overall creation of value that is expected to be achieved in a strategy execution cycle. Therefore, the difference between the current situation and the target future situation sets the value gap, which is the difference between current value and desired future value, and which should be fulfilled by a portfolio of initiatives defined by the organization in their strategic plan (Kaplan and Norton 2008). These strategic initiatives, normally executed in the form of projects and programs, are expected to deliver the outputs that will enable new capabilities or promote required changes. Each new capability or change to existing capabilities is expected to create new value for the business, gradually filling the value gap.

Projects have clearly defined outputs, which should be delivered in a specific time frame (Chittendon and Bon 2006). These project outputs are the products, capabilities, or results (PMI® 2013a) expected to enable positive changes in the

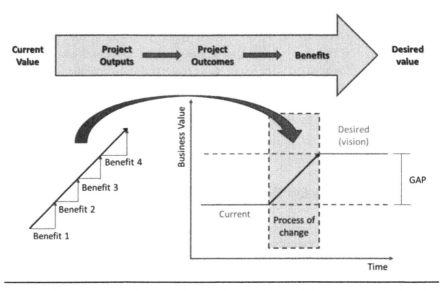

**Figure 3-1**   Filling the value gap. [*Source:* Serra, C. E. and M. Kunc. (2015). "Benefits Realisation Management and its influence on project success and on the execution of business strategies." *International Journal of Project Management* 33(1). Used with permission.]

business, and these changes should be related to the achievement of business objectives (APM 2012; PMI® 2013c). The improvement caused in the business by these changes is called a "benefit" (Chittendon and Bon 2006). Therefore, benefits are increments in the business value from the shareholders' perspective (Zwikael and Smyrk 2011). Furthermore, benefits can also flow to other beneficiaries of projects, such as customers, suppliers, or even the society (Zwikael and Smyrk 2011) (see Figure 3-1).

Programs are a way to ensure the alignment between corporate strategy, changing processes, and day-to-day business (OGC 2011). Although project managers manage individual projects, the program manager ensures the delivery of expected benefits from a program (APM 2012). These benefits are enabled by the successful completion of a program's related projects (APM 2012; Chittenden and Bon 2006).

Both programs and projects intend to deliver outcomes to their customers to satisfy their needs (APM 2012; PMI® 2013c). The value created by a program or by a project can be calculated by the relationship between the satisfaction of needs and the use of resources to obtain that satisfaction (BSI 2000). The satisfaction of needs can be tangible or not, depending on the outcome expected (BSI 2000). However, even if intangible, everything is measurable since the object of measurement is clearly defined (Hubbard 2007). Then, the satisfaction of needs should be translated into a numeric measure in order to enable its valuation (BSI 2000).

Whenever possible, program and project objectives should be measurable by using key performance indicators (KPIs) defined for strategic objectives (OGC 2011). However, since KPIs are often not suitable for measuring end benefits or intermediate benefits, other indicators can supplement them in order to be able to measure benefits (OGC 2011). Measures of process performance are very often suitable to the measurement of benefits even when these are not KPIs defined for strategic objectives. It happens because the achievement of strategic objectives is often achieved by the improvement of process performance.

For example, a strategic objective of increase in revenue from sales, which would be measured by a KPI called *financial revenue from sales,* could have its achievement supported by the realization of some intermediate benefits such as an increase in market share, an increase in number of sales, and an increase in production. These three could also be broken down into more granular and operational levels until the level affected by the change initiative is reached. In this scenario, the success of a project to increase the sales workforce could be measured by the increase in staff-hour capacity, which supports the achievement of an increase in number of sales and consequently also the target growth for the KPI *financial revenue from sales.*

Once the benefits criteria and benefits measures are defined, scoring systems such as the Balanced Scorecard are useful to clarify the relationship between business objectives and expected benefits and to track the execution of their strategy (Melton et al. 2008). In large organizations, corporative strategic objectives can be cascaded to divisions, business and support units, and departments to make it easier to create and manage local value-creation initiatives (Kaplan and Norton 2008). In the context exemplified earlier in the chapter, the increase in staff-hour capacity might be a local need of one single office within a global organization. All other offices might need to take different actions, such as achieving an increase in market share, without needing an increase in staff-hour capacity. Therefore, each office should be able to cascade the corporate objectives by identifying the changes required within their own remit that would support the achievement of the corporate objectives and then defining their own local objectives. However, all cascaded objectives need vertical and horizontal integration inside the organization (Kaplan and Norton 2008).

As observed in the previous paragraphs, many initiatives can deliver value, but organizations do not have infinite money to invest. Executives should select the most relevant projects by following a strategy. Initiatives are then selected based on their value for business, which should be measured in terms of a numeric figure that states how it contributes to filling the value gap. Therefore, more than mere outputs, successful projects deliver the required value or the required benefits.

### 3.2.3 Project Benefits Deliver the Value
### That Businesses Need

As discussed in previous chapters, benefits can be defined as being the measurable improvements that are perceived by stakeholders as adding value to the business (Chittendon and Bon 2006; OGC 2011). Improvements can be understood as new capabilities or as enhancements made to existing capabilities. These improvements are mainly the outcomes of changes, which are usually managed using program and project management techniques. Therefore, the successful execution of business strategies and the consequent creation of value to the business strongly depend on programs and projects delivering their expected benefits.

Benefits Realization Management enables planning and delivering benefits as well as communicating the progress of the benefits realization to stakeholders in order to support effective benefits realization (Chittenden and Bon 2006). Therefore, the management of benefits during projects' life cycles establishes the link between business and projects (Melton et al. 2008).

Therefore, the delivery of the expected benefits in order to create strategic value to the organization is the clearest evidence of a project being successful. Conversely, individual projects may deliver benefits that do not support the fulfillment of the complex benefits dependency network that leads to the achievement of business objectives. Because of that, benefits realization managed on an organizational level is instrumental for the execution of business strategies and achievement of the business vision. In addition, on program and project levels, careful management of each program's and project's contribution to the realization of the organizational benefits realization strategy should be performed to ensure that programs and projects deliver outputs, enable outcomes and then support the realization of the needed benefits. Therefore, although benefits are not the only criteria to evaluate project success, they are certainly the best to measure how valuable a program or project is to its sponsoring organization.

### 3.2.4 How Benefits Realization Management
### Can Support Project Success

The previous section presented a set of criteria to assess project success from the strategic perspective. Then this section discussed in more depth the relationship between benefits and strategic value for business. Since benefits increase business value, Benefits Realization Management practices support the successful creation of value by enabling effective delivery of benefits. Critical Success Factors (CSFs) for project success, if achieved, enable the creation of value for the business and are associated with Benefits Realization Management practices (see Table 3-2).

**Table 3-2 Business Value CSFs Supported by Benefits
Realization Management Practices**

| Criteria | CSF influenced by Benefits Realization Management | How Benefits Realization Management supports? |
|---|---|---|
| Expected outcomes | Structured processes are required to ensure the integration of project outputs into the business.<br><br>Expected outcomes and benefits should be frequently reviewed. | It ensures the embedding of project outputs in the day-to-day business.<br><br>It ensures frequent review and re-alignment among plans, actions, actual results, and expectations. |
| Undesired outcomes | Undesired outcomes should be identified and managed. | It monitors and manages disbenefits on the same way as benefits. |
| Return on investment | Measurement of the return on investment considering the value created for the business. This value can be measurable only when combining the results of several projects or in the long term. | It stimulates the assessment of project success based on the value delivered to the business. The understanding of the full chain of outputs, outcomes, and benefits enables measuring of the value of complex and interrelated results. |
| Business case | Business cases should adhere to business strategies, or they will be meaningless and unstable.<br><br>The adherence of actual results to the business case needs frequent assessment during the project life cycle and after closeout. | It maps the links between project objectives and business strategies and then enables the approval of meaningful business cases.<br><br>It frequently reviews benefits, as part of the project scope as well as after project closeout. |

Data derived from Serra, C. E. *Benefits Realisation Management and Its Influence on Project Success, Project Governance, and Execution of Business Strategy: Analysis of Brazil, the United Kingdom, and the United States of America.* Dissertation submitted in partial fulfillment for the degree of Master of Science in Programme and Project Management. Coventry, UK: University of Warwick, 2012.

In contrast, Benefits Realization Management was suggested as not being a CSF for the assessment of success from the perspective of project management performance (Cooke-Davies 2002). However, since there is an assumption that it increases the effectiveness of project governance, it can influence the project management performance perspective as well. Some CSFs are recommended for project performance; various Benefits Realization Management practices are associated with each of these CSFs (see Table 3-3).

Table 3-3  Project Performance CSFs Supported by
Benefits Realization Management Practices

| Criteria | CSF influenced by Benefits Realization Management | How Benefits Realization Management Supports? |
|---|---|---|
| Budget goals | Forecasting accuracy. Financial discipline. | It indirectly influences cost management, since it makes objectives clearer and provides tools to improve resources and scope management. |
| Schedule goals | Prioritization and availability of required resources. | It enables selection and prioritization of the most valuable actions. Then, it makes stakeholders aware and supportive to project needs. |
| Required outputs | Clear understanding of outputs needed to enable the realization of the expected benefits. Strong communication and alignment with customer. | It provides ways to clarify the desired output. It makes it easier to align expectations through the clear definition of final objectives. |

Data derived from Serra, C. E. *Benefits Realisation Management and Its Influence on Project Success, Project Governance, and Execution of Business Strategy: Analysis of Brazil, the United Kingdom, and the United States of America.* Dissertation submitted in partial fulfillment for the degree of Master of Science in Programme and Project Management. Coventry, UK: University of Warwick, 2012.

The Benefits Realization Management practices that are suggested to increase the effectiveness of project governance and in consequence to provide support to the achievement of project success as summarized in Tables 3-2 and 3-3, as well as the roles and responsibilities that are associated with these good practices, will be explained in the next chapter.

## 3.3 Chapter Summary: Project Success and Creation of Value to the Business

The previous chapter discussed how to be successful in the execution of business strategies by applying project, program and portfolio management. It also discussed objective setting and different types of strategies to achieve such business objectives. This chapter got into a deeper level of detail on how to measure success.

Program and project success are important—this is a point of almost unanimous agreement. But how are program and project success measured and evaluated? Firstly, it is important to understand program and project success as being things that can be evaluated based on measures but also as including a strong component of judgment. Therefore, clear and well-defined measures support the evaluation and decision making about success or failure. However, there is no single set of measures that can evaluate program and project success in one go. Several sets of measures can be applied, although they can be split into two basic main groups. The first group, project management success, evaluates how successful the project management team is in managing the project according to a set of constraints—mainly scope, schedule and cost. The second group, creation of value to the business, evaluates how successful the same project management team is in creating new value aligned to the business strategies. The two set of criteria measure two different things that can be achieved together or separately. Although the best scenario is to achieve both, we can say that is meaningless to achieve success in project management performance without achieving success in creating strategic value to the business.

In such a context, Benefits Realization Management builds the bridge between project and program management and business strategies. It ensures that project objectives are aligned to business objectives and therefore will support the achievement of strategy objectives. We can say that Benefits Realization Management is probably the best set of practices and techniques to support successful strategy execution.

To explain how to apply Benefits Realization Management to support the execution of business strategies and the achievement of strategic objectives, Part II of this book presents in more detail a set of Benefits Realization Management practices split into four groups: Establishing the Environment for Benefits Realization (Chapter 4), Planning Benefits (Chapter 5), Realizing Benefits (Chapter 6), and Reviewing and Evaluating Benefits (Chapter 7). Such practices can be applied by any organization to effectively support the execution of business strategies through strategically aligned portfolios of programs and projects.

## 3.4 End-of-Chapter Review Questions—Chapter 3

In this section, a set of end-of-chapter review questions are provided to enable a self-assessment of the understanding of the Chapter 3. The answers to all questions can be found at the end of the book in *Appendix A*.

1. What is project success?
2. How project success is usually assessed?
3. What is success in terms of project management performance?
4. What is success in delivering benefits to the organization?
5. How can we define project success criteria from a strategic perspective?

6. Can organizations execute an unlimited number of projects? Why?
7. What values do businesses need?
8. What is the *value gap*?
9. How are projects linked to the achievement of business strategic objectives?

# PART II

# Enterprise Benefits Realization Management (eBRM)

# Chapter 4

## Establishing the Environment for Benefit Realization

The second part of this book starts in this chapter by discussing a set of best practices for Benefits Realization Management that are recommended to be applied along with organizations' project, program, and portfolio management processes. This chapter presents the way Benefits Realization Management practices can enhance the effectiveness of project management in creating value to the business (Serra and Kunc 2015), mostly by making clear the value of each project and then strengthening the link between project management governance and business strategy.

To do so, this chapter and the following ones bring to our attention a series of project program and portfolio management practices that should be applied in association with Benefits Realization Management practices, although this book does not get into a lot of depth into the utilization of each of those project program and portfolio management practices. Our main focus is to clarify the association between the practices that support effective project governance and are instrumental in achieving project success. Therefore, instead of suggesting the replacement of any existing best practices, Benefits Realization Management practices are to be applied *in addition to* most of the existing project, program, and portfolio management best practices, most times working as strong and clear linking elements between different areas of expertise, functional areas, and organizational levels across the business.

Table 4-1  The Four Groups of BRM Practices

| Group of Practices | Description | Chapter |
|---|---|---|
| I | Establishing the environment for benefits realization | 4 |
| II | Planning benefits | 5 |
| III | Realizing benefits | 6 |
| IV | Reviewing and evaluating benefits | 7 |

The Benefits Realization Management practices are split into four groups throughout this Part II of this book. Each of these four groups is approached in a specific chapter, as listed in Table 4-1, where it is associated with one of four key governance processes. Chapter 4 (this chapter) sets the environment for effective realization of strategic aligned benefits, explains the role of project governance on the organization, and presents its responsibility in aligning business strategies, projects, programs, and portfolios. Chapter 5, on planning benefits, explains some fundamental steps of project governance necessary to composing portfolios, starting changes, and supporting their relevance. Chapter 6, on realizing those benefits, discusses the preparation required to ensure successful benefits realization, the project closeout, embedding changes, and then the realization of expected benefits. Chapter 7, the last in the book, addresses reviewing and evaluating benefits, discussing the required control and constant strategic realignment of the ongoing portfolio of initiatives.

Each chapter starts with a section introducing the area of project governance for which Benefits Realization Management practices are instrumental. After that, a number of sections present the Benefits Realization Management practices in association with some project, program, and portfolio management practices upon which these depend—or that are dependent upon them. Then, a section provides a summary of the chapter and highlights a set of key Benefits Realization Management practices that are fundamental to the effectiveness of the governance area approached by the chapter; also listed are a set of key templates that are associated with the chapter and which are available at the end of this book as *Appendices D* (Blank Templates) and *E* (How to Use Guidance). At the end of each chapter, end-of-chapter review questions are included to provide means for a self-assessment of the understanding. The answers to all questions can be found at the end of the book in *Appendix A*. At the end of this book, recommendations for further reading for each chapter are also provided in *Appendix B*.

As discussed in Part I of this book, Benefits Realization Management is about ensuring the successful execution of business strategies and therefore the creation of meaningful value to the business. To accomplish this, benefits management strategies should become an important linking element of a hierarchy of organizational strategies. This chapter discusses these strategies as well as ways to establish them; therefore, the chapter discusses ways to set up the appropriate environment to enable effective Benefits Realization Management. It also introduces the main roles and responsibilities that are associated with Benefits Realization Management and, therefore, are responsible for producing and executing such strategies. After an organization has identified its strategic goals and defined its strategies, the implementation of these strategies will require an appropriate and integrated set of processes and tools, which will be discussed in the following chapters.

## 4.1 Introduction: Developing and Aligning Strategies

Corporate governance establishes the relationships between an organization's stakeholders, shareholders, and executive board (APM 2004), sets objectives, creates strategies to achieve these objectives, and then monitors the execution of these strategies (Amason 2011; APM 2004) to assure investors that they obtain the return on their financial investment (Shleifer and Vishny 1997). As explained in Chapters 2 and 3, changes to the current status enable the creation of value to the business and then the achievement of the objectives, which will take the organization to the desired future status.

While business strategies are the plans to go from a current to a desired status, corporate governance is responsible for managing the entire journey. Governance strategies ensure the execution of all changes in a cohesive way to ensure the achievement of the business objectives and then the successful transition from the current to the expected future status—the business vision.

| Subsection | Subject |
|---|---|
| 4.1.1 | Planning the Route for Strategy Execution: A Hierarchy of Strategies |
| 4.1.2 | Small, Medium, or Large, Projects Are All About Strategy Execution |
| 4.1.3 | Investment Criteria: How to Select What Is Valuable |

### 4.1.1 Planning the Route for Strategy Execution: A Hierarchy of Strategies

In this scenario, many different models and approaches are suggested to manage changes, ranging from long-term and massive planned changes to emergent

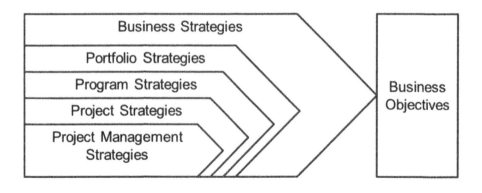

**Figure 4-1**   Hierarchy of strategies: business, portfolio, program, project, and project management strategies.

dynamic changes (Burnes 2004; Todnem 2005). However, although changes have different types and objectives, a major strategy should align the execution of all the changes to be performed by an organization. As discussed in Chapters 2 and 3, such strategy is a high-level plan, which is set by the Senior Executive Board and later will be replicated and executed throughout the entire organization. In large organizations, corporate strategies are often cascaded down and further refined to make them applicable to the various organization's divisions or lines of business. After the strategies have been cascaded down and refined to the most appropriate level of the organizational structure, program and project management are usually the sets of processes, tools, and techniques utilized by organizations to manage each and every single change. Therefore, as discussed in Chapter 2, the business strategies are further decomposed into program and project strategies in order to enable portfolios of programs and projects to carry on the execution of such strategies in a coherent and planned fashion.

At this stage, project governance is the part of corporate governance responsible for ensuring the alignment between business strategies and projects, and consequently for ensuring timely, effective, and relevant delivery (APM 2004). Effective project governance ensures projects, programs, and portfolios enable the changes required by business strategies and then support the realization of benefits and the consequent the creation of value expected by the corporate governance.

The management of a portfolio of initiatives requires well-defined projects, programs, and day-to-day business activities as well as a formal and standardized portfolio management system, including processes, templates, and guidance (Jenner, 2010).

### 4.1.2 Small, Medium, or Large, Projects Are All About Strategy Execution

Another relevant aspect is that different types and sizes of change can be needed to move from the current state to the desired state, ranging from improvements in local processes and procedures to major changes across the organization or even transformations involving elements from the environment outside the organization (Chittenden and Bon 2006). However, most organizations do not pay enough attention to their small projects, because it is hard to manage a portfolio of several small projects (Gray and Larson 2010). Although each one does not request a large amount of money, they compete together for scarce resources and consume a large total amount of money; effective governance is necessary in order to keep them focused on the business vision (Gray and Larson 2010).

### 4.1.3 Investment Criteria: How to Select What Is Valuable

Organizational leaders have also to define their investment criteria, which will be used later, to appraise all proposed investments (Jenner 2010). Several financial methods can be applied to appraise investments, such as payback, cost-benefit analysis, accounting rate of return, net present value (NPV), internal rate of return (IRR), discounted cash flow, economic value added (EVA), opportunity cost, and real options. Since projects are considered a type of investment, these techniques are employed for project appraisal; Chapter 5 describes these methods during the discussion about the composition of project portfolios.

## 4.2 Creating or Enhancing the Environment for Effective Benefits Realization Management

Although Benefits Realization Management is not yet largely employed, it has been increasingly studied in the past few years as a link between portfolios, programs, and projects (Breese 2012). Several best practices have been developed and tested by academics, management consulting companies, and organizations in general, connecting Benefits Realization Management to project governance processes as well as to several roles inside an organization. Research shows that some best practices are already heavily utilized by organizations, while Benefits Realization Management strategies are not so frequently put in place (Serra and Kunc 2015). At the same time, organizations report low maturity in benefits realization and consequent negative impact on strategy execution (PMI® 2014). This scenario suggests that a large set of tools and best practices cannot be effective if they are not implemented in a planned way focusing on achieving clearly defined goals.

Thereby, organizational leaders should plan their way to manage benefits in order to ensure investment in the right initiatives and the delivery of the needed benefits. This rhetorical statement can be easily misunderstood, because of the variety of levels and extents to which Benefits Realization Management strategies can be applied. As discussed in previous chapters, strategies are plans to achieve goals. The next sections will discuss some strategies to effectively employ Benefits Realization Management to achieve organizational goals.

| Subsection | Subject |
|---|---|
| 4.2.1 | Implementing Benefits Realization Management Practices or Enhancing Maturity in Benefits Realization Management |
| 4.2.2 | Developing an Enterprise Benefits Realization Strategy (eBRS) |

## 4.2.1 Implementing Benefits Realization Management Practices or Enhancing Maturity in Benefits Realization Management

As a starting point, which may have to some extent been left aside by some of the existing literature in Benefits Realization Management, organizations need to produce a strategy to implement a structured Benefits Realization Management set of processes that will consequently enhance the organization's maturity through Benefits Realization Management.

Some companies, especially startups, will not have a standard process for Benefits Realization Management, so they will need a strategy in terms of how to develop and implement those practices. The implementation of Benefits Realization Management can be treated as a program, a project, or just as a set of tasks. Nevertheless, as any type of change initiative, it will require a strategy to be successful, as discussed in Chapter 2. Therefore, the development of this strategy is strongly recommended to enable the implementation of Benefits Realization Management in a new business.

Another scenario that requires a specific strategy is the enhancement of Benefits Realization Management capabilities in an existing business. Different from the green-field scenario presented before, this second scenario requires previous analysis to enable the understanding of the current situation and then to support the development of the best strategy to reach the vision. It will be based normally on the results of an analysis of the current situation—also known as an *as-is* analysis—and will determinate how to progress to a desired higher level of maturity planned by an analysis of the expected future situation—also known as a *to-be* analysis. The results from assessments of project, program, and portfolio management maturity and capability can provide valuable inputs to recognize the areas that are requiring improvement. Some of the existing maturity or capability assessment frameworks may not assess Benefits Realization Management separately as a single discipline—which is to some extent understandable, since it happens to integrate several other existing disciplines. Several issues are related to change management or project management can be addressed by the implementation or improvement of Benefits Realization Management practices (Bradley 2010). Therefore, the analysis of the organizational issues affecting the effectiveness of project management can provide valuable inputs to support the business case for the implementation of or for the maturity or capability enhancements in Benefits Realization Management. The application of a specific model to identify benefits realization maturity levels is even more recommended, since it gives direct input for the incremental improvement of the benefits realization techniques applied by an organization (Gartner 2011b). We can mention an example of such a model, which is the Benefits Management Maturity diagnostic developed by Ward and Daniel (2012).

After gaining an understanding of the strengths and weaknesses of the current Benefits Realization Management environment (for example, by applying a maturity assessment) and internally agreeing on the desired level of maturity in Benefits Realization Management to be achieved, two key deliverables are recommended for implementation as part of both types of strategies to provide sound support for the utilization of Benefits Realization Management practices across the organization. The two documents are an Enterprise Benefits Realization Management Framework (eBRMF) and a Measures Dictionary (or Benefits Dictionary). Both documents are described in the following two subsections. Figure 4-2 presents a generic Enterprise Benefits Realization Management Maturity Enhancement Strategy.

## Developing an Enterprise Benefits Realization Management Framework (eBRMF)

The execution of an organizational level or portfolio level benefits realization strategy will be supported by a Benefits Realization Management framework, which provides tools and techniques to the enable the entire organization to adopt similar practices across different areas of the business to manage the realization of benefits. It increases the productivity and effectiveness of benefits management practitioners in their activities by providing a set of recognized best practices.

A framework is an overview that outlines a set of associated items to support a particular approach to achieve specific objectives. It works as a general

| TEMPLATE | | | |
|---|---|---|---|
| **Enterprise Benefits Realization Management Maturity Enhancement Strategy** | | | |
| **Organization:** | *<Name of the organization and/or division>* | | |
| **Version:** | *<X.X>* | **Version Type:** | *<Final/Draft>* |
| **Issued by:** | *<Name, Surname>* | **Issue date:** | *<DD-MM-YY>* |
| **Department:** | *<Department>* | **Job title:** | *<Job title>* |
| **Approved by:** | *<Name, Surname>* | **Approval date:** | *<DD-MM-YY>* |
| **Department:** | *<Department>* | **Job title:** | *<Job title>* |

| **I. Rationale and Background** |
|---|
| *<Add text>* |
| **II. Objectives** |
| *<Add text>* |
| **III. Approach** |
| **a. Planning** |
| *i. AS-IS Analysis*<br>　　*<Add text>*<br>*ii. TO-BE Analysis*<br>　　*<Add text>*<br>*iii. GAP Analysis*<br>　　*<Add text>*<br>*iv. Changes to Be Implemented*<br>　　*<Add text>* |
| **b. Implementation** |
| *i. Documentation (Processes and Procedures)*<br>　　*<Add text>*<br>*ii. Training in Systems and Tools*<br>　　*<Add text>*<br>*iii. General Communications and Training in Systems and Tools*<br>　　*<Add text>*<br>*iv. Senior Management Communications and Training*<br>　　*<Add text>*<br>*v. Go-Live*<br>　　*<Add text>* |

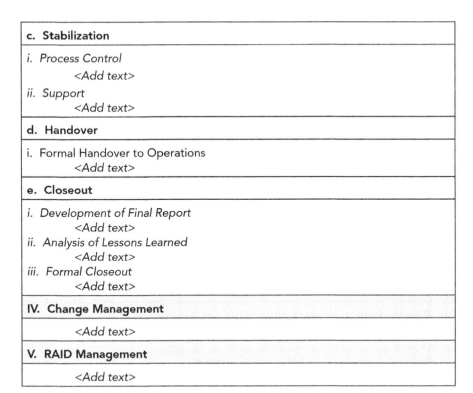

| **c. Stabilization** |
| :--- |
| *i. Process Control*<br>    *<Add text>*<br>*ii. Support*<br>    *<Add text>* |
| **d. Handover** |
| i. Formal Handover to Operations<br>    *<Add text>* |
| **e. Closeout** |
| *i. Development of Final Report*<br>    *<Add text>*<br>*ii. Analysis of Lessons Learned*<br>    *<Add text>*<br>*iii. Formal Closeout*<br>    *<Add text>* |
| **IV.  Change Management** |
| *<Add text>* |
| **V. RAID Management** |
| *<Add text>* |

**Figure 4-2**   Template: Enterprise Benefits Realization Management: Maturity Enhancement Strategy.

guidance, which can be updated and modified as required by adding new items, amending existing items, or retiring obsolete or no longer appropriate items. To support adoption and to maximize the utilization of the framework, documents such as handbooks, pocketbooks, booklets, or leaflets can be produced to make the most relevant information from the framework available to practitioners for quick access or in a more attractive display.

A Benefits Realization Management framework (see template in Figure 4-3) can include categories of benefits to support the assessment of eligibility to be part of the portfolio, procedures for assessment of benefit cases during stage-gate reviews and other portfolio level reviews, arrangements for the continuity of the Benefits Realization Management activities after the program and/or project closeout, standard procedures and templates for consolidated benefits tracking and reporting, and the activities associated with the utilization of post-implementation reviews and lessons learned to support the enhancement of processes and benefits realization forecasts (OGC 2011a).

| TEMPLATE | | | |
|---|---|---|---|
| **Benefits Realization Management Framework** | | | |
| **Organization:** | *<Name of the organization and/or division>* | | |
| **Version:** | *<X.X>* | **Version Type:** | *<Final/Draft>* |
| **Issued by:** | *<Name, Surname>* | **Issue date:** | *<DD-MM-YY>* |
| **Department:** | *<Department>* | **Job title:** | *<Job title>* |
| **Approved by:** | *<Name, Surname>* | **Approval date:** | *<DD-MM-YY>* |
| **Department:** | *<Department>* | **Job title:** | *<Job title>* |

| |
|---|
| **I. Introduction** |
| *<Add text>* |
| **II. Benefits Realization Management: Theoretical Background** |
| *<Add text>* |
| **III. Benefits Realization Management Life Cycle** |
| *<Add graphical representation of the life cycle >* |
| **IV. Benefits Realization Management Processes** |
| ***a. Enterprise Benefits Realization Strategy*** |
| *<Add text>* |
| ***b. Planning Benefits*** |
| *<Add text>* |
| ***c. Realizing Benefits*** |
| *<Add text>* |
| ***d. Reviewing and Evaluating Benefits*** |
| *<Add text>* |
| **V. Roles and Responsibilities** |
| *<Add text>* |

**Figure 4-3**   Template: Benefits Realization Management Framework.

## Developing a Measures Dictionary (or Benefits Dictionary)

To simplify the identification of benefits that are associated with their existing business processes, organizations can adopt a practice that supports the identification of the benefits, which is the use of an organizational measures dictionary (see template, Figure 4.4) that lists all measures

# TEMPLATE

## Measures Dictionary

| Organization: | <Name of the organization and/or division> | | |
|---|---|---|---|
| Version: | <X.X> | Version Type: | <Final/Draft> |
| Issued by: | <Name, Surname> | Issue date: | <DD-MM-YY> |
| Department: | <Department> | Job title: | <Job title> |
| Approved by: | <Name, Surname> | Approval date: | <DD-MM-YY> |
| Department: | <Department> | Job title: | <Job title> |

| Measure Name/Code | Measure Owner | Measure Type | Measure Objective | Associated Business Functions | Associated Business Processes | Associated Tools or IT Systems | Measurement Method | Measurement Periodicity | Benefit Measurer |
|---|---|---|---|---|---|---|---|---|---|
| | | | | | | | | | |
| | | | | | | | | | |
| | | | | | | | | | |
| | | | | | | | | | |
| | | | | | | | | | |
| | | | | | | | | | |

Figure 4-4   Template: Measures Dictionary.

being tracked by the organization (Bradley 2010). The dictionary lists all measures in use throughout the organization and identifies information about each measure, such as the measure's owners, the person responsible for taking the measures (measurer), the source of the data, any calculation required to generate the measure, the method for capturing the data, the periodicity of measurement, and other relevant information. Such a document, which can be also called a Benefit Dictionary, supports the identification of benefits that are measurable and can be associated with any strategic objectives or change initiatives.

## 4.2.2 Developing an Enterprise Benefits Realization Strategy (eBRS)

The third scenario is a different type of strategy. Rather than implementing or enhancing the Benefits Realization Management practices, this strategy involves developing an organizational strategy to achieve the organization's strategic goals supported by the structured utilization of Benefits Realization Management processes and tools in a preplanned way. Although the next three chapters will discuss Benefits Realization Management techniques that contribute to the establishment of connections between strategy and change initiatives, these techniques can be of little effect if not properly utilized in a preplanned fashion.

At this point, we should refer to Chapter 2. Organizations have a variety of strategies aiming to achieve different objectives at different level. Projects, programs, and even portfolios all need strategies. All program and project strategies should be connected to one main organizational business strategy that takes its place at the project portfolio level, which can be achieved by using a variety of techniques that are described in the next subsections.

Therefore, prior to adopting any top-down or bottom-up approach to the connection between investment initiatives and business strategies, a high-level Benefits Realization Strategy should guide an entire organization or an entire portfolio to the achievement of the desired end benefits and to the creation of the expected value to the business. Such strategy defines priorities and provides means to the achieve benefits required by the business strategy. It provides a method organizational leaders can use to identify the benefits needed by the business strategies and that will be expected to be realized from the outputs and outcomes delivered by projects and from wider business changes enabled by programs. The first required step to produce this strategy is the understanding of the organizational drivers, which will be discussed in the next subsection.

## Understanding Organizational Drivers: Gathering Ideas

As already discussed in Chapter 2, benefits, projects, programs, and portfolios are ways of executing business strategies that depend on internal and external issues and opportunities. The business strategies define business drivers, which will guide all change initiatives. Project benefits are linked to strategic objectives through the satisfaction of the organizational drivers (OGC 2011b). Therefore, by knowing their organizational drivers as well as the actions that are needed to perform each specific change, it is easier to identify the required benefits (Melton 2007). The organizational drivers can be better understood by performing a driver analysis, which makes clear the drivers that require the organization to make changes to the way it performs its activities or even to what the organization does (Ward and Daniel 2012). After the organizational drivers have been clearly defined, understood, and communicated, benefits can be linked to them.

Several techniques available for the analysis of the organizational drivers, such as fishbone or Ishikawa diagrams, mind mapping, and root-cause analysis, analyze and map their issues to identify causes related to their current situation (Melton et al. 2008). An important remark is that organizational drivers should incorporate both strategic needs, mostly driven by an external analysis and by a shareholder-driven analysis of needs and wants and also operational needs (and if possible wants) that are driven by the day-to-day needs of the business. The utilization of a top-down but also bottom-up approach to the identification of organizational drivers helps to ensure that no important needs will be missed or overshadowed (see Figure 4-5).

As an example of how to analyze strategic drivers that is suggested as specific for IS/IT projects, but can perhaps be applicable to other areas too, Ward and Daniel (2012) suggest the existence of three types of drivers for IS/IT projects: *content,* when a specific deliverable is needed; *context,* when an internal or external issue or opportunity has to be addressed; and *outcome,* when an outcome is expected—usually verifiable and measurable in terms of performance improvement. From these three types, which can be applied to other sectors apart from IS/IT, the outcome would be certainly the type of driver that clearly associates a program or project

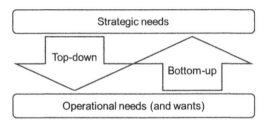

**Figure 4-5**   Top-down/bottom-up strategic analysis.

with the required outcomes, since they are the main objective behind the initiative. In contrast, the other two types of drivers demand additional effort from the program or project management team and business managers to identify the benefits. The context type requires more analysis, since a broader set of options will need to be taken into consideration to address the situation. Conversely, the content type, the most common one, does not require a lot of analysis because the required products are already known. The content type then can be said to some extent a "tricky" type since, although, the project management team may know what is expected from the project in terms of deliverables, there may be a tendency for benefits to be overshadowed by the required deliverables and then perhaps left aside.

The final outcome from the driver analysis will be a list of changes needed by the organization, which is based on internal and external drivers. Some changes can be available from the strategic planning process, although it is important to have this process cascaded down to reach all levels of the organization where investment in change can take place. A better investment decision can be made if it is based on a sound understanding of all needs.

## Developing an Enterprise Benefits Realization Strategy (eBRS)

Having analyzed and understood the internal and external organizational drivers, the Portfolio Governance Board has to make decisions about what to achieve and where to focus its efforts. Several needs as well as opportunities will have been identified, but the resources available are limited. Therefore, the Portfolio Governance Board has to clearly define the strategic objectives of the organization as well as the benefits associated with each objective.

This process is strategic planning, and it has already been discussed in previous chapters. However, now we are discussing a slightly different and integrated approach for strategy execution that is totally driven by the realization of the benefits required by the business strategy as the main and only way to achieve the strategic objectives of an organization. Rather than simply identifying projects and initiatives that will help to achieve these strategic objectives, we are starting the whole process of strategy execution by asking the question:

- What are the main end benefits that are required to achieve the objectives determined by the business strategies?

The answer to this question will help us answer further questions, such as:

- Which are the KPIs to be employed to evaluate the achievement of each strategic objective of the organization?
- Which initiatives are relevant and which ones are not?
- How can change initiatives be prioritized?

| TEMPLATE | | |
|---|---|---|
| **eBRS: Enterprise Benefits Realization Strategy** | | |
| **Organization:** | <Name of the organization and/or division> | |
| **Version:** | <X.X> | **Version Type:** <Final/Draft> |
| **Next review:** | <DD-MM-YY> | **Next full review:** <DD-MM-YY> |
| **Issued by:** | <Name, Surname> | **Issue date:** <DD-MM-YY> |
| **Department:** | <Department> | **Job title:** <Job title> |
| **Approved by:** | <Name, Surname> | **Approval date:** <DD-MM-YY> |
| **Department:** | <Department> | **Job title:** <Job title> |

| I. Key Strategic Drivers |
|---|
| <Add text> |
| **II. Strategic Objectives** |
| <Add text> |
| **III. End Benefits** |
| <Add text> |
| **IV. Changes Required** |
| <Add text> |
| **V. Ideas** |
| <Add text> |
| **VI. Selection Criteria** |
| <Add text> |
| **VII. High-Level Governance Process** |
| <Add text> |
| **VIII. Initiatives Selected for Implementation** |
| <Add text> |
| **IX. Benefits Dependency Network** |
| <Add text> |

**Figure 4-6**  Template: eBRS: Enterprise Benefits Realization Strategy.

Therefore, an Enterprise Benefits Realization Strategy (see template, Figure 4-6) starts by identifying and defining the benefits associated with each strategic objective. Then it defines ownership for the objectives as well as for the benefits. It defines ways to perform benefits measurement, tracking, and recording, and attributes ownership to these activities. It defines the process of periodic review and governance of the organizational Benefits Realization Management as the highest level governance of the strategy execution process. It defines criteria for the analysis and selection of programs and projects to get into the portfolio. And, finally, it defines the process of governing the execution of the portfolio of changes with the view of realizing the expected end benefits required by the business strategy.

After the business strategies have clearly defined the business objectives (what) and the reasons behind these objectives (why), the Enterprise Benefits Realization Strategy (Figure 4-6) provides an extremely important—and perhaps missing—link between the strategy level and the execution level.

## 4.3 Key Roles and Responsibilities for Benefits Realization Management

This section identifies the key roles that are responsible for executing the key Benefits Realization Management practices and for enabling effective governance. Although each company can have a different organizational architecture with different functions, this chapter presents a set of key important roles and their responsibilities. To make comprehension easier, the full set of roles is split into three groups, each one discussed in one subsection. These three groups are: (1) benefits realization governance roles; (2) program and project management roles; and (3) benefits ownership roles (see Figure 4-7).

| Subsection | Subject |
|:---:|:---|
| 4.3.1 | Benefits Realization Governance Roles |
| 4.3.2 | Program and Project Management Roles |
| 4.3.3 | Benefits Ownership Roles |

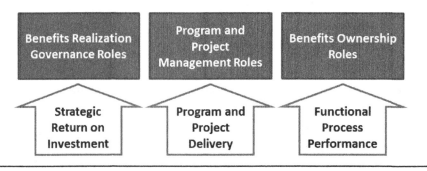

**Figure 4-7** Three main groups of roles involved in benefits realization management.

## 4.3.1 Benefits Realization Governance Roles

This first subsection identifies some roles that are directly involved in the governance of benefits realization. These are basically portfolio, program, and project governance roles, which are responsible for executive leadership, strategic alignment, prioritization, and funding of programs and projects. These are roles can be also directly involved with the governance of strategy execution in broader terms and with project portfolio management. As Benefits Realization Management is a common element that links all areas of the business, this group may include senior representatives from all business areas. In addition, it also includes a set of supporting roles that support the senior executives in making strategic decisions, in managing performance, and in managing change on steering level.

Benefits realization governance roles in an organization can be identified in a number of organizational positions—for example, CEO, Management Board, Portfolio Governance Board, Project Portfolio Management (PPM) Governance Council, Portfolio Board, Steering Group, Sponsoring Group, Project Sponsors, Office of Strategic Management, and Business Change Manager. The next topics break down benefits realization governance roles into the two most common subgroups found in organizations in general.

### Executive Leadership Roles

The executive leadership roles include a number of senior lever individual, which are in the highest hierarchical level of an organization, such as Chief Executive Officers, Chief Financial Officers, Chief Operating Officers, and Chief Information Officers. These are key people that accountable for the successful execution of an organization's business strategy.

- **Senior Executive Board (CEO, CFO, COO, CIO, etc.).** Executive leadership plays an important management role, defining strategy, communicating, supporting the implementations, and being aware of strategic changes (Kaplan and Norton 2008). The CEO and the Senior Executive Board are responsible for seeing the big picture and then for creating business strategies, supported by people working closer to the daily routine (Amason 2011). They are responsible for integrating the business in order to execute the plan and generate value for their customers (Amason 2011). Moreover, since the strategy can be deliberate and emergent, rather than planned by a traditional approach, the executives should be aware of the necessity to continually review and adapt their plans in order to maintain their validity in a constantly changing environment (Amason 2011).

## Project, Program, and Portfolio Steering Roles

The project program and portfolio steering roles include the roles responsible for directly steering the management of projects, programs, and portfolios. These roles mostly approve funding for programs and projects, sign off the business cases, and ensure the return on the investment. Because of that, these roles are directly responsible for the governance of projects, programs, and portfolios.

- **Portfolio Governance Board.** The Portfolio Governance Board (Kendall and Rollins 2003), which is also known as Project Portfolio Management (PPM) Governance Council (Levine 2005), or the Portfolio Board, Steering Group, or Sponsoring Group (Bradley 2010), is a group that can be created just below the Senior Executive Board level, with the responsibility for making key decisions on the project portfolio.

  Senior executives or their representatives take part in this group (Bradley 2010, Kendall and Rollins 2003; Levine 2005). They meet regularly to make decisions usually related to approving new projects, authorizing initiation, deactivating projects, terminating projects, or prioritizing and reallocating resources (Kendall and Rollins 2003). They can request information about projects and should communicate relevant information (Kendall and Rollins 2003).

- **Project Sponsorship.** The project sponsors are usually responsible for initiating and funding each project (PMI® 2013a) representing the organization (APM 2012). They can be considered as the closest representatives of business leadership that each project has. More than providing funding, senior business managers usually have a deep knowledge about the strategic plan and are accountable for its execution. Therefore, attention from middle and top managers is required to manage the link between the business strategies and programs projects (Gray and Larson 2010). Because of that, business sponsors or senior responsible owners are ultimately accountable for the achievement of benefits (Bradley 2010), even when they are not assigned to the role of *benefit owner*, which will be discussed in another section of this book.

## Strategy Management Roles

Strategy management roles provide support in planning and managing the execution of business strategies.

- **Strategy Management Office.** Corporate headquarters approve and integrate local strategies from different business and service areas, because they are cascaded components of the corporate strategy (Kaplan and Norton 2008). Organizations often have employees or even entire departments (in large organizations) that are fully or partially dedicated to support the strategy planning process, as well as strategic alignment between different areas of the business. Similarly, these same teams involved in strategic planning also track the execution of business strategies by overseeing the performance of the various business processes affected by the business strategies.

These teams can be allocated to an organization department usually called a Strategy Management Office (or Office of Strategy Management). Typically, organizations that have implemented such a new unit at a corporate level have managed to sustain their strategy focus throughout the strategy execution process, not limiting their efforts mainly to strategy planning (Kaplan and Norton 2005). A Strategy Management Office is responsible for the philosophy of performance management, for ensuring the execution of the processes needed to manage the strategy, and for ensuring the integration between different areas and the strategy (Kaplan and Norton 2008). The membership of a Strategy Management Office can include a strategy management manager, strategy management officers, strategy management advisors, and others depending on the structure and size of the organization.

## Business Management Support Roles

Another group of roles that is involved in providing support to the governance of benefits realization is composed of roles involved in supporting business management. Although these roles will most times not have ownership over the business processes and their improvement, they provide the means to design, implement, control, and improve business process all across the organization. In many cases, they will also monitor performance of existing processes toward the achievement of predefined business process performance goals. Therefore, these roles are instrumental and influential in identifying the need for change, as well as in monitoring the benefits that result from any strategic change implemented to existing processes.

- **Business Process Management Office.** Business process management roles support organizations to perform strategically-aligned creations of value according to their value chains. They do so by applying a systematic approach to an organization's work flow in order to increase its effectiveness and efficiency. They also aim to make organizations capable of adapting fast and effectively to an ever-changing environment. These activities include planning business processes, assisting the implementation of new business processes, and perhaps more importantly having an active role in supporting business process optimization. They support the identification of options and solutions and ensure the overall fit of any new processes into the organizational business architecture. Therefore, this function supports the implementation and embedding of any change to existing business processes.

- **Business Performance Management Office.** Business performance management roles support organizations in managing their performance toward the achievement of strategic objectives. They do so by applying management and analytic processes. Different from the business process management roles, business performance management roles focus on the management of the performance of existing processes. These roles manage organizational KPIs to identify variations in business process performance against planned service levels. The management of performance supports the achievement of business objectives by ensuring that the existing processes meet their targets. This role provides information to decision-making boards regarding needs or opportunities for improvement. It also supports the benefits realization processes by measuring the performance of new or improved business process and then providing input to benefits monitoring and controlling.

## Organizational Change Supporting Roles

Organizational change supporting roles provide support to the organization in managing change. These can vary significantly from one organization to another in terms of the approach taken and the depth of involvement with programs and projects.

- **Business Change Management.** The business change manager is a key role, reporting to program managers the responsibility of the senior managers of the affected business areas and being responsible for providing support to benefits realization (Chittenden and Bon 2006), by coordinating business changes (Bradley 2010) and incorporating the new capabilities in the routine of the organization (OGC 2011b).

  The role can be performed by a business change manager, business change officers, or business change advisors, depending on the structure and size of the organization.

- **Project, Program, and Portfolio Management Office (PMO).** PMO is normally an acronym for Project Management Office, but it can also represent a Program Management Office and/or a Portfolio Management

Office. Sometimes the PMO will fulfill the roles of all three. The PMO can work on monitoring projects and reporting to the Portfolio Governance Board (Levine 2005). Apart from the reporting role, it may also have an important role in executing a number of project portfolio management activities. Because of that, it performs a pivotal role in supporting the Benefits Realization Management process.

Nevertheless, it is important to keep in mind that the role of a PMO can vary between several different models (Hill 2004; Kendall and Rollins 2003; Kerzner 2003). Therefore, each organization has to find the most appropriate PMO model to support its program and project delivery. In addition, it is suggested that the PMO and the Corporate Governance Office have different approaches to what is more important in a project; the first should focus on project management issues, and the second on the business (Levine 2005). As a result, these two complement each other, one by focusing on program and project delivery and the other by focusing on creation of strategic value to the business.

This role can be performed by a PMO manager, PMO officers, PMO analyst, and PMO administrators, depending on the structure and size of the organization.

- **Enterprise Benefits Realization Management Office.** Another business function that is still not commonly found in organizations but can be instrumental to the implementations and execution of Benefits Realization Management practices is an Enterprise Benefits Realization Management (eBRM) function. An Enterprise Benefits Realization Management Office (eBRMO) is basically a department or part of a department—such as a corporate level PMO—composed of a group of specialists in benefits management.

  The eBRMO works in a similar way to a business performance management department; however, instead of managing business process performance, it manages the performance of the execution of the enterprise Benefits Realization Strategy. These roles can work on an organizational level, divisional level, departmental level, or program level.

  Several roles can be part of this group, for example:

  ○ *Benefits Realization Management Managers* are responsible for overseeing the end-to-end benefits realization lifecycle for a project, program or, more likely, portfolio, and manages the other roles listed below.

  ○ *Benefits Realization Management Leads, Analysts or Advisors* are responsible for benefits analysis and control and provide support and guidance to other roles on the benefits realization process.

- *Benefits Realization Management Administrators* provide administrative support in benefits measurement and control.
- *Benefits Management Consultants* perform any of the roles above and/or provide advice and support to the eBRM function and/or to the business.

All the roles above work on ensuring that benefits are aligned to the organizational or departmental strategic objectives, supporting the production of benefits profiles, supporting benefits definition, identifying an appropriate means of measurement, tracking benefits utilizing appropriate tools and techniques, supporting development and continuous improvement of the Benefits Realization Strategies, and supporting benefits realization.

## 4.3.2 Program and Project Management Roles

This second subsection identifies some roles that are directly involved in the actual delivery of outputs and outcomes that are expected from programs and projects. Additionally, program and project management roles are responsible for delivering the required outputs, satisfying the stakeholders' needs, being aware of the project success criteria, and maintaining the alignment between the project plans and their ability to meet the stakeholders' expectations. These roles are responsible for enabling change and, therefore, for making benefits realization achievable.

Although the program and project management roles are extremely important, they do not participate in the process throughout the entire benefit realization life cycle. Their work usually starts after the organizational level benefits planning, which provides means to the investment in the program or project.

Program and project management roles into an organization can be identified in a number of organizational positions, for example: program manager, program management team member, project manager, and project management team member. The next topics break down the Program and Project Management roles into the two most common subgroups found in organizations in general.

### Project Management Roles

Project management roles are responsible for project delivery, or in other words for the execution of the project strategy.

- **Project Management.** Project managers are responsible for managing the project and the project team, which undertake the project work

(Buttrick 1997). They should understand the strategy of the organization in order to be able to evaluate and demonstrate how their projects can deliver value (Gary and Larson 2010). Project team members and stakeholders need to understand the relevance and priority of a project's outcomes based on their value for the execution of business strategy (Gary and Larson 2010). Full understanding about the expected outcomes is fundamental in order to ensure their delivery.

The involvement of project management roles in benefits realization typically ends after project delivery, mostly at project closeout. Therefore, they often do not have the opportunity to experience the actual realization of benefits. In summary, they usually plan a benefit realization process, which will not executed by them, of a benefit—typically one in which they have not been involved with the identification. As a result, it is important to make these roles fully aware of the rationale behind each benefit and also on all interfaces and dependencies associated with its realization.

- **IS/IT Project Management.** In IS/IT projects, the project management roles may be split between the business and the IS/IT team by having a business project manager responsible for the business change and an IS/IT project manager or project lead responsible for the solution development and delivery (Ward and Daniel 2012). A similar scenario can be applicable to other disciplines in which the business change is managed by the business and the solution development is delivered by a separate team or department.

## Program Management Roles

Similar to the project management roles but on another level, program management roles are responsible for program delivery: in other words, for the execution of the program strategy.

- **Program Management.** The program manager should manage the day-to-day activities of the program, ensuring that all projects' deliveries are meeting the program's requirements (OGC 2011b). The program manager is also responsible for planning and implementing the stakeholders' engagement strategy (Chittendon and Bon 2006), which is extremely important to ensure the continuous alignment of expectations between multiple project teams and other program stakeholders.

  Those who serve in program management roles often find that they realize benefits that can last much longer than their involvement in the specific role. PMI® (2013c), for example, recommends a program to include activities for benefits delivery and transition, which take place before program closeout. These activities cover part of the benefits realization lifecycle and are designed to ensure the effective handover of the benefits realization activities to the business operations. Since the program management plan includes activities to manage part of the benefits realization life cycle and the effective handover of benefits realization activities to operations (PMI® 2013c), the program manager and the program's stakeholders are responsible for managing benefits and the enabling their realization (Chittenden and Bon 2006).

However, this is an approach that has been evolving in the last decade or so, and therefore its adoption by organizations may still vary. Some organizations may consider benefits realization to be out of the remit of program management teams and to be a set of activities assigned to other organizational departments, for example to business change departments or business performance management departments.

### 4.3.3 Benefits Ownership Roles

This third and last subsection identifies some roles that own benefits and therefore are directly involved in the actual identification, planning, and realization of benefits. These roles should be involved in the benefit realization management process very early, from the definition of program and project strategies to the end of the realization of all expected benefits. They can provide input to the strategic planning process, by identifying required or desired changes to the day-to-day business processes as well as identifying benefits that are desirable and achievable in relation to their areas of expertise within the organization or that are external to the organizational environment.

Throughout the program and project delivery processes, benefit owners are responsible for receiving project outputs and then starting the realization of the required benefits. Different from the roles involved in program and project management, the benefit owners' work will most of the time have its emphasis after the end of program and project delivery life cycles.

Whenever project outputs are delivered incrementally during the project lifecycle, the responsibilities for benefits realization have to be clearly described in the benefits realization strategy. When working fully independently from business as usual (BAU) operations, the project manager may have responsibility for benefits realization during the project life cycle. Another option is to hand over benefits incrementally to the benefit owner. The strategy to be adopted in these cases will depend on the characteristics of the project and on the structure of the organization.

Benefits ownership roles in an organization can be identified in a number of organizational positions, for example: heads of department and senior business managers, top and middle managers and functional leads, business sponsors, senior responsible owners, and program and project customers. The next topic discusses in more details the benefits ownership roles in association with their more common occurrence in an organizational structure, which is as a functional management role.

### Functional Management Roles

- **Benefit Owner.** A key point to ensure the achievement of the desired benefits is to define clear and individual ownership of benefits (OGC 2011b; Chittenden and Bon 2006). Since benefits are often expected to be realized by business operations (Ward and Daniel 2012), ideally one person in the business area that is affected by the changes should be accountable for successful benefits delivery (OGC 2011b). This role can be called benefit owner (Bradley 2010). More often than not, program and project customers (people who receive the project outputs) have the responsibility to ensure that the outputs delivered by projects or programs will realize the required benefits.

  Benefits owners may not exactly be program and project customers; rather, they are operational or support groups in the organization that will receive project outputs and then be responsible for the realization of expected benefits. In these cases, the formalization of their responsibilities is very important. Although a senior executive or senior manager may be assigned to become the benefit owner, the responsibility for the realization of the expected benefits should be cascaded to the appropriate level, so that there is ownership in place to enable effective control.

## 4.4 Case Study: Benefits Realization Management at ProjectEng Civil Engineering Services Ltd.

Throughout the second part of this book, a case study will exemplify most of the concepts to be presented and discussed. At the end of each chapter the reader will find a case study section featuring examples associated with the contents of that chapter. The case study analyzes the strategy execution process of ProjectEng, a global organization that can be considered as a newcomer into the Benefits Realization Management environment (see Table 4-2). The case study will follow the steps recommended by this book to the implementation and execution of an eBRS. The utilization of some templates will be exemplified throughout the case

**Table 4-2 ProjectEng Fact Sheet**

| Fact Sheet: ProjectEng Civil Engineering Services Ltd. |
| --- |
| • *Organization:* ProjectEng Civil Engineering Services Ltd. |
| • *Market:* Infrastructure, Building and Construction |
| • *Geographies:* 37 countries spread across 4 regions: Americas, Europe, Africa/Middle-East, and Asia-Pacific |
| • *Headquarters:* New Jersey, United States |
| • *Services:* Civil infrastructure, oil and gas, chemicals, power and mining |
| • *Divisions:* Sales and marketing, project delivery, managed services, procurement and logistics, business support, information systems, shared services |
| • *Number of employees:* 6,383 direct employees |
| • *Number of project managers:* 220 |
| • *Total revenue:* US $5.2 billion (2015)<br>  ○ *Revenue in the European Market:* US $1.5 billion<br>  ○ *Revenue in the American Market:* US $1.8 billion<br>  ○ *Revenue in the Asia-Pacific Market:* US $1 billion<br>  ○ *Revenue in the African and Middle Eastern Markets:* US $0.9 billion |
| • *Total Operating Costs:* US $4.8 billion. |

study to support the understanding of the process. The information used to fill in the templates is detailed enough to enable to understanding of the process, although more detailed information may be required in a real-life situation.

Although the case study happens within a fictional organization, the examples described are recreations of real-life situations observed within several different organizations. To ensure the anonymity of the organizations, the case study uses fictional parameters and nomenclatures for all the examples given.

This first case study section introduces ProjectEng to the reader by describing the business environment and strategic context for the case study, providing the basic characteristics of the organization and describing its current scenario, which is driving it towards the development of Benefits Realization Management capability. After that, it describes the way ProjectEng is going to enhance its maturity in Benefits Realization Management by developing and applying an Enterprise Benefits Realization Strategy, associated to a Benefits Realization Management framework. These new practices are expected to enhance the levels of project success and consequently improve the budgetary efficiency of the business.

| Subsection | Subject |
|------------|---------|
| 4.4.1 | Organization Profile |
| 4.4.2 | Planning the Enhancement of Benefits Realization Management Maturity |
| 4.4.3 | Developing a Benefits Realization Management Framework |
| 4.4.4 | Developing an Enterprise Benefits Realization Strategy (Step 1) |

## 4.4.1 Organization Profile

Our case study takes place at ProjectEng Civil Engineering Services Ltd., a large organization with global presence in the infrastructure, building, and construction market. It operates across 37 countries spread across all continents. The work is delivered to clients mostly through projects or managed services, which have their management broken down by regions and business streams. In the financial year of 2015 (from January 1, 2015, to December 31, 2015) ProjectEng recorded total revenue of US $5.2 billion, employing around 6,000 people.

In 1935, ProjectEng started its activities in New Jersey, in the United States, focusing only on the local market. The company expanded initially through the U.S. east coast and later to the west coast. In the second half of the 20th century, it rapidly expanded, initially to Europe and then later to the Middle East and North Africa, boosted by reconstruction efforts after World War II and a series of infrastructure contracts with local governments. In the last two decades of the 20th century, the company expanded to Asia and Australia, being heavily involved in the construction of shipyards, manufacturing plants, and power systems.

### Strategy Execution Environment

Since ProjectEng delivers most of its services to external clients through programs and projects, the clients' success is fundamental to business success. Apart from the management of revenue-generating programs and projects, program and project management are also utilized all across the business to manage change.

The strategy execution within ProjectEng is managed by a hierarchical structure of nine PMOs that are responsible for overseeing both investment projects and revenue-generating projects. In terms of project management capabilities, ProjectEng has 220 professional project managers working on revenue-generating projects and on investment projects. It has also more than 400 staff working on diverse project management support roles across the

**Table 4-3 ProjectEng: Summary of the Strategy Execution Environment**

| ProjectEng: Summary of the Strategy Execution Environment |
| --- |
| • *Number of Project, Programs and Portfolio Management Offices (PMOs):* 9 |
| • *Number of project managers:* 230 |
| • *Number of project management support staff:* over 400 |
| • *Level of overall maturity:* Unknown, but expected to be high in some divisions, low in others |
| • *Project Management Information Systems:* Three different solutions; two are off-the-shelf software, and one is in-house developed software |

business, including planners, controllers, PMO officers, PMO managers, project quality analysts, and project finance analysts, among others.

To support effective program and project delivery, the organization has a PMO hierarchy, as described below (also see Table 4-3):

1. A *Project Management Center of Excellence* is the policy maker regarding project management best practices, project management tools and technology, and project management competence development. It sits under the chief finance officer's structure, aiming to provide best practices and tools to ensure creation of value and return on investment through the application of a standard set service delivery and strategy execution best practices.

2. An *Enterprise PMO* is the central hub of information and governance. It works alongside the strategic management department and the corporate investment department to ensure the successful execution of business strategies, as well as the achievement of the expected targets in terms of return on investment and in terms of revenue from external projects. It sits under the chief finance officer's structure because of its strategic characteristics in ensuring that projects generate value to the business and provide the expected return on investment. Its team works very closely with the project management center of excellence to ensure the development and application of the best set of practices all across the business.

3. An *IS/IT PMO* supports the Software Development, IT Infrastructure and the Service Desk departments, being responsible for project management as well as service-level management, resource management, and the enforcement of the service delivery framework, in addition to the Information Technology Infrastructure Library (ITIL) best practices.

4. A *shared services' PMO* supports projects within the shared services division, which includes HR, infrastructure, procurement, accounting, and finance.

Table 4-4  ProjectEng's Mission Statement

| ProjectEng: Mission Statement |
| --- |
| To deliver world-class civil engineering services with focus on innovative solutions and services by applying high-end technology in infrastructure and construction. |

Table 4-5  ProjectEng's Vision Statement

| ProjectEng: Vision Statement |
| --- |
| To be the global market lead in innovative solutions with application of new technologies and materials for the infrastructure and construction sector. |

5. Four *regional PMOs* cover the operations in the three regions where the organization has activities Americas, Europe, Africa/Middle-East, and Asia-Pacific.

6. A *PMO* supports an ongoing, long-term business change program called "Redefine-ProjectEng" by providing administrative support to the program and reporting.

## Mission, Vision, and Strategic Leadership

The organization brands itself as a provider of innovative high-end infrastructure and construction technology solutions and services. It aims to be the global market lead in the application of new technologies and materials for the provision of solutions and services to the infrastructure and construction sector.

ProjectEng has a Senior Executive Board composed of the senior directors of each of its divisions. Once a year, the Senior Executive Board meets to review the performance during the previous years and to revise the business strategy for the following years.

Tables 4.4 and 4.5 present ProjectEng's mission and vision statements.

## 4.4.2 Planning the Enhancement of Benefits Realization Management Maturity

To achieve the business objective of operational excellence, the Senior Executive Board identified the need for more robust Benefits Realization Management practices to enhance the efficiency and effectiveness of the strategy execution projects. The Enterprise PMO was assigned the responsibility to implement this change initiative. An eBRM Maturity Enhancement Strategy template, available in *Appendix C* of this book, is employed to exemplify the way the initiative was planned. The first step of the process is the identification of the owner of this plan, which in this case is the Enterprise PMO Director, John Johnson. The approver of the plan is another important stakeholder, Michael Clark, ProjectEng's CFO.

The next step is the clarification about the rationale and background for the initiative. It is important to make the reasons behind the execution of the initiative clear, so that all stakeholders can recognize why the work is being done. Another important point is the definition of the objectives of the initiative that in this case are directly associated with efficiency and effectiveness—clearly aiming to achieve higher cost efficiency.

Having defined the objectives, the next step is determining the approach to be adopted to achieve the objectives.

In *Appendix C,* the templates provided in this chapter are completed for this case study example. The high-level approach suggested in the template is followed, which splits the initiative into five consecutive stages: planning, implementation, stabilization, handover, and closeout. In addition, the strategies regarding Management of Change and Risks, Assumptions, Issues, and Dependencies (RAID) management are described in a following section.

The document provides the key items of a high-level strategy for the enhancement of the Benefits Realization Management practices. It can be expanded and then transformed into a complete project management plan by including other sections such as budget, schedule, and other plans (e.g., a communications plan, stakeholder engagement plan, quality management plan, etc.). It can also have the information detailed into a more in-depth level, if needed.

### 4.4.3 Developing a Benefits Realization Management Framework

As described in the Enterprise Benefits Realization Management—Maturity Enhancement Strategy, one of the key deliverables of the initiative for the implementation of more effective Benefits Realization Management practices is the development of an eBRMF. This collection of theory, terminology, definitions, processes, and templates includes processes to define the annual Benefits Realization Strategy, as well as processes for benefits planning, realization, and review and measuring. It includes also a measures dictionary, which identifies all appropriate measures that are available for benefits tracking across the organization. *Appendix D* of this book includes blank templates for the development of the Benefits Realization Management Framework and the Measures Dictionary.

### 4.4.4 Developing an Enterprise Benefits Realization Strategy (Step 1)

In accordance with its Benefits Realization Management Framework and organizational policies, ProjectEng reviews its eBRS (Enterprise Benefits Realization Strategy) every quarter, with a full review taking place once a year, prior to the beginning of the next financial year (which happens in July). This process ensures the frequent review of priorities and therefore the appropriate review of expected realized benefits according to any changes to the key business drivers. Reviewing this strategy is crucial to support the decision to sustain investment on projects that are currently under execution and to start a new project. As a result of the quarterly review process, projects can be delayed, canceled, put on hold, or have their start date pushed forward.

In the same way as happened with the Benefits Realization Management maturity enhancement strategy (discussed in a previous session), the first step for the preparation of an eBRS is the assignment of the correct ownership to it. In this case, the strategy was again issued by John Johnson, enterprise PMO director, because his team has the necessary business analysis and project portfolio management skills to liaise with the strategic management team in order to identify the best set of alternatives to achieve the strategic objectives defined by the Senior Executive Board. The strategy was approved by Michael Clark, chief financial officer, since the enterprise PMO sits under his structure based on ProjectEng's views of the strong link between project governance and corporate governance from the perspective of ensuring that projects will enable the organization to provide return on investment to its shareholders, both via revenue-generating projects and investment projects.

For the 2015–2016 strategy review cycle, ProjectEng has five key business objectives derived from its strategic drivers described above: (1) market diversification, (2) operational excellence, (3) professional registration, (4) knowledge management, and (5) internal training.

Based on the strategic drivers, strategic objectives were defined by the Senior Executive Board as part of the strategic planning process. Although this process happened outside of the scope of Benefits Realization Management, the summary information about the key drivers and the strategic objectives is extremely relevant to provide rationale to the rapid and appropriate realignment in case the situation changes.

The achievement of the strategic objectives can be measured by the realization of some end benefits. A general rule of thumb suggests that around three KPIs should be associated with each strategic objective in order to enable the evaluation of their achievement. These same KPIs can be also applicable measures for the success criteria associated with any strategic initiatives that are intending to support the achievement of a strategic objective. However, our case study has only one KPI associated with each strategic objective. The relationship between benefits and strategic objectives is identified by applying techniques such as benefits mapping, which was discussed in the previous chapter and will be described in more depth in the next chapter.

In *Appendix C,* a template provided in this chapter is completed for this case study example. This is the first step of the development of a Benefits Realization Management strategy. At this point, Sections I to III are completed. Sections IV to VIII will be updated after benefits mapping, which will be explained in the next chapter. This first draft of a Benefits Realization Management strategy is a key input to the identification of benefits, and its production continues in the next chapter.

## 4.5 Chapter Summary: Establishing the Environment for Benefits Realization

A Benefits Realization Strategy is required to enable effective management of project benefits, ensuring that all the financial resources employed aim to support the execution of the business strategy. Some key practices (Serra and Kunc 2015) discussed in this chapter are focused on ensuring the effectiveness of benefits realization, which is instrumental for effective project governance and consequently in supporting project success (see Table 4-6).

Three key groups of roles are directly involved in Benefits Realization Management activities within an organization (see Table 4-7).

**Table 4-6 Key Benefits Realization Management Practices to Support Project Success: Developing and Implementing Benefits Realization Management Strategies**

| Governance Process | Benefits Realization Management Process | Benefits Realization Management Key Practice |
|---|---|---|
| Aligning strategies of change | Developing and implementing an eBRS | A Benefits Realization Strategy supported by a Benefits Realization Management framework provides a main set of strategic drivers as well as standard processes and tools to be applied throughout the entire organization. |

Adapted from Serra, C. E. *Benefits Realisation Management and Its Influence on Project Success, Project Governance, and Execution of Business Strategy: Analysis of Brazil, the United Kingdom, and the United States of America.* Coventry, UK: University of Warwick (2012); and Serra, C. E. and M. Kunc. "Benefits Realisation Management and its influence on project success and on the execution of business strategies." *International Journal of Project Management* 33(1) 2015. (Used with permission.)

**Table 4-7 Organizational Roles Responsible for Key Benefits Realization Management Practices**

| Group of Roles | Description | Subgroups | Roles |
|---|---|---|---|
| Portfolio, Program, and Project Governance | Perform the required executive leadership, establishing strategic alignment, providing program and project support and prioritization, and then ensuring program and project success. | • Executive Leadership Roles | • Senior Executive Board |
| | | • Project, Program and Portfolio Steering roles | • Portfolio Governance Board<br>• Project Sponsorship |
| | | • Strategy Management Roles | • Strategy Management Office |
| | | • Business Management Support Roles | • Business Process Management Office<br>• Business Performance Management Office |
| | | • Organizational Change Supporting Roles | • Business Change Management<br>• PMO<br>• Enterprise Benefits Realization Management Office |
| Program and Project Management | Responsible for delivering the required outputs in order to satisfy their stakeholders' needs.<br><br>They are required to be aware of their program's or project's success criteria, and should then maintain the alignment between the program or project and the expectations, in order to ensure program or project success. | • Project Management Roles | • Project Management<br>• IS/IT Project Management |
| | | • Program Management Roles | • Program Management |
| Benefits Owners | Receive project outputs and then are accountable for delivering the required benefits. They are usually business managers. | • Functional Management Roles | • Benefit Owner |

Data derived from Serra, C. E. *Benefits Realisation Management and Its Influence on Project Success, Project Governance, and Execution of Business Strategy: Analysis of Brazil, the United Kingdom, and the United States of America.* Coventry, UK: University of Warwick. 2012.

The process of planning benefits includes the set of activities discussed in this chapter and produces a series of outputs that can be also called management products:

### eBRS Implementation or Enhancement Strategies

- Benefits Realization Management Implementation Strategy
- Benefits Realization Management Enhancement Strategy

### eBRS and Benefits Realization Management Framework

- Benefits Realization Management Framework
- Measures Dictionary
- eBRS: Enterprise Benefits Realization Management

The next chapters present a general framework for managing benefits delivery, including some tools and techniques. Organizations may apply all or only some of them by using their own definitions and processes.

## 4.6 End-of-Chapter Review Questions—Chapter 4

In this section, a set of end-of-chapter review questions are provided to enable a self-assessment of the understanding of Chapter 4. The answers to all questions can be found at the end of the book in *Appendix A*.

1. List five different strategies associated with the achievement of strategic objectives.
2. Do both large and small projects require governance? Why?
3. What types of strategies can be applied to establish the environment for benefits realization? What are the different scenarios which require these different strategies?
4. List and describe the three groups of roles involved in Benefits Realization Management within an organization.

# Chapter 5

## Planning Benefits

This chapter discusses the activities associated with the preparation needed before executing any changes required to realize the expected benefits. These pre-execution steps are needed to different extents in portfolio, program, and project levels. Throughout this chapter, a set of Benefits Realization Management practices is introduced, and the link between these activities and the project, program, and portfolio management processes is established.

First, an introduction briefly discusses the way these practices are integrated with project governance. The second section presents the steps required to the complete understanding of each of the expected benefits, which are identified through a discovery and analysis process that starts with the business strategy drivers defined and described in the Enterprise Benefits Realization Strategy (eBRS). The third section focuses on the steps that follow after identifying the expected benefits that will enable achievement of business objectives. At that point, a project portfolio is composed by identifying, appraising, and selecting programs and projects that will be responsible for delivering the outputs, outcomes, and changes that will enable the realization of the expected benefits. In the last section, the key points of this chapter are summarized.

## 5.1 Introduction: Composing Portfolios of Initiatives

The changes required to execute business strategies have to be identified, defined, and classified in order to be appraised. Based on the results of the appraisal, they are selected and prioritized for execution. Although several techniques are available to support these activities as part of project portfolio management, the following sections present an overview of the key steps that are closely linked to Benefits Realization Management. These steps are fundamental to establish the links between Project Governance and further Benefits Realization Management practices, and then to provide the necessary inputs to enable a controlled and effective process to realize the expected benefits. Therefore, some of the steps required to compose a cohesive and effective portfolio are presented in topics in this chapter.

## 5.2 Translating Business Strategy Drivers into Expected Benefits

Planning benefits is the first step to implementing any Benefits Realization Strategy. It uses inputs from the Benefits Realization Strategy discussed in the previous chapter. The first step of benefits planning is the process of identifying the expected benefits to be later realized. To do so, it starts from the organizational drivers.

After the organizational drivers are analyzed, a number of techniques can be employed to identify the ways to address the existing issues and to exploit the opportunities, as previously discussed in Chapter 2. As an example, Ward and Daniel (2012) suggest a framework that associates business drivers with investment objectives and then to organizational issues that may affect the portfolio of change initiatives (see Figure 5-1). This framework makes clear that projects are investments, and as such, they have objectives that are driven towards business drivers. The drivers can be internal or external and dictate how the budget will be invested. Organizational issues feed into this mix as the existing hurdles for the achievement of the business drivers and, therefore, will have to be resolved by the projects, so that the business drivers can be achieved. In such context, any project that is not linked to the achievement of one or more business drivers will not have a credible business case and therefore tend to have low priority.

**Figure 5-1**  Framework for drivers and objectives analysis. (*Source:* Adapted from Ward, J. and E. Daniel. *Benefits Management: How to Increase the Business Value of Your IT Projects*, 2nd ed. Chichester, UK: John Wiley & Sons Ltd. 2012.)

By drilling down from the organizational drivers, business objectives, and changes required to achieve the objectives, ideas of initiatives are identified to enable the changes or even to directly achieve the business objectives. On another route, ideas generated on operational level can be linked to the achievement of business objectives. The better way, though, to link initiatives to the achievement business objectives is to identify benefits associated to each element of that network.

The identification process covers all the steps from producing and analyzing benefits dependency networks (also known as benefit maps or benefit chains), to classifying benefits, defining measures and targets to be achieved, and then creating benefit profiles to capture all the information associated with each and every single benefit that organizational leaders expect to realize. The results of these activities reveal how much each project contributes to the achievement of the organizational goals and will later feed directly into the process described in Section 5.3 regarding project identification, definition, classification, appraisal, selection, and prioritization.

| Subsection | Subject |
|:----------:|---------|
| 5.2.1 | Identifying Benefits |
| 5.2.2 | Mapping Benefits |
| 5.2.3 | Creating Benefits Matrixes |
| 5.2.4 | Classifying Benefits |
| 5.2.5 | Setting Benefits Measures and Targets |
| 5.2.6 | Defining Benefits Ownership |
| 5.2.7 | Creating Benefit Profiles |

## 5.2.1 Identifying Benefits

After having identified the strategic drivers that motivate the business in the implementation of its strategy and also some of the change initiatives that are required, it is time to identify the benefits to be expected from each change initiative. During this process, new strategic initiatives may be suggested or required to enhance the business's potential to achieve benefits or even to enable the business to achieve additional required benefits. Some of the initiatives will be implemented by adopting a program management approach and others—usually the less complex or smaller ones—by adopting a project management approach. Regardless of whether a program or a project is used, all change initiatives will have benefits associated with them, so their contribution to the business can be appraised and later evaluated. To enable the pre-project appraisal and post-project evaluation, each change initiative must be understood as an investment, which consequently aims to achieve investment objectives. Therefore, one or more benefits will be expected to be realized as a consequence of the change, and the financial value of these benefits will be expected to repay the investment made.

For the business changes associated with improvements on the performance of existing processes, the benefits of those changes can be easily associated with existing performance measures, which will be later employed to support the business case for the investment. The benefits dictionary or measures dictionary, discussed in the previous chapter, are useful tools that are part of the Enterprise Benefits Realization Management Framework (eBRMF).

Some changes will be associated with processes that are not currently monitored or do not exist. Business changes that are associated with creating new capabilities for the business may not be associated with existing performance measures, and then new measures will have to be identified before the performance of the process can be managed. Every time a new measure is created, it must be added to the dictionary; otherwise, there is a risk of ending up with an outdated dictionary (Bradley 2010).

In addition to these two types, there are compliance initiatives, which usually deliver benefits associated with risk avoidance. These initiatives ensure the continuity of the business in face of drivers that are out of the organization's control but that might affect the ability of the business to carry on its operations.

External projects, which are also called client-facing projects or revenue-generating projects, basically deliver outputs and outcomes to some entity outside of the organization. In these cases, benefits are usually associated with the financial income of profit to be made as a result of the work performed. Apart from financial benefits, other benefits can also be associated with this type of initiative; in most cases they will be associated with marketing performance measures, such as brand value, market share, and client retention.

All four types of initiatives are part of an organization's portfolio, and all four have to be taken into consideration during benefits identification. Although the four types have different objectives, they can deliver the same or similar benefits and will frequently share organizational resources. Therefore, except for compliance projects, which are usually not optional, the projects for the other three types will typically compete for prioritization, funds, and resources. Some of the next subsections will discuss ways to assess and compare the value associated with each project, so that a project portfolio can be prioritized in an efficient and effective way.

## 5.2.2 Mapping Benefits

After having identified the expected benefits, they are mapped, identifying then the relationships between them according to the business strategy (as explained in Section 3.2). The benefits map shows the desired business objectives and then all end benefits, intermediate benefits, business changes, and project outputs or enablers (OGC 2011b). In addition, it can support the design of a schedule for the benefits realization plan (OGC 2011b).

There are two suggested ways to develop a benefits map: top-down mapping and bottom-up mapping (Melton et al. 2008). The first approach recommended is top-down mapping, identifying the top levels of the benefits hierarchy and thus making it easier to later expand the main benefits tree by aggregating additional elements in a bottom-up analysis.

### Top-Down Benefits Mapping

Ideally, the benefits mapping should start from the strategic objectives, going through the identification of the required benefits, business changes, and enablers (Bradley 2010; OGC 2011b). The enablers are the project outputs, which enable a business change or the realization of benefits. In turn, the business change creates outcomes that prepare operations to realize benefits, and may even realize those benefits straight away. In top-down mapping, organizational goals should be broken down until the last steps are reached, which are identified benefits and their associated measures (Melton et al. 2008). The first step is the identification of end benefits associated with the achievement of a strategic objective (see Figure 5-2). These end benefits are identified on an organizational level, become part of the enterprise Benefits Realization

**Figure 5-2**    Benefits mapping: Top-down first step—end benefits.

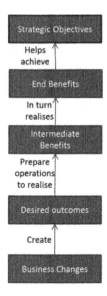

**Figure 5-3**    Benefits mapping: Top-down second step—outcomes and business changes.

Management (eBRM) strategy and are unlikely to change until the strategic objectives are achieved or until the business strategies change because of changes to the strategic drivers.

The next step is to identify the business changes and desired outcomes that enable operations to realize the end benefits (see Figure 5-3). However, as previously discussed, end benefits may not be achieved immediately from the outcomes of business changes. Typically, they require a combination of changes and outcomes. Then intermediate benefits that are associated with the realization of end benefits will be also identified during this step. They are likely to change or to be identified later, during other steps of the benefits planning process, because benefits mapping is an iterative process that requires constant review of the entire map whenever new benefits are identified and may impact on other benefits previously added to the map. This main route to achieve strategic objectives should be incorporated into the eBRM strategy. It will become the main route map and a baseline for strategy execution.

The last step is identifying outputs that will be delivered by programs and projects to enable the business changes. Projects will most times deliver outputs and then hand over the further steps of the benefits realization life cycle to the benefits owner as part of the regular business operations. In turn, programs will usually also manage the business changes, ensure the creation of the expected outcomes, and then manage part of the benefits realization life cycle until the further steps of the benefits realization lifecycle are fully handed over to the Benefits Owner. By grouping projects in a way that maximizes the efforts toward the achievement of the same set of benefits, programs provide a better structure to support the management of the benefits realization process. If projects aiming to realize the same set of benefits are managed separately, it very often complicates the measurement of benefits associated with each project and can result in double counting, in which the same benefit is counting twice when analyzed on portfolio level.

Although project outputs can directly realize benefits too, as explained in the previous paragraph, measurement of benefits on the project level may increase the overall complexity of measuring benefits. Managing benefits on the project level may also take to a much larger number of measures to be controlled by the organization. Because of that, it is highly recommended that organizations group their initiatives into programs, if possible. However, if the initiative that will support the achievement of a strategic objective can be managed as a standalone project, there is no need for the organization to compose a program. This is also the case for example when revenue-generating (also acknowledged as external or client-facing) projects generate benefits associated with revenue and profit that count to the achievement of revenue-related business objectives. This last step is shown in Figure 5-4.

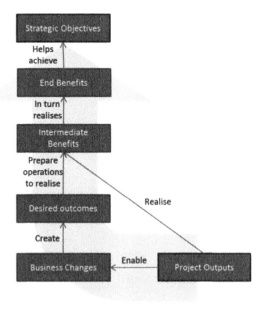

**Figure 5-4**  Benefits mapping: Top-down third step—project outputs.

## Bottom-Up Benefits Mapping

Alternatively, when project outputs (enablers) are already given, the map can begin from them and later join the strategic objectives (OGC 2011b). It usually happens in cases where projects are already in progress and need to be connected to the business strategy.* However, it also happens when changes are required by business units, but they need connection to organizational level business strategies in order to support their business cases. The benefits associated with these changes are identified by the appropriate business process owners and will be part of the business cases to assess the viability of the investment. In these cases, the benefits will many times not be produced by the direct decomposition of end benefits, but by aggregating (connecting) benefits to the end benefit most closely associated. In this bottom-up mapping, measurable benefits are associated with business objectives (Melton et al. 2008). If no link can be established, more appropriate benefits will need to be identified, or the initiative may be canceled since it does not link to the business strategy.

Conceptually, the bottom-up benefits chain (see Figure 5-5) starts with a project delivering outputs; these outputs enable business changes or directly

---

* If portfolio management is practiced, projects would be connected to the business strategy from their inception. Therefore, this situation should only happen when portfolio management is not practiced.

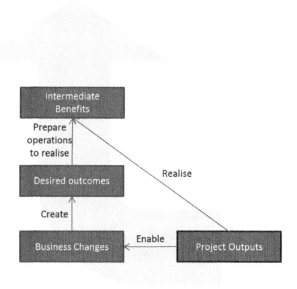

**Figure 5-5** Project outputs enabling business changes and realizing benefits.

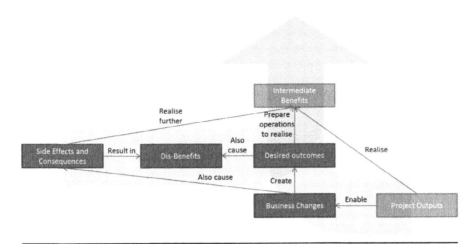

**Figure 5-6**   Business changes causing side effects and consequences that result in DisBenefits.

realize intermediate benefits (OGC 2011b). The business changes are expected to create outcomes that prepare operations (also acknowledged as business-as-usual) to realize benefits. Moreover, the same business changes can also realize intermediate benefits straight away, regardless of whether they are enabled by project outputs (Serra 2012).

The same business changes mentioned in the previous paragraph can also cause side effects and consequences—the negative outcomes of the business change, which could be, for example, the business process requiring additional skills or being subject to cost increases (Chittenden and Bon 2006; OGC 2011b). However, these same side effects and consequences can also realize additional intermediate benefits as well (Serra 2012). Moreover, desired outcomes can also cause disbenefits (see Figure 5-6). A more practical example is provided in the case study section and in *Appendix D.*

Intermediate benefits are expected to contribute to the achievement of end benefits (Bradley 2010; OGC 2011b). Usually, an end benefit is the result of a process of business change, which is composed by several projects that are managed together as a program (Bradley 2010; OGC 2011b). For example, in Figure 5-7, most of the activities required to ensure the realization of the intermediate benefits may be part of a program.

End benefits are expected to directly contribute to the achievement of one or more strategic business objectives (OGC 2011b). Figure 5-8 illustrates a complete theoretical benefits chain starting from projects and going through the several steps discussed in the previous paragraphs until finally reaching the achievement of strategic business objectives.

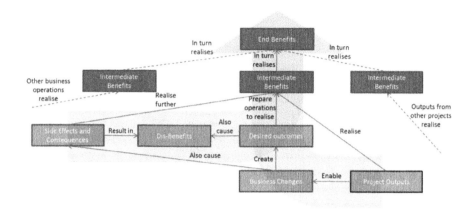

**Figure 5-7**    Intermediate benefits realizing end benefits.

Organizations can map benefits in both ways, but the most important is to make sure all benefits are consistently connected so that organizational leaders clearly know all benefits are supporting the achievement of strategic objectives.

## Benefits Map/Benefits Dependency Network

As an example of a completed benefits map, Figure 5-9 shows a benefits map that starts with initiatives delivering outputs/enablers, which leads to business changes

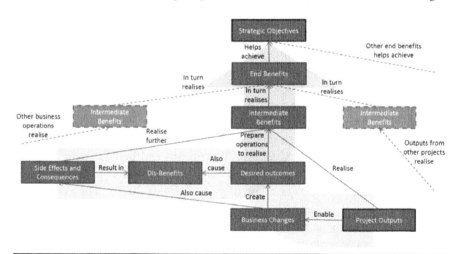

**Figure 5-8**    Chain of Benefits. [*Source:* **Reproduced** from Serra, C. E., and M. Kunc. "Benefits Realisation Management and Its Influence on Project Success and on the Execution of Business Strategies." *International Journal of Project Management,* 33, no. 1 (2015). Used with permission.]

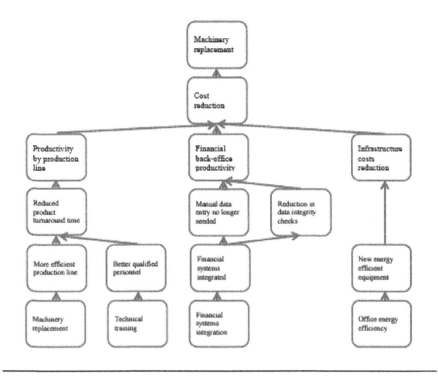

**Figure 5-9**    Benefits map or benefits dependency network.

that prepare operations to realize intermediate benefits that in turn realize end benefits that contribute to the achievement of business objectives. In the example presented in Figure 5-9, the introduction of new energy-efficient equipment generates infrastructure cost reduction, which does not require any kind of business change, by considering that the new equipment has the same operating standards as the previous one and will not introduce any changes to the business operations. There are cases when some steps such as business changes and intermediate benefits will be not needed. In these cases, such steps can be skipped. Figure 5-10 presents a generic Benefits Map/Benefits Dependency Network template.

## 5.2.3 Creating Benefits Matrixes

After having developed the benefits map and the activity map, organizations can use a benefits matrix to identify activities related to one or more benefits (Melton et al. 2008). The matrix enables the identification of all process or activities that are associated with a single benefit as well as all benefits that are associated with a process or activity (see Figure 5-11). It can provide a valuable

| Template | |
|---|---|
| **Benefits Map / Benefits Dependency Network** | |

| | | | |
|---|---|---|---|
| Organization: | <Name of the organization and/or division> | | |
| Version: | <X.X> | Version Type: | <Final/Draft> |
| Issued by: | <Name, Surname> | Issue date: | <DD-MM-YY> |
| Department: | <Department> | Job title: <Job title:> | |
| Approved by: | <Name, Surname> | Approval date: | <DD-MM-YY> |
| Department: | <Department> | Job title: <Job title:> | |

| Initiatives | Outputs / Enablers | Business Changes | Intermediate Benefits | End Benefits | Business Objectives |
|---|---|---|---|---|---|
| | | | | | |

Figure 5-10   Template: Benefits Map/Benefits Dependency Network.

| Benefits/Activities Matrix | | | |
|---|---|---|---|
| Processes / Activities | Benefits | | |
| | Benefit 1 | Benefit 2 | Benefit 3 |
| Process / Activity A | Strong/Medium/Low | Strong/Medium/Low | Strong/Medium/Low |
| Process / Activity A | Strong/Medium/Low | Strong/Medium/Low | Strong/Medium/Low |
| Process / Activity A | Strong/Medium/Low | Strong/Medium/Low | Strong/Medium/Low |
| Process / Activity A | Strong/Medium/Low | Strong/Medium/Low | Strong/Medium/Low |

**Figure 5-11**    Template: Benefits/Activities Matrix.

| Benefits/Stakeholders Matrix | | | |
|---|---|---|---|
| Stakeholders | Benefits | | |
| | Benefit 1 | Benefit 2 | Benefit 3 |
| Stakeholder A | Strong/Medium/Low | Strong/Medium/Low | Strong/Medium/Low |
| Stakeholder B | Strong/Medium/Low | Strong/Medium/Low | Strong/Medium/Low |
| Stakeholder C | Strong/Medium/Low | Strong/Medium/Low | Strong/Medium/Low |
| Stakeholder D | Strong/Medium/Low | Strong/Medium/Low | Strong/Medium/Low |

**Figure 5-12**    Template: Benefits/Stakeholders Matrix.

input to benefits mapping by making the association clear and easily replicable in a more complex network. This technique is also useful for selecting and prioritizing activities or ideas, grouping them in projects, and identifying dependencies (Melton et al. 2008).

Another matrix links benefits and disbenefits to related stakeholders, which enables more effective stakeholders' engagement (OGC 2011b). It can provide a valuable input to the benefits stakeholder engagement planning process (see Figure 5-12).

## 5.2.4 Classifying Benefits

The needed benefits are identified by using tools such as the issues map, the benefits map, or the benefits dependency network. Nevertheless, it is important to keep in mind that different types of benefits can occur, and each type of benefit can be associated with different processes, techniques, or other assessment criteria, for example, investment appraisal and benefits tracking and evaluation. Therefore, once the benefits are identified, they can be classified in different ways, for example by category, by change type (Bradley 2010), by stakeholder, by business impact (Bradley 2010; OGC 2011b), by business area (OGC 2011b), or by any other classification system that is meaningful and relevant to each organization. As an example, Remenyi, Money, and Twite (1995) recommend grouping benefits into regulatory benefits, financial benefits, quality of service benefits, customer perception of the firm benefits, and internal management benefits, and also includes a group that is associated with disbenefits. Remenyi et al. (1995) associate each benefit group with a series of benefit types, which helps organizations to clarify the objectives expected to meet the return on the investment, as summarized in the following bullet points:

- **Customer perception of the firm.** Increased customer confidence; increased staff confidence
- **Disbenefits.** Related to people; related to the job; related to computers
- **Financial.** Improved productivity; reductions in the cost of failure; improved cash flow and reduced bad debts; reduced computer costs; reduced overhead costs.
- **Internal management benefits.** Improved decision making; improved management productivity.
- **Quality of service.** Improved interface with clients; improved response times; improved resource utilization.
- **Regulatory benefits.** Regulatory compliance.

The management of disbenefits has been clearly linked to the achievement of the desired return on investment, and their early identification and management are becoming increasingly more relevant. As discussed in a previous chapter, projects can also create undesirable outcomes (Zwikael and Smyrk 2011), which can also be called negative outcomes. These negative outcomes can be called disbenefits (Bradley 2010; OGC 2011b). They are not risks that can occur or not, and they have to be identified and managed in order to minimize their impact (OGC 2011b). Therefore, their identification and classification are extremely important to enable further control.

Similarly, several other classification systems can relate benefits to the type of value that each benefit is expected to generate, which is a relevant way to classify benefits. It directly associates the benefits with the type of measures that will be applied to measure the realization of the benefit. Such measure types are extremely important to enable the organization to group project and then to identify how the benefit of each type is expected to be realized. This type of classification leads directly into the next step, which is setting benefits measures and targets. Measures and targets enable the organization to ascertain how much benefit has been realized at a given moment in time and then to evaluate the effectiveness of the benefit realization process.

In another example, Bradley (2010) and the British Office for Government Commerce (OGC 2011b) recommend a classification system that is widely used in the United Kingdom, especially in the public sector. It categorizes benefits based on value types as summarized in the following bullet points:

- *Tangible/Definite.* Value is predictable with certainty.
- *Tangible/Expected.* Value is predictable on historic basis, with high levels of confidence.
- *Tangible/Anticipated.* Value is not reliably predictable, but benefit is anticipated.
- *Intangible.* Value is difficult to substantiate, but may be anticipated, and evidence of its realization can be gathered from the measurement of other causally related benefits.

Another example, the Pereira Diamond (Teixeira and Pereira 2015), classifies the value created depending on what organization issue or problem it will resolve or mitigate. It groups these organizational issues or problems into four groups, which are:

- Business increase—or growth
- Cost reduction
- Efficiency increase
- Legal compliance

Although the type of value is important to support further activities and decision making depending on each organization's Benefits Realization Strategy, it could be worth cross-referencing different classification systems. An example of a classification matrix is suggested by Ward and Daniel (2012) to classify benefits by their types, in terms of "how to achieve" (do new things, do things better, and stop doing things) and by their increasing degree of explicitness or "how to track" (observable, measurable, quantifiable, and financial).

Another model, developed by Giaglis, Mylonopoulos, and Doukidis (1999), classifies benefits from information systems and applies a matrix with four quadrants, which classifies benefits as *indirect, strategic, hard,* and *intangible.* Across the horizontal axis, it scores the benefits from hard (bottom left) or indirect (top left) to intangible (bottom right) or strategic (top right) by assessing their measurability in terms of quantifiable or nonquantifiable characteristics. Across the vertical axis, it scores the benefits from hard (bottom left) or intangible (bottom right) to indirect (top left) or strategic (top right) by assessing if the benefits are attributable to the information system in terms of being strongly or weakly attributed.

In the model above (Giaglis et al. 1999), *hard benefits* are quantifiable and strongly attributable to the information system—for example, the cost reduction associated to the automation of a business process, which enables staff reduction or reallocation. *Indirect benefits* are quantifiable but weakly attributable to the information system—for example, infrastructure projects enable high performance for a number of applications, but they depend on the introduction and utilization of such applications. *Intangible benefits* cannot be easily quantified, although they can be attributable to the information system—for example, employee satisfaction due to the introduction of a new and more user friendly system. *Strategic benefits* are realized over a long term and are enabled by a combination of a number of contributing factors—for example, new revenue due to the implementation of a new system. Although the new system supports the achievement of new revenue, it may require a number of staffing, marketing, and sales investments that will also contribute to the achievement of the benefit, but are not necessarily managed as part of the same project or maybe even program.

Therefore, based on the examples presented above, various models can be applied to classifying benefits. Each model has a different proposition, but all of them can provide relevant information to support further activities in terms of managing the benefits realization journey. Independently from the model employed, the most important remark at this stage is to have the selected classification model aligned to all further processes associated with the composition and execution of project portfolios. They will be discussed in the following section.

## 5.2.5 Setting Benefits Measures and Targets

After having identified the benefits category, the following consequent step is the identification of benefit measures. Some benefit types can be easily measured, but others are much more complex. However, as previously discussed, all of them have to be measurable in order to make them achievable and verifiable. Benefits have to be measurable, because otherwise the management of their realization is impossible (OGC 2011b). Preferably, benefits should be measured in financial terms, but in cases for which this is impossible, another kind of numerical measure should be defined (Chittenden and Bon 2006)—a benefit that cannot be measured nor tracked, and the achievement of which cannot be verified (Chittenden and Bon 2006). In the same way, negative or undesirable benefits also have to be measured so that the negative impact to the business can be clearly quantified; then any appropriate mitigating or preventing actions can have their financial viability assessed. The valuation of disbenefits is done by calculating the sum of undesirable outcomes times the notional market value of each one (Zwikael and Smyrk 2011).

Although there may be several different ways to measure the same benefit, it is strongly recommended that the business employ measures that are already in use to measure business performance. Since benefits are directly associated with improvements in business performance and value, these performance and value measures are likely to be applicable to the measurement of the benefit. The process of measurement itself can involve a series of models and techniques that can be sector specific, as it is possible for one to find some sector-specific guidance books available in the marketplace, for example, *Effective Measurement and Management of IT Costs and Benefits* (Remenyi et al. 1995), *Measuring and Valuing Health Benefits for Economic Evaluation* (Brazier 2007), *The Measurement of Environmental and Resource Values: Theory and Methods* (Freeman and Herriges 2003), and *Recognizing Public Value* (Moore 2013).

Since several projects can contribute to the realization of the same sets of benefits, it is possible for us to assume that some projects can be responsible for a percentage of the benefit that is going to be realized as a result of a program. Therefore, a percentage of the program's benefits can be attributed to each project. The same can happen between projects and subprojects. Whenever a large project is composed of a number of smaller projects, each project contributes to some extent to the achievement of the benefits expected from the overarching project. For example, the construction of an oil platform can be broken down into a number of projects, although the results from all subprojects will ensure the conclusion of the overarching project and therefore the realization of benefits. Similarly, it happens between benefits, intermediate benefits and end benefits. The benefits delivered by a project may group with benefits from other projects and thus contribute to the realization of intermediate benefits. In turn, these may be combined with others to support the realization of end benefits—those directly associated to the achievement of business objectives.

As discussed before, there are some models available to support the analysis of the relationship between strategic objectives, benefits, and project outputs, such as Benefits Breakdown Structures, Benefits Dependency Networks, and Benefit Maps. These techniques are useful tools to clarify the way benefits are cascaded, which makes it easier to identify benefits and also to set targets for benefits when several initiatives contribute to the same end benefits. Table 5-1 exemplifies the decomposition of end benefits into intermediate benefits and then benefits for an Operational Efficiency Program, which is composed by four projects and focus on cost reduction.

Table 5-1 Example: Benefits Decomposition for an Operational Efficiency Program

| End Benefit | Intermediate Benefit | Benefit | Project |
|---|---|---|---|
| Cost reduction | Productivity by production line | Productivity by equipment | Machinery replacement |
| | | Productivity by employee | Technical training |
| | Infrastructure costs reduction | Energy cost reduction | Office energy efficiency |
| | Financial back-office productivity | Reduction in data entry | Financial systems integration |

By following the concept of decomposition, Bradley (2010) recommends a process called *ranking benefits,* in which benefits maps are incremented with weighted paths and scores. The element at the far right of the map receives a score (e.g., 1,000) that is decomposed across the map. The weighted paths are the percentages by which the decomposition is made, and the scores are the results of the decomposition. Figure 5-13 presents a benefits network that breaks down the cost reduction end benefit shown in Table 5-1, identifying the contribution of each benefit with the following level and the weight of each intermediate benefit with the achievement of the end benefit.

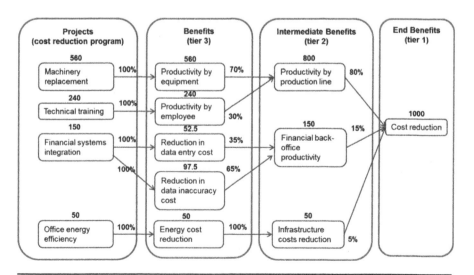

**Figure 5-13** Benefits dependency network: Percentages of contribution to the following level.

Another relevant aspect at this point is the decision as to whether the benefit is worth being measured only on the project level. Since some small projects can generate small amounts of benefits, the effort involved in measuring the benefits may be not worth the costs involved. Therefore, in these cases, benefits can be grouped and measured on a program or a portfolio level. It reduces the effort and expenses of measuring and analyzing results, although it still provides a means to show the contribution from each project by using weighted decomposition techniques.

After defining the variables that will measure the realization of the benefits, the next step is setting the target measures that are expected to be achieved (OGC 2011b). Before the execution starts, the current situation should be assessed in order to enable a future evaluation of whether the benefits have been achieved (Chittenden and Bon 2006).

At this point, one important aspect is avoiding double counting benefits, which happens when the same benefit is attributed to more than one source and targets are associated with each source without considering any aggregation. It normally causes an unrealistic total benefit amount, which would be unachievable. Double counting can cause, for example, an unrealistic goal of expecting the operational costs to be reduced by more than 100 percent because the benefits expected from all cost-reduction initiatives are summed. Double counting can be minimized by using the benefits mapping technique and by applying the benefits measures dictionary (Bradley 2010).

## 5.2.6 Defining Benefits Ownership

The identification, mapping, and classification of benefits may happen without having an assigned benefit owner. However, the next steps require someone who is responsible and accountable for the benefit realization and who will champion the benefit realization process. The *benefit owner* is an individual who will take direct advantage from the benefit and is willing to work or to assign a resource from his or her team to work toward the realization of the expected benefits (Ward and Daniel 2012). Therefore, an important step of benefits planning is identifying benefit owners. The benefit owner, a role that has been already described in the previous chapter, will be ultimately accountable for the realization of benefits after program and project closeout.

## 5.2.7 Creating Benefit Profiles

The *benefit profile* describes the benefit, presenting information such as its interdependencies, its ownership, and its measurements (Bradley 2010; Chittenden

| TEMPLATE | | | |
|---|---|---|---|
| **Benefit Profile/Benefit Identification Sheet** | | | |
| *Organization:* | <Name of the organization and/or division> | | |
| *Version:* | <X.X> | *Version Type:* | <Final/Draft> |
| *Issued by:* | <Name, Surname> | *Issue date:* | <DD-MM-YY> |
| *Department:* | <Department> | *Job title:* <Job title> | |
| *Approved by:* | <Name, Surname> | *Approval date:* | <DD-MM-YY> |
| *Department:* | <Department> | *Job title:* <Job title> | |

| **Benefit Basic Details** | |
|---|---|
| **Benefit Code / Name** | |
| **Benefit Definition** | |
| **Benefit Category** | |
| **Type of Benefit** | |
| **Strategic Objective Associated** | |
| **Benefit Dependency Network Diagram** | |
| <Insert the benefit dependency network diagram> | |
| **Benefit Measurement Details** | |
| Is the Benefit Measurable? | |
| Is the Benefit Financially Quantifiable? | |
| Measure | |
| Total Financial Amount | |
| Total Non-Financial Amount | |
| Total Budget Associated | |
| Cost/Benefit Ratio | |
| Frequency of Measurement | |
| Measure Owner | |
| Measurement Technique | |
| Source of Measurements | |
| Disbenefits Associated | |

| Benefit Realization and Ownership Details | |
|---|---|
| Benefit Owner | |
| Business Areas Responsible for Realizing the Benefit | |
| Realization Start Date (Planned/Actual) | |
| Realization End Date (Planned/Actual) | |
| Total Benefit Expected (Baseline) | |
| Total Benefit Expected | |
| **Program(s) and/or Projects Associated** | |
| Program Code/Name | |
| Program Sponsor | |
| Program Manager | |
| Project Code/Name | |
| Project Sponsor | |
| Project Manager | |
| Project Start Date (Planned/Actual) | |
| Project End Date (Planned/Actual) | |

**Figure 5-14**   Template: Benefit Profile/Benefit Identification Sheet.

and Bon 2006; OGC 2011b). The benefit profiles are composed by the information produced during the benefits planning process and should be periodically reviewed and updated. Most of the information required for a business case can be generated from the benefit profiles (Bradley 2010). Figure 5-14 presents a generic Benefit Profile/Benefit Identification Sheet template.

## 5.3 Composing a Project Portfolio to Realize the Expected Benefits

After performing the preliminary steps to structure project governance, the first step to implement the strategy is selecting projects to compose the organization's project portfolio (Gray and Larson 2010). As discussed in the previous chapter, the end benefits required by the business strategies are the main driver for the identification, selection, and prioritization of projects to compose a project portfolio. The following subsections identify some critical steps for the composition of a project portfolio that are common across a group of methodologies and sets of best practices.

| Subsection | Subject |
|---|---|
| 5.3.1 | Identifying Projects |
| 5.3.2 | Defining Projects |
| 5.3.3 | Classifying Projects |
| 5.3.4 | Appraising Projects |
| 5.3.5 | Selecting and Prioritizing Projects |

### 5.3.1 Identifying Projects

The first required step to compose a project portfolio is identifying the organizational needs for projects. That is because projects should be undertaken in order to deliver business needs and then support the execution of business strategies (Buttrick 1997). Therefore, after planning business strategies, defining business objectives, and starting to map the benefits that are needed to reach the business vision, organizational leaders are then able to identify the projects that can deliver the required outcomes to enable realization of the expected benefits.

### 5.3.2 Defining Programs and Projects

As many would expect based on the previous chapters, when defining a project, the extremely important first step is to understand the business needs that make the project relevant. When projects are part of programs, it is easier to do since the program is already linked to business objectives. Nevertheless, many projects are standalone, and regardless if a project is part of a program, it needs to support the achievement of business objectives. As Chapter 2 discusses, project strategies will be produced to deliver a scope that supports the achievement of program objectives and business objectives. Such objectives will sometimes be clearly and directly translatable into project objectives, but other times it will not be easy to establish clear links, which then makes it difficult to identify the appropriate scope.

The process of defining project objectives is complex and driven by two perspectives, uncertainty and certainty; these influence project objectives and the methods that will be applied to the achieve them (Melton et al. 2008). Both objectives (what to achieve) and methods (how to achieve) can be scored from relative uncertainty to relative certainty. In both cases, the amount of uncertainty increases complexity with the increase in uncertainty.

The preferable scenario refers to situations when the objectives are clearly defined, and the ways to achieve them are also clear, a situation most project managers and their team members assume is the case for their projects (Melton et al. 2008). However, if the objectives are clear, but the methods are not, then it is necessary to identify the different options and select the one that seems to be the best (Buttrick 1997; Melton et al. 2008). In the third scenario, unclear objectives and clear methods occur when managers have already decided that some type of project can be positive to the organization but do not know exactly why or how to measure its benefits, which can lead to benefits being defined only to justify the investment (Melton et al. 2008). The last scenario presents unclear objectives and also unclear methods, which is the case when the strategy is not well established, and managers have a budget to spend to look for opportunities (Melton et al. 2008). This kind of project sometimes is closed and does not deliver any benefits (Buttrick 1997). From the strategic point of view, it is probably the most distant from being the best scenario (Melton et al. 2008). Therefore, uncertainty will generally add risks to the realization of expected benefits, and then it will become a relevant input for project selection and prioritization.

Another aspect to be considered is the usual inability of a single project to deliver an end benefit alone. As explained in a previous section, benefits that directly contribute to the achievement of business objectives are called *end-benefits* (Bradley 2010; OGC 2011b). It is important to keep in mind that most projects do not deliver alone the end-benefits needed, or even deliver outcomes that are unable to deliver benefits by themselves (OGC 2011b). Often, projects deliver intermediate benefits, which support the achievement of the desired end benefits (Bradley 2010; OGC 2011b). In these cases further benefits mapping is useful during project definition.

Therefore, as soon as the project objectives have been identified and a clear link with business objectives or program objectives has been established, further benefits mapping is required to update the organizational benefits map. It will provide a clear understanding of the dependencies between all projects in the portfolio and also of the way each project contributes to the achievement of the business objectives. By having the project objectives and benefits identified as well as a high-level scope, the projects are ready for classification, appraisal, and selection.

### 5.3.3 Classifying Projects

Projects in an organizational portfolio can meet different perspectives (Gray and Larson 2006; Levine 2005). Therefore, it is useful to classify projects in order to establish different investment criteria. Otherwise, the investment budget focuses only on the most profitable initiatives, leaving needed ones with less priority to be executed (Jenner 2010). To be able to measure the value of each

Table 5-2 Investment Types: Type of Value to Be Created by the Project

| Author | Types of Investment |
|---|---|
| Kendall and Rollins (2003) | Increase throughput, that is to increase the value of organizations' products or services minus the operational costs |
| | Reduce the investment needed in capital or inventories |
| | Reduce operating expenses |
| Jenner (2010) | Revenue generation—to increase income |
| | Cost savings/efficiency—to reduce costs |
| | Strategic contribution—to enable the achievement of some strategic objectives |
| | "Must do" projects—to comply with regulatory or legal requirements or also to support business continuity |
| Gray and Larson (2006) | Manage regular operations |
| | Manage strategic initiatives |
| | Manage compliance initiatives |
| Levine (2005) | Improve and maintain required business capabilities |
| | Create new products or services |
| | Deliver outputs to external customers |

project, a first step is to identify the types of value a project intends to deliver in terms of return on the investment. Authors suggest a variety of criteria to classify projects according to the type of investment (see the examples presented in Table 5-2). Interestingly, although each author suggests slightly different sets of criteria, they all focus on similar investment objectives.

Based on the analysis of these examples, it is clear that investments (or projects) can be associated with different types of business objectives. This separation is important, because to move from the actual state to the business vision, the organization needs to maintain its regular operations while it implements the portfolio of planned changes (Gray and Larson 2010). Therefore, projects can be classified in the four groups, depending on the business objective associated to the investment, as illustrated in Table 5-2 and Figure 5-15.

## Strategic Initiatives: Development of New Capabilities

Strategic initiatives, which can also be described as initiatives for the development of new capabilities, are investments focused on implementing planned changes to the existing operations. The strategic initiatives aim to enable new

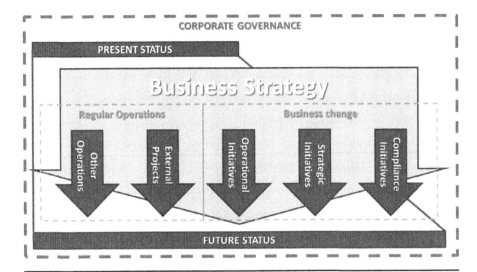

**Figure 5-15**    Corporate governance and investment types.

capabilities such as the development of new products, processes, or technologies. They can also focus on developing and implementing new business process that do not exist in the organization. As an example, we can consider a project that starts from scratch to develop an entirely new product or process, and then to create an entirely new value to the organization, as shown in Figure 5-16.

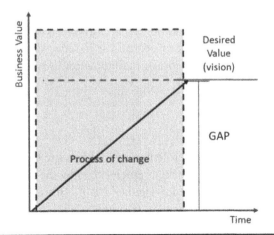

**Figure 5-16**    Strategic initiatives: Illustrative example. (*Source:* **Reproduced** from Serra, C. E. "Benefits Realisation Management and Strategic Project Success: Analysis of UK, USA, and Brazil." *PMI Global Congress EMEA 2015 Proceedings*. London, UK: Project Management Institute, 2015. Used with permission.)

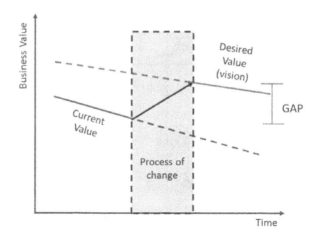

**Figure 5-17**   Operational initiatives: Illustrative example. (*Source:* Reproduced from Serra, C. E. "Benefits Realisation Management and Strategic Project Success: Analysis of UK, USA, and Brazil." *PMI Global Congress EMEA 2015 Proceedings.* London, UK: Project Management Institute, 2015. Used with permission.)

## Operational Initiatives: Enhancement of Existing Capabilities

Operational initiatives, which can also be described as initiatives for the enhancement of existing capabilities, are investments made to support or maintain ongoing businesses operations or to improve existing routines, also known as business-as-usual. It is related to products, services, and/or business processes that already exist in the organization. As an example, consider an existing process, or equipment, that has been decreasing in value during the last several years, but with some improvements or maintenance, its value could increase, as displayed in Figure 5-17.

## Compliance Initiatives

Compliance initiatives are investments required because of regulatory or unexpected issues, which are often seem as emergencies by the Portfolio Governance Boards. They can rarely be avoided (Jenner 2010). This investment type is different from the previous two because it complies with emergent needs, such as regulatory changes, technological changes, natural disasters, trade unions' pressures, and the like. In these cases, the main objective is not associated with the creation of value but with business continuity—for example, compliance with a new regulation that can stop sales of a product or service. Although they may enable change, they may not create any new value, as exemplified in Figure 5-18.

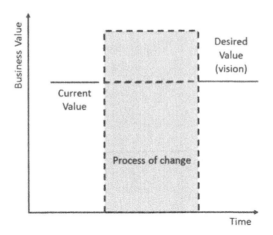

**Figure 5-18**   Compliance initiatives: Illustrative example. (*Source:* Reproduced from Serra, C. E. "Benefits Realisation Management and Strategic Project Success: Analysis of UK, USA, and Brazil." *PMI Global Congress EMEA 2015 Proceedings.* London, UK: Project Management Institute, 2015. Used with permission.)

## External Projects

External projects can be considered as investments, focused on delivering benefits that are required by the business strategies of external organizations or even by people, government or society. This group can be considered as part of the organization's regular operations, and the primarily benefit, which it delivers to its own organization, is the financial income paid in by the customer (Levine 2005).

These projects are different from all the previous ones, because many times they may not enable any change to the organization but focus on changes to other external organizations or people. This investment type usually aims to satisfy external customers by delivering outputs to customers and then generating financial income or intangible benefits, which are mostly related to marketing performance measures such as brand image, market share, client retention, and the like. This investment type can be considered quite different from the other three investment types since it is usually part of an organization's regular operations, as part of the main stream of an organization's value chain.

For example, construction projects temporarily allocate resources to the construction of something that is often going to be handed over to a third party. Therefore, the construction company basically realizes income plus other eventual benefits, such as increase in market share and expertise or brand strengthening. This example is illustrated in Figure 5-19.

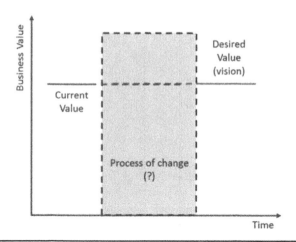

**Figure 5-19**   External projects: Illustrative example. (*Source:* Reproduced from Serra, C. E. "Benefits Realisation Management and Strategic Project Success: Analysis of UK, USA, and Brazil." *PMI Global Congress EMEA 2015 Proceedings.* London, UK: Project Management Institute, 2015. Used with permission.)

## 5.3.4 Appraising Projects

Different strategies need to be appraised in order to identify those projects that will be implemented (Johnson and Scholes 2002). However, depending on the type of project and on its objectives, different criteria can be employed in the assessment. Although project appraisal commonly assesses financial and non-financial aspects, there is no fully comprehensive or standard set of criteria. Therefore, each project can be evaluated by using specific criteria previously agreed upon among stakeholders, as already discussed in previous chapters.

Since projects are investments and the objective of investments is to maximize return (Jenner 2010, Levine 2005), the first step to select the best investments is performing a financial appraisal (Jenner 2010; Levine 2005). Although most companies recognize that most financial methods are not fully reliable and can fail, they need to perform investment appraisal in order to support the project selection (Jenner 2010). Several techniques are available for financial appraisal, and some of them are briefly described in this section and summarized in Table 5-3.

However, the process of project appraisal is much more complex than simply applying a financial model to evaluate a single project (Jenner 2010; Levine 2005). The return of an investment in change comes from the realization of project benefits and the creation of value for the business (Jenner 2010; Levine 2005). If projects are not related to organizational strategic needs, they can be meaningless (Jenner 2010). Other drivers than the financial ones should

Table 5-3 Summary of Financial Models

| Financial models | Summary Description |
|---|---|
| Payback | Time to recover the investment in the project. |
| Discounted Cash Flow | Total profit or loss during the period under analysis brought to present value by using an annual discount rate. |
| Cost-Benefit Analysis | Comparison of expected benefits to the associated costs in monetary terms. |
| Accounting Rate of Return | Profit divided by the cost of the investment. |
| Net Present Value (NPV) | Cash flow considering a minimum rate of return that is established by the organization. |
| Internal Rate of Return (IRR) | The minimum rate to be applied to a cash flow that gives a NPV of zero. |
| Economic Value Added (EVA) | The economic profit or value added to the organization. |
| Opportunity Cost | Cost of missing an opportunity. |
| Real Options | Analysis of different options available to a proposed implementation. |

influence the decisions taken over one project (Levine 2005). Therefore, although financial appraisals are important, by themselves they are not enough to qualify a project. Financial and nonfinancial models should be applied together in order to estimate the expected return on investment. Nonfinancial models are mostly based on multiweighted scoring models (described in this section and summarized in Table 5-4).

Furthermore, most projects do not deliver changes by themselves, because their outcomes will enable capabilities that, combined with outcomes from other projects, with capabilities enabled by other projects, or even with capabilities enabled by regular business operations, will then create value (Jenner 2010).

Table 5-4  Summary of Nonfinancial Models

| Nonfinancial Models | Description |
|---|---|
| Multiweighted scoring models | Multiattribute or multicriteria analysis that consists of the identification of factors that are important for the objective of the appraisal, the allocation of weights associated to the relevance of each factor, and then the allocation of scores to reflect how much the project performs in relation to each factor. |

Therefore, a project appraisal, more often than not, will only be possible after evaluating a set of projects together (Levine 2005).

An important artifact produced during project appraisal is the *business case*, a document developed to establish a clear understanding of the investment and its motivations (Jenner 2010) as it describes the value for business of the expected outcomes (OGC 2011b). It covers the achievability and affordability of the investment as well as the attractiveness, explaining whether the investment will result in cashable savings or non-cashable efficiency savings, or whether it will have strategic impacts (Jenner 2010).

- *Payback.* The payback model, the simplest and most applied method, calculates how long it will take to recover the investment in the project by purely analyzing the expected cash flow (Gray and Larson 2010; Jenner 2010). The payback period can be calculated by using a nondiscounted cash flow, which sums each individual cost and revenue expected in the period of analysis, or a discounted cash flow, which sums the individual costs and revenues after they are adjusted by an annual discount rate. By considering that revenues generated by the project recover the investment made, the payback period is the period of time required for the revenue to recover the capital invested in the project.

  When applying the payback model, it is important to consider that projects usually go through a period where only costs incur and there is no revenue. This period is usually followed by a period where revenues—which are usually the benefits that are expected from the project—start to happen. In some projects, costs and revenues can happen concurrently; in such cases, the net revenue is calculated by summing all the revenues minus all the costs for the period.

- *Discounted Cash Flow.* The value of a project is calculated as the benefits provided by the project minus taxes and cost of ownership, and then divided by an annual discount rate, which is calculated based on time and risk (Levine 2005). It determines the value of future estimated cash flows by discounting them of the appropriate capital cost. It is based on the idea that the value of money today is higher than the estimated value in the future.

- *Cost-Benefit Analysis.* The cost-benefit analysis compares the benefits that are expected from a program or project, expressed in monetary terms, to the costs associated to the same program or project, also expressed in monetary terms. It then produces an indicator, which is called the cost-benefit ratio.

  An important aspect of the cost-benefit analysis is that both the benefits and costs must be expressed in present values. Since benefits are realized primarily after all the expenditures are made and the project is completed, it is important to calculate the present value of the expected cash flow to achieve a more realistic cost-benefit ratio.

- **Accounting Rate of Return.** The accounting rate of return calculates the profit generated by the project divided by the cost of the investment (Jenner 2010). It is the relationship between the amount of money earned (or lost) as result of an investment and the amount of money invested. Different from the cost-benefit ratio, the accounting rate of return does not take into account the concept of time value of money.

- **Net Present Value (NPV).** The net present value (NPV) analyzes the cash flow considering an expected rate of return that is established by the organization as a minimum desired return for any investments (Gray and Larson 2010). It provides the monetary value of the project from its inception until the end of the benefits realization lifecycle brought forward to the present date, where net costs and net benefits are discounted by a predefined discount rate. Due to the application of a discount rate, any costs or benefits accrued in the future have less value than the same amount if accrued in the present. Therefore, it enables the contrast between investments made in the present and benefits realized over a longer period of time. Because of that, it is a measure frequently used to justify the investment in a program or project based on economic principles.

  In other—and perhaps simpler—words, it is the difference between discounted cash flows for benefits and for costs (Bradley 2010). In summary, a positive NPV means that the program or project will provide positive financial return, and thus is economically acceptable. A negative NPV, on the other hand, means that the program or project is not going to provide positive financial return, and thus is not acceptable in economic terms.

- **Internal Rate of Return (IRR).** Similar to the NPV, the IRR calculates the rate of return on the investment, enabling consideration of the organization's cost of capital (Jenner 2010). The IRR is the discount rate according to which a sequence of costs and benefits has an NPV of zero.

- **Economic Value Added (EVA).** The EVA measures the economic profit, which reflects the return over or above that expected related to the value of capital or assets employed, including the cost of capital (Amason 2011). This measure is important to let investors know the real financial return they will have on their investment in any project.

- **Opportunity Cost.** Opportunity cost is the situation when the managers decide whether to implement a project based on a comparative basis, selecting the options that can bring more financial return (Melton et al. 2008). It is a term used in economics to indicate the costs caused by missing an opportunity as well as the benefits that could be achieved by exploiting the same opportunity. It can also be used to consider the higher income that could be achieved by investing the money in another way.

- **Real Options.** The value of any proposed implementation can be measured in terms of options, where some options can be more profitable from the current situation (Amason 2011). Real option valuation or real options analysis is a decision-making supporting technique to compare the financial value in terms of return on investment for different investment options—for example, options relating to project size, to project life and timing, or to project operation. Many suggest that organizations should keep—and manage—their portfolio of alternative options, because in different scenarios these options can turn out to be even more profitable than the current chosen ones (Amason 2011).

- **Nonfinancial Models.** Weighted scoring models assign a weight to each of several different qualitative or quantitative criteria to enable scoring and ranking projects (Gray and Larson 2010; Jenner 2010). Especially in cases where benefits are not easily quantifiable in financial terms, the utilization of weighted models provides an effective way to translate several attributes into a single quantitative measure that enables the comparison and contrast between several different options (see Table 5-4).

  Another advantage of using nonfinancial models for project appraisal is the ability to mix and match several different aspects that otherwise might be not comparable. It enables organizations to balance several different and perhaps even antagonistic perspectives when selecting and prioritizing projects. Because of the possibility of fitting together strategic relevance, financial measures, and other criteria, these models are the most useful for prioritizing projects (Gray and Larson 2010).

## 5.3.5 Selecting and Prioritizing Projects

After being appraised based on a set of measures, usually projects will be selected by a balanced and fair ranking system (Levine 2005) (see Table 5-5). As explained before, most organizations do not have sufficient funds to execute all projects. The ranking is composed by a weighted score based on the results of all the appraisals performed (Levine 2005). The viability, the priority, and the availability of funding will affect the selection (Buttrick 1997). The analytic hierarchy process (AHP) and other methods are available to support the decision process for ranking projects, including the efficient frontier, pairwise comparison matrices, and structured decision analysis methodologies (Levine 2005). Program optimization models are also available to support the identification of the best project mix and the dependencies between projects (Buttrick 1997). Most of these models are associated with the Modern Portfolio Theory, which aims to maximize return and minimize risk by selecting a balanced portfolio of investment. This financial theory can be applied to support the composition of balanced project portfolios. After finishing this process, executive dashboards are useful to communicate the data used as drivers as well as the decisions made (Levine 2005).

Kendall and Rollins (2003) expand on this topic. They explain that business objectives are normally split into sub-objectives to be achieved by functional areas, where many sub-objectives will address different areas. Most of the time these goals compete for resources, and functional managers should decide where to focus their efforts and what criteria to use for prioritization. Furthermore,

Table 5-5 Techniques for Portfolio Selection and Prioritization

| Technique | Description |
|---|---|
| Analytic Hierarchy Process (AHP) | The AHP applies pairwise comparisons and judgments of experts to produce priority scales. These scales enable measuring intangibles in relative terms. |
| Efficient Frontier | The Efficient Frontier is a method that enables plotting a chart that graphically displays a set of investment options for a defined level of risk or the lowest risk for a given level of expected return. A curve displayed in the chart represents the frontier between the best investment options. Such a curve is called the efficient frontier, because portfolios positioned below the curve or on its right-hand side are not expected to provide enough return on the investment or are considered to be of a high level of risk. |
| Pairwise Comparison Matrices | Pairwise comparison matrices are a tool to support the process of comparing pairs of entities to enable judgment on which entity is preferred or has a greater amount of some quantitative characteristic. |
| Structured Decision Analysis Methodologies | Structured decision analysis methodologies are a series of procedures, methods, and tools to support the decision-making process. They include the identification and assessment of the relevant inputs for a decision to be made. |

one area of the business can prejudice other areas in achieving their goals when focusing on different objectives, which could take organizational departments or divisions to work in opposite ways, very incompatibly. For example, if two departments need new IT equipment to enable the achievement of their strategic objectives, but the IT department has a limited budget that allows the provision of this equipment to only one department, the one receiving new equipment will have to receive higher priority from the Portfolio Governance Board. Then, the different objectives should be sequenced and aligned in the organizational plans to make their achievement feasible and valuable for the organization. When analyzed inside functional areas, projects expecting more return can be prioritized, but it is important to pay attention to the value of the entire set of business objectives for the various departments of the business.

Kendall and Rollins (2003) also mention that most of the time, single projects can have small or no financial return, but they are needed to enable the achievement of a business goal. If these projects are not performed, organizations may fail to achieve their business objectives. However, they spend large amounts of money working to achieve only parts of them. Then, more than analyzing each project, organizations should plan how to obtain the whole system of inputs needed to achieve each business objectives.

Finally, Kendall and Rollins (2003) emphasize that executives from different areas should understand the whole business strategy and perform more projects that are relevant in order to achieve the most valuable business objectives. If they focus only on the needs of their functional areas, they will probably fail in supporting the execution of the business strategy. Measures and policies should also comply with the whole business; otherwise, functional areas can be led to prioritizing needs that are not a priority for the business as a whole. Furthermore, strategic projects should be aligned with operational projects, because it is often necessary to stabilize a process before improving it.

Therefore, although several techniques are available to support project appraisal, their objective is to generate information to support the decision-making process where decision makers consider several relevant issues until they determine which will be the approved set of projects (Gray and Larson 2010). The Business Case is an important tool for capturing the reasoning for initiating a project or task and is widely used by organizations for the assessment of a project as an investment option. Figure 5-20 presents a generic Business Case template.

## 5.4 Case Study: Enterprise Benefits Planning

This section demonstrates the way ProjectEng planned the realization of the benefits that are required by its business strategy. It will be exemplified by focusing on one strategic objective of the business: the reduction of operating costs.

| TEMPLATE | | | |
|---|---|---|---|
| **Business Case** | | | |
| *Organization:* | <Name of the organization and/or division> | | |
| *Version:* | <X.X> | *Version Type:* | <Final/Draft> |
| *Issued by:* | <Name, Surname> | *Issue date:* | <DD-MM-YY> |
| *Department:* | <Department> | *Job title:* <Job title> | |
| *Approved by:* | <Name, Surname> | *Approval date:* | <DD-MM-YY> |
| *Department:* | <Department> | *Job title:* <Job title> | |

**I. Introduction**

*<Add text>*

**II. Motivation**

*<Add text>*

**III. Expected Benefits and Success Criteria**

*<Add text>*

**IV. Options**

*Option A: <Add text>*

*Option B: <Add text>*

**V. Recommendations**

*<Add text>*

**VI. Initial Assumptions and Constraints**

| | |
|---|---|
| *Assumption A: <Add text>* | *Constraint A: <Add text>* |
| *Assumption B: <Add text>* | *Constraint B: <Add text>* |

**VII. High-Level Costs**

*High-level cost – type A: <Add text>*

*High-level cost – type B: <Add text>*

**VIII. Impact Analysis**

*Impact A: <Add text>*

*Impact B: <Add text>*

**IX. Risk Analysis**

*Risk A: <Add text>*

*Risk B: <Add text>*

*(Continued on next page)*

*(Template: Business Case, Continued)*

| X. High-Level Plan |
| --- |
| *<Add text>* |
| **XI. Governance and Rules of the Organization** |
| *<Add text>* |

**Figure 5-20**   Template: Business Case.

The other strategic objectives will not be discussed in more depth in this section. The section starts by explaining the way that the programs and projects were selected and the expected benefits were identified and baselined. Then, it exemplifies the benefit profile, which provides all relevant information that is associated with a specific benefit.

| Subsection | Subject |
| --- | --- |
| 5.4.1 | Finalizing the Enterprise Benefits Realization Strategy (Step 2) |
| 5.4.2 | Composing the Project Portfolio |
| 5.4.3 | Creating a Benefit Profile |

## 5.4.1 Finalizing the Enterprise Benefits Realization Strategy (Step 2)

The first step of benefits planning uses a key input from the eBRM strategy. Starting from the list of key benefits required by the business strategy, the next step of this process is the identifying changes that can enable benefits realization and achievement of the strategic objectives. At this point, suitable changes are identified through a business analysis activity. However, any changes identified at this point will still be subject to further appraisal, prior to being part of the pipeline of change initiatives.

A number of tools are applied for this analysis, as shown in the example Benefits versus Processes/Activities Matrix (Table 5-6). It supports the identification of the functional dependencies for the realization of each strategic end benefits. By identifying the processes and activities associated with the realization of each end benefit, the organization can focus on a set of specific functional areas to identify possible enablers for each of the benefits required by the business strategy.

Another tool applicable to supporting this analysis is a Benefits versus Stakeholders Matrix (see Table 5-7). In the same way as the Benefits versus

Table 5-6 ProjectEng's Benefits/Activities Matrix

| Processes / Activities | Benefits | | |
|---|---|---|---|
| | Cost Reduction | New revenue | Competitive Advantage |
| Manufacturing | Directly Associated | Not Directly Associated | Directly Associated |
| Sales | Directly Associated | Directly Associated | Not Directly Associated |
| Recruitment | Directly Associated | Not Directly Associated | Not Directly Associated |
| Systems Development | Directly Associated | Not Directly Associated | Directly Associated |

Activities Matrix, this matrix supports the identification of dependencies between benefits and key organizational roles. By identifying such dependencies, the organization can start engaging early with the key stakeholders associated with each benefit. There individual are very likely to be key players to support the benefits planning process.

The final step is the identification of ideas to implement the changes and to achieve the business objectives by realizing the expected benefits. All ideas will be subject to further appraisal, as discussed in the previous chapter and described in Section 5.3.

Table 5-7 ProjectEng's Benefits/Stakeholders Matrix

| Stakeholders | Benefits | | |
|---|---|---|---|
| | Cost Reduction | New Revenue | Competitive Advantage |
| Operations Manager | Directly Associated | Not Directly Associated | Directly Associated |
| Business Development Manager | Directly Associated | Directly Associated | Not Directly Associated |
| Head of Human Resources Management | Directly Associated | Not Directly Associated | Directly Associated |
| External Client ABC | Not Directly Associated | Directly Associated | Not Directly Associated |

A fully worked example of the refined Benefits Realization Management strategy is presented in *Appendix D,* using the scenario above as a contextual reference. At this point, the template should have all sections completed, including Sections IV to VIII.

## 5.4.2 Composing the Project Portfolio

All the ideas identified in the previous section were fed into the project portfolio funnel, which is part of ProjectEng's Project Portfolio Management Process. After a few rounds of assessment, some ideas were canceled or put on hold, and others were authorized to progress. Some ideas were grouped into a program, such as (for example) the Renewables Market Strategic Program, which includes two initiatives: (1) mobilization of the renewables specialists' resource pool in Europe and Americas, and (2) business development in the European and American renewables markets. Some other ideas were selected for execution as standalone projects, such as the Professional Registration Project. Table 5-8 summarizes the outputs of this process of assessment, prioritization, and portfolio level planning.

All initiatives selected for implementation were then assigned success criteria and expected financial benefits. The compliance initiatives were directly associated with financial benefits, but they could be achieved through the adoption of the concepts of risk avoidance or business continuity (see Table 5-9). The Professional Registration Project, for example, does not represent any additional income or reduction in costs. Nevertheless, if it were not successful, the business risks would comprise US $200 million in revenue, which is equivalent to about US $18 million in profit. By considering the risk impact of 50 percent and the probability of 75 percent, we can translate the failure of the project into a reduction of US $6.75 million profit (50% × 75% × US $18 million = US $6.75 million).

## 5.4.3 Creating a Benefit Profile

The following benefit profile sheet identifies the characteristics of the Benefit B002 Operating Costs, the realization of which is required to the achieve ProjectEng's strategic objective SO002 Operational Excellence. It is presented as an example of the information required to enable the complete understanding of each benefit. The template presented below summarizes the general information related to the benefit as well as identifies all the initiatives that will enable its realization. It is led by Jeff Stuart, a seasoned Program Manager, who

Table 5-8  Changes Required, Ideas, and Initiatives Selected

| Change Required | Idea | Initiative Selected |
|---|---|---|
| Development of the capability to generate income from the renewables market sector in Europe and the Americas. | Mobilization of renewables specialists' resource pool in Europe and the Americas. | Renewables Market Strategic Program |
| Development of new clients and contracts in the renewables market sector in Europe and the Americas. | Business development in the European and American renewables markets. | |
| Optimization of the benefits realization from investment projects and revenue-generating projects. | Benefits Realization Management Maturity Enhancement. | Operational Excellence Program |
| Increase in efficiency of project delivery, including investment projects and revenue-generating projects. | Business process mapping, improvement and standardization. | |
| Increase in efficiency of back office operations (finance, accounting, procurement, human resources management, etc.). | Organizational architecture redesign. IT systems integration. New ERP. (canceled) | |
| Standardization of service delivery activities across different geographies, supported by the appropriate documentation and training. | Development of competence frameworks for the business core competences. Review of career pathways for service delivery roles (put on hold) | Organizational Competence Program |
| Identification of key skills needed for service delivery and development of self-service eLearning capability. | Global proactive eLearning program | |
| Development of a new employees' qualification program. | New employees program | |
| Professional registration of all employees according to local regulations. | Professional registration program | Professional Registration Project |

Table 5-9 Initiatives, Project Types, Associated Benefits, and Investment

| Initiative | Project Type | Financial Benefit (value to be created) | Investment |
|---|---|---|---|
| Renewables Market Strategic Program | Strategic Initiative | US $330 million new gross revenue per year | US $5 million |
| Operational Excellence Program | Operational Initiative | US $240 million cost reduction per year | US $100 million |
| Organizational Competence Program | Operational Initiative | | US $45 million |
| Professional Registration Project | Compliance Initiative | US $6.75 million profit per year (risk avoidance) | US $0.1 million |

has extensive experience in change management but also has a background in business analysis and performance improvement. The program, which affects all areas of the business, is sponsored by the Haji Aljaid, Chief Finance Officer.

A fully worked example of the creation of a benefit profile by using the template provided in this chapter is presented in *Appendix D,* using the scenario above as a contextual reference.

# 5.5 Chapter Summary: Planning Benefits

Outcomes and benefits should be measurable; otherwise, it would be impossible to evaluate the value of each project and whether its objectives have been achieved. Organizational leaders should appraise all projects by considering project benefits in order to calculate how much value each project can create for the business. The portfolio management staff should provide the Portfolio Governance Board with clearly mapped relationships between outputs, outcomes, intermediate benefits, end benefits, and business objectives in order to determine the relationship between all different initiatives in the portfolio, as well as each initiative's contribution to the achievement of strategic objectives. All the information about benefits, outcomes, and outputs should be stated in the in the benefits profile and later in the business case; this information is necessary to enable the Portfolio Governance Board to select, prioritize, and support the most relevant group of projects. Table 5-10 summarizes some key practices (Serra and Kunc 2015) discussed in this chapter to ensure the effectiveness of benefits realization, which are instrumental for effective project governance and consequently in supporting project success.

**Table 5-10  Key Benefits Realization Management Practices to Support Project Success: Planning**

| Governance Process | Benefits Realization Management Process | Benefits Realization Management Key Practices |
| --- | --- | --- |
| Composing and prioritizing portfolios of changes | Planning benefits | Expected outcomes are clearly defined. |
| | | The value created to the organization by project outcomes is clearly measurable. |
| | | The strategic objectives that project outcomes are expected to support the achievement of are clearly defined. |
| | | A business case is approved at the beginning of the project, describing all outputs, outcomes and benefits that are expected from the project. |

*Source:* **Adapted from** Serra, C. E. *Benefits Realisation Management and Its Influence on Project Success, Project Governance, and Execution of Business Strategy: Analysis of Brazil, the United Kingdom, and the United States of America.* Coventry, UK: University of Warwick (2012); and Serra, C. E. and M. Kunc. "Benefits Realisation Management and Its Influence on Project Success and on the Execution of Business Strategies." *International Journal of Project Management* 33(1) 2015. (Used with permission.)

The process of planning benefits includes a set of activities, which were discussed in this chapter. These activities produce a series of outputs that also can be called management products, which are summarized as follows:

## Benefits Identification and Analysis Management Products

- Benefits List
- Benefits Map
- Benefits Matrix
- Benefit Profile
- Business Case

# 5.6 End-of-Chapter Review Questions—Chapter 5

In this section, a set of end-of-chapter review questions are provided to enable a self-assessment of the understanding of the Chapter 5. The answers to all questions can be found at the end of the book in *Appendix A*.

1. What is the first required step for planning benefits at the organizational level? In summary, what happens in this step?
2. What is benefits mapping, and why is it important?
3. Why are benefits classified?
4. Why do we need benefits to be measureable?
5. Why is the benefits owner important?
6. What is a benefit profile?
7. Why are projects identified?
8. Why are uncertainty and certainty relevant to define project objectives and methods?
9. What are the four types of initiatives suggested in this chapter?
10. What is a business case and what is its association with project appraisal?
11. Why do organizations need to prioritize projects?

# Chapter 6

# Realizing Benefits

After benefits are planned, they have to be realized. This process will involve several steps, such as the delivery of outputs, the production of outcomes, and the implementation of changes, which can happen in different ways as described in Chapters 3 and 5. Benefits realization is the process of making expected benefits become real while also making people aware of their achievement. It will preferably involve some type of financial measurement of the value actually created to the business.

This chapter begins by describing the context of the point of a project portfolio management life cycle when a project has delivered outputs, and then when the same project or its overarching program or even business operations have the required enablers to start realizing the benefits. The second section moves one step back to plan the benefits realization. Although benefits have been already planned on a corporate level, the realization itself has to be planned on a program or even a project level. The third section discusses some of the project, program, and portfolio management practices that enable the realization of expected benefits. The fourth section explains the realization itself, which is when the value is created according to the plan. The fifth and last section summarizes this chapter and presents some key Benefits Realization Management practices that are associated with the realization of benefits.

## 6.1 Introduction: Delivering Outputs, Business Changes, and Outcomes to Realize Benefits

Before starting this chapter, it is important to revisit the meaning of benefits realization. When referring to benefits realization, we are doing it based on the description provided in the paragraph below.

> *[Benefits] realization is a process to make benefits happen and also to make people fully aware of them throughout the entire process of realization in order to ensure the creation of strategic and measurable value to the business* (Serra 2015).

To do so, after benefits have been planned on organizational level, a group of processes ensures the execution of the benefits realization plans during program and project life cycles. In addition, after project delivery is complete, the processes guarantee that the project closeout occurs in an appropriate and pre-planned way to ensure the realization of all expected benefits. It also ensures the benefits handover takes place to secure ownership and accountability for benefits realization after project closeout. Therefore, from a project governance perspective, we can summarize benefits realization as a process to deliver outputs, business changes and outcomes to realize benefits.

The following sections present these processes, which are required to ensure the effective delivery of the expected benefits during program and project life cycles and also after program and project closeout.

## 6.2 Planning Benefits Realization

To ensure the realization of the benefits required by their business strategies, organizational leaders should plan the whole process, including the delivery of the capability, the realization of benefits as well as their related costs and risks (OGC 2011b). Although the traditional focus on benefits realization happens during program and project delivery (Glynne and Stubbs 2014), the benefits realization plan should cover the period after program and project closeout if needed during transition and sustainment to ensure the entire realization of the expected benefits (see Figure 6-1). Therefore, programs need to plan the benefits realization during the program planning process (Chittenden and Bon 2006). The same applies to projects that are not part of a program, since they often lack a benefits realization plan. These benefit realization plans should include the activities required during and after program and project closeout to ensure the realization of the benefits required by the business strategies.

The following two subsections discuss what should be part of program and project Benefits Realization Strategies. The subsequent two subsections focus

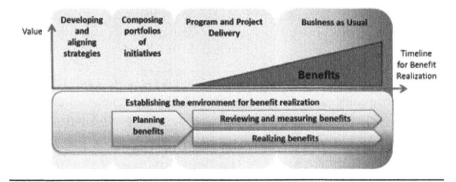

**Figure 6-1**    Benefits realization and the timeline for strategy execution.

on activities to be planned to ensure the realization of benefits after handover or outputs to business operations, plans to manage risks that may affect benefits realization, and then plans to manage benefit stakeholders.

| Subsection | Subject |
|---|---|
| 6.2.1 | Developing a Program-Level Benefits Realization Strategy |
| 6.2.2 | Developing a Project-Level Benefits Realization Strategy |
| 6.2.3 | Planning the Management of Benefit Risks |
| 6.2.4 | Planning Benefits Stakeholder Engagement |

## 6.2.1 Developing a Program-Level Benefits Realization Strategy

In Chapter 5, benefits were identified to support the achievement of business objectives. Then initiatives were identified to deliver those benefits. Many of the initiatives will be delivered as programs. Each program will be expected to enable the realization of a set of benefits, intermediate benefits, or even end benefits. Most of these benefits will be realized as a result of the changes enabled by project outputs and outcomes. Therefore, a formal strategy is needed to define how to manage the whole process of benefits realization (OGC 2011b). The whole process to ensure the realization of all expected benefits is much more than just planning the benefits and tracking their realization.

According to OGC (2011b), a program-level benefits realization strategy is a plan that (a) defines how the program will identify and define benefits; (b) links benefits to strategic outcomes; (c) makes the business areas responsible for delivering defined benefits (or even more); (d) performs benefits measurement, tracks, and records progress; (e) delivers change by managing initiatives based on the dependencies between their expected benefits; and (f) establishes a clear relationship between initiatives (vision and desired benefits) and the strategic objectives of the organization.

The benefits realization strategy also includes defining the roles and responsibilities, frequency of reviews, measurement techniques, processes employed, and ways to establish the needed ownership and commitment (Chittenden and

| Template | | | |
|---|---|---|---|
| **Program Benefits Realization Strategy** | | | |
| **Organization:** | <Name of the organization and/or division> | | |
| **Program:** | <Name of the program> | | |
| Program Manager | *<Name, Surname>* | **Department:** | **<Department>** |
| Program Sponsor | *<Name, Surname>* | **Department:** | **<Department>** |
| Version: | *<X.X>* | Version Type: | *<Final/Draft>* |
| **Issued by:** | *<Name, Surname>* | **Issue date:** | *<DD-MM-YY>* |
| **Department:** | *<Department>* | **Job title:** | *<Job title>* |
| **Approved by:** | *<Name, Surname>* | **Approval date:** | *<DD-MM-YY>* |
| **Department:** | *<Department>* | **Job title:** | *<Job title>* |

| **I. Initiatives** |
|---|
| *<Add text>* |
| **II. Benefits Dependency Network** |
| *<Add graphical representation of the benefits dependency network>* |
| **III. Benefits to Be Realized** |
| *<Add text>* |
| **IV. Disbenefits to Be Managed** |
| *<Add text>* |
| **V. Management of Change Strategies** |
| *<Add text>* |
| **VI. Handover Strategies** |
| *<Add text>* |

**Figure 6-2**   Template: Program Benefits Realization Strategy.

Bon 2006; OGC 2011b). It has to treat disbenefits as well (Chittenden and Bon 2006) to manage and try to avoid them.

In addition to the activities to be performed as part of the program and its projects, benefits realization strategies—or plans—include all activities that should be performed by the business to ensure the realization of benefits. Some of these activities will happen during the program life cycle, and others will occur after the program closeout. These activities can include reorganizing the work of a team or providing training (Chittenden and Bon 2006). These activities should be agreed upon by the program management team and the functional managers, since the responsibility for their execution can be assigned to business functions, and the program team will lack involvement. Figure 6-2 presents a generic Program Benefits Realization Strategy template.

## 6.2.2 Developing a Project-Level Benefits Realization Strategy

A project-level benefits management strategy can be similar to a program level one or one with less detail. The main driver for determining the detail in the plan will depend on whether the project is part of a program or not. If the project is part of a program, the program-level strategy will usually take care of the realization of any benefits that are expected to be realized after project closeout. Conversely, projects that are not part of a program are likely to require a more complete and comprehensive Benefits Realization Strategy, perhaps similar to one required at the program level—especially if the project is critical to the organization's portfolio and has numerous complexities associated with it.

When it is expected that benefits will be realized as a result of changes enabled by project outputs, one important aspect will be the incorporation of some change management activities into the project management plan. These activities, which many times would be executed on program level instead, will be part of the project scope or delegated to the benefits owners. Although large projects can easily incorporate these activities by having extended life cycles with a strong focus on postdelivery activities, small projects may have to balance the relevance of these activities with the viability of the investment. Figure 6-3 presents a generic Project Benefits Realization Strategy template.

## 6.2.3 Planning the Management of Benefit Risks

Organizational and business change risks have to be taken into consideration because they can affect the business's capability to successful carry out the changes that will enable the realization of the expected benefits (Ward and

| Template | | | |
|---|---|---|---|
| **Project Benefits Realization Strategy** | | | |
| **Organization:** | *<Name of the organization and/or division>* | | |
| **Project:** | *<Name of the project>* | | |
| Project Manager | *<Name, Surname>* | **Department:** | *<Department>* |
| Program Sponsor | *<Name, Surname>* | **Department:** | *<Department>* |
| **Department:** | *<Department>* | **Job title:** | *<Job title>* |
| **Approved by:** | *<Name, Surname>* | **Approval date:** | *<DD-MM-YY>* |
| **Department:** | *<Department>* | **Job title:** | *<Job title>* |

| **I. Benefits to Be Realized** |
|---|
| *<Add text>* |
| **II. Disbenefits to Be Managed** |
| *<Add text>* |
| **III. Management of Change Strategies** |
| *<Add text>* |
| **IV. Handover Strategies** |
| *<Add text>* |

**Figure 6-3**　Template: Project Benefits Realization Strategy.

Daniel 2012). Financial risks can also have an impact on financial benefits due to the unpredictability of associated costs. All these risks that might have an impact on the realization of the expected benefits will be added to the program and project risk management plans and then managed accordingly. Although these risks are managed by program and project management teams during the program and project life cycles, the management of these risks will be handed over to the benefits owner during the program and project closeout stage.

Other types of benefit risks are not associated with uncertainty that can affect the realization of the expected benefits, but with the impact of not realizing the expected benefits to the business. The achievement or nonachievement of any benefits will generate a risk to the business. These benefit risks are owned by the benefits owner and can be managed by the program and project teams during the program and project delivery life cycles, but they have to be fully handed over to the benefits owner after the program or project closeout. Figure 6-4 presents a generic benefits risk log template.

## Template

### Benefits Risk Log

| Organization: | <Name of the organization and/or division> | | |
|---|---|---|---|
| Version: | <X.X> | Version Type: | <Final/Draft> |
| Issued by: | <Name, Surname> | Issue date: | <DD-MM-YY> |
| Department: | <Department> | Job title: | <Job title> |

### Benefits Change Log

| Benefit Code/Name | Description of the Risk | Risk Identifier/ Risk Owner | Probability | Impact | Response Type | Response Strategy | Status |
|---|---|---|---|---|---|---|---|
| <Add text> | <Add text> | Risk Identifier: <Add text> Risk Owner: <Add text> | <Add text> | <Add text> | <Add text> | Action: <Add text> Action Owner: <Add text> Action due date: <Add text> | <Add text> |
| | | | | | | | |
| | | | | | | | |
| | | | | | | | |
| | | | | | | | |
| | | | | | | | |
| | | | | | | | |

Figure 6-4   Template: Benefits Risk Log.

### 6.2.4 Planning Benefits Stakeholder Engagement

In the same way that programs and projects have stakeholders to be managed, benefits realization has stakeholders too. Most or all of the benefits stakeholders may be the same stakeholders identified on program and project levels. However, some activities relevant to ensure stakeholders actively supporting the realization of the expected benefits may be missed, since stakeholder engagement plans usually focus only on program and project delivery. Some stakeholder engagement strategies may go beyond the program and project closeout. Additionally, some stakeholders that will be important after project closeout may be missed in a stakeholder engagement strategy that focuses solely on program and project delivery. Figure 6-5 presents a generic Benefit Stakeholder Engagement Plan template.

## 6.3 Enabling the Realization of Strategic Benefits

Benefits realization is planned on portfolio, program, and project levels, as discussed in the previous chapter. According to those plans, a series of prerequisites will have to be met during project and program life cycles to enable the realization of any expected benefits, which will happen mostly after project closeout. Therefore, during the project delivery or execution stages, program and project management teams have to follow the benefits realization plan, making sure it is updated whenever changes affect it.

Another important aspect is the procedures associated to program and project closeout. Programs and projects may close in different ways, which depend on the closeout procedures. In each specific case, benefits realization will start, continue, be handed over, concluded or even canceled.

| Subsection | Subject |
|------------|---------|
| 6.3.1 | Change Control |
| 6.3.2 | Project Closeout |
| 6.3.3 | Managing Transition |

### 6.3.1 Change Control

All changes required to projects should follow management of change systems adopted by the organization (PMI® 2013a). Then all the documents related to the Benefits Realization Management life cycle will also need to have their versions controlled. In addition, any changes to these documents have to be

## Benefit Stakeholder Engagement Plan

| Organization: | <Name of the organization and/or division> | | |
|---|---|---|---|
| Program or project: | <Name of the program or project> | | |
| Version: | <X.X> | Version Type: | <Final/Draft> |
| Issued by: | <Name, Surname> | Issue date: | <DD-MM-YY> |
| Department: | <Department> | Job title: | <Job title:> |
| Approved by: | <Name, Surname> | Approval date: | <DD-MM-YY> |
| Department: | <Department> | Job title: | <Job title:> |

| Stakeholder | Goals, motivations, expectations, and interests | Influence | Interest | Impact | Level of involvement | Action type / stakeholder category | Strategies |
|---|---|---|---|---|---|---|---|
| | | | | | | | |
| | | | | | | | |
| | | | | | | | |
| | | | | | | | |

Figure 6-5   Template: Benefit stakeholder engagement plan.

managed according to a formal and structured process. Business cases, for example, have to be updated for every change approved, and then new versions should be created in order to maintain a log of changes (Buttrick 1997). This is a key point for evaluating project success, since project sponsors can evaluate success based on the achievement of the benefits defined in the business case (APM 2012).

To keep track of the changes to each specific benefit from its identification to the end of the benefit realization life cycle, program and project managers can use a benefit change log that captures all changes made to the benefit. Such changes may include changes to its description, measures, benefit ownership, measurement process, and targets for benefit realization, among others. Without keeping the log of changes, situations can occur such as the misunderstanding of realization patterns due to changes to measurement procedures or even missing historical data based on changes of storage procedures for the measures database. Figure 6-6 presents a generic benefits change log template.

## 6.3.2 Project Closeout

Since projects are periodically assessed, decisions can be made concerning their status based on their performance or the current relevance of their objectives (Levine 2005). Decisions related to project closeout are taken or approved as part of the governance process. Closed projects are removed from the portfolio when they are completed or when they are no longer viable (Buttrick 1997). Some suggested classifications of project closeout are presented below.

- *Normal.* Project activities are completed, and then all the outputs have been delivered to the customer (Gray and Larson 2010). Even in a program, the outputs are handed over when each project is concluded (Chittenden and Bon 2006). Then the ownership of the outputs is totally transferred to the customers, and they are incorporated into the regular operations (Gray and Larson 2010).

- *Premature.* Some activities are excluded from the scope; then the project is finished early, which can make the benefits become illusory or unsustainable (Gray and Larson 2010). This happens, for example, when there is a severe reduction of funding due to circumstances external to the project. In this case, the scope of the solution could be reduced so severely that it will no longer enable the realization of the expected benefits. The project will deliver its products and then be closed out, but the products will be usually less or lower in quality than originally planned.

## Template

### Benefits Change Log

| Organization: | <Name of the organization and/or division> | |
|---|---|---|
| Version: | <X.X> | Benefits changed in this version: | Benefit code(s) |
| Issued by: | <Name, Surname> | Issue date: | <DD-MM-YY> |
| Department: | <Department> | Job title: | <Job title:> |

### Benefits Change Log

| Benefit Code/Name | Description of the Change | Reason of the Change | Originator | Date Received | Date Required | Impact | Stakeholders Notified |
|---|---|---|---|---|---|---|---|
| <Add text> | <Add text> | <Add text> | <Add text> | <Add text> | <Add text> | <Add text> | <Add text> |
| | | | | | | | |
| | | | | | | | |
| | | | | | | | |
| | | | | | | | |
| | | | | | | | |
| | | | | | | | |
| | | | | | | | |

**Figure 6-6** Template: Benefits Change Log.

- **Perpetual.** Project managers need to force closeout by limiting budget or compressing the schedule if projects are delayed several times or have their scope increased and changed, when it may seem that they will never end (Gray and Larson 2010).
- **Failed project.** This situation occurs if the project proves to be unnecessary or unfeasible and then is canceled (Gray and Larson 2010).
- **Changed priority.** When business strategies change and projects are not as necessary as they were, they may lose priority and then should be closed (Gray and Larson 2010).

Project closeouts are key decisions that should be based on inputs coming from the constant assessment of stakeholders, business needs, and project status. An important activity in this process is the transference of the ownership of project outputs, which can compromise the benefits realization if not performed correctly.

### 6.3.3 Managing Transition

A transition plan should be followed in order to ensure the actual implementation of project outputs (Chittenden and Bon 2006). This plan should aim to maximize benefit realization by using the appropriate management of change strategies (Bradley 2010). Whenever benefits realization depends on changes to existing processes, it is important that the changes will be understood and accepted by the key stakeholders. In addition, in order to ensure the realization of the expected benefits, cultural aspects should be managed, especially when benefits realization is dependent on acceptance by different cultures across various geographies; this adds extra complexity to the process of managing changes. For example, perhaps the company wishes to introduce a policy that provides free office lunch and reduces the lunch break from one and a half hours to one hour.

This policy can be seen as a positive in various cultures, because it may increase productivity and enable people to go home earlier in the evening. Conversely, the same new policy can be perceived in a negative way in other cultures that value longer lunch breaks, such as in the Latin American (Moran et al. 2011) and Spanish cultures (Remland et al. 2015). In such cultures, such a policy could lead to employee dissatisfaction and even increase in employee turnover. Therefore training, events, and the participation of HR professionals should occur whenever necessary (Chittenden and Bon 2006). Communications strategies should also support the acceptance of the changes by taking into consideration all the different target audiences, the objectives of the communication, and the communication channels available.

| Template | | | |
|---|---|---|---|
| **Benefits Handover Form** | | | |
| Organization: | <Name of the organization and/or division> | | |
| Version: | <X.X> | Version Type: | <Final/Draft> |
| **Project Manager:** | <Name, Surname> | **Issue date:** | <DD-MM-YY> |
| **Department:** | <Department> | **Job title:** | <Job title> |
| **Benefit Owner:** | <Name, Surname> | **Approval date:** | <DD-MM-YY> |
| **Department:** | <Department> | **Job title:** | **<Job title>** |

| |
|---|
| **I. Program/Project Manager** |
| <Add text> |
| **II. Benefit Owner** |
| <Add text> |
| **III. Benefit Code/Name** |
| <Add text> |
| **IV. Benefit Measure** |
| <Add text> |
| **V. Measurement Baseline** |
| <Add text> |
| **VI. Frequency of Measurement** |
| <Add text> |
| **VII. Measure Owner** |
| <Add text> |
| **VIII. Benefit Reporting Recipients** |
| <Add text> |
| **IX. Expected Benefit (Baseline from Business Case)** |
| <Add text> |
| **X. Expected Benefit (Reviewed Baseline)** |
| <Add text> |
| **XI. Benefit Realization Timeline** |
| <Add text> |

**Figure 6-7** Template: Benefits Handover Form.

Another key step of the transition process is the formal handover of benefits to the benefits owners. It happens after the conclusion of program and project delivery. It means that the business no longer depends on the program or project activities to realize the benefits. A formal handover marks the end of the program or project's partial accountability for the benefit, which makes the benefit owner fully accountable for the realization. A benefit handover can be applicable to formalize the handover from program or project teams to benefit owners. Figure 6-7 presents a generic benefits handover form template.

## 6.4 Making Benefits Happen

After being planned, benefits have to be realized. In a well-structured and mature organization, benefits are the steps to be taken in order to successfully execute business strategies. Therefore, benefits realization goes beyond the remit of program and project managers. At the organizational level, benefits realization is instrumental for business success, as it part of project governance and of project portfolio management (Chittenden and Bon 2006).

The benefits realization process can start during project execution, since it is the stage of a project life cycle when projects start to deliver outputs and outcomes. Nevertheless, most of it happens after project closeout, when all the project outputs have already been delivered. In many cases, the project management team will have little if any association with the actual process of benefit realization. Although they must be involved with, if not made responsible for, the production of benefits realization strategies, they tend to hand over such strategies to benefits owners at the closeout stage of their projects. In these cases, the role of project governance and project portfolio management are important to ensure the continuity and effectiveness of the process.

In programs, benefits realization occurs continuously during the program life cycle (OGC 2011b). Different from standalone projects, programs have responsibility for managing the benefits realization process. In these cases, benefits realization can be managed on the program level or on the strategic or corporate level as well (OGC 2011b).

The benefits are delivered as long as programs and projects are being executed, but often they occur only after all the outcomes are delivered. After delivery, new capabilities should be incorporated into the business in order to produce the effects of the change (OGC 2011b). Therefore, benefits realization is an organizational process that ensures project outcomes are embedded into the normal business operations.

Sometimes businesses need support in employing new capabilities or services in order to achieve the desired benefits (OGC 2011b). In this case, it is recommended that the business receive support even after the program or project closes (OGC 2011b). This support can be provided by the program or project structure or by a functional area specially focused on ensuring the realization of benefits and coordinating the delivery of benefits by the whole portfolio of initiatives (OGC 2011).

During the entire process of benefits realization, even after program or project closeout, the benefits realization plans should be frequently reviewed (OGC 2011b). to ensure that they are still applicable and effective. These reviews will have input from the benefits reviewing and evaluating process discussed in the next chapter.

## 6.5 Case Study: Enterprise Benefits Realization

This section demonstrates the way ProjectEng realizes the benefits that are required by its business strategy. It is exemplified by focusing on one strategic initiative of the business: the operational excellence program. The selected program has three projects that aim to reduce operating costs. Since cost reduction is driven by a set of different factors that may overlap, the measurement of the financial benefit at the program level significantly reduces the risk of double-counting benefits. Nevertheless, a set of intermediate benefits will also be realized; therefore, they were previously identified and will have their realization monitored and evaluated. This is important because they will support the realization of the end benefit; should they not happen, the end benefit is also unlikely to be achieved.

| Subsection | Subject |
|:---:|:---|
| 6.5.1 | Developing a Program-Level Benefits Realization Strategy |
| 6.5.2 | Realizing Benefits |
| 6.5.3 | Handing Over Benefits |

### 6.5.1 Developing a Program-Level Benefits Realization Strategy

The first required step to ensure the realization of program benefits is the development of a program-level benefits realization strategy. To demonstrate how to perform this activity, the following example depicts a benefits realization strategy for the operational excellence program. The program aims to redesign the organization's operating model to avoid unnecessary costs by increasing efficiency and effectiveness. The scope includes improvement of the maturity in Benefits Realization Management, business process mapping and improvement, and the optimization and integration of information technology (IT) systems. The program organizational structure spans several business departments such as human resources, IT, finance, and others.

A fully worked example of the program-level benefits realization strategy for this case study is provided in *Appendix D*, using the scenario above as a contextual reference.

## 6.5.2 Realizing Benefits

After the benefits realization strategy has been prepared and approved, the benefits are realized by the respective benefit owners with support from the program team. According to the benefit profile, Hans Braun, Chief Operating Officer, is responsible for the realization of the benefit B002 Operating Costs. However, this benefit will be achieved by the realization of a series of intermediate benefits. Therefore, the benefits owners responsible for the realization of such benefits will play an important role in the realization of the end benefit, since they need to produce the benefits that are expected to contribute to the realization of the end benefit required to achieve the organization's strategic objectives.

## 6.5.3 Handing Over Benefits

The benefits handover form is produced by the program or project manager and approved by the benefit owner or benefit recipient to formalize the handover of the benefit. From the moment this document is approved, the benefit owner takes full and exclusive ownership for realizing the benefit and becomes responsible for controlling and reporting the performance of the benefit realization process, no longer depending on the program(s) or project(s) to enable its realization. The handover form should capture some key information about the benefit as well as any changes to the expected amount of benefit to be realized and the period of benefit realization. The following example formalizes the handover of the benefit B002 Operating Costs from Jeff Stuart, Program Manager, to Hans Braun, Chief Operating Officer. In this example, the benefit handover happens at the program closeout stage, after all outputs have been delivered and all changes imbedded into business as usual (BAU). Although all changes were complete prior to the beginning of 2017, the program continued to support change management activities for another six months to ensure the realization of the benefits. During these six months, the program management team monitored and controlled the realization of the expected benefits. From the handover onward, the benefits owner becomes fully responsible for ensuring the continuation of the benefits realization at least until all the expected benefits are realized.

Table 6-1 Key Benefits Realization Management
Practices to Support Project Success: Realizing

| Governance Process | Benefits Realization Management Process | Benefits Realization Management Key Practices |
|---|---|---|
| Concluding and embedding changes to realize benefits | Realizing benefits | A benefits realization strategy is applied to the project and/or program. |
| | | Activities to ensure the integration of project outputs to the regular business routine are executed as part of the project's scope |
| | | From the first delivery to the project's closeout, the organization performs a preplanned, regular process to ensure the integration of project outputs into the regular business routine |
| | | After project closeout, the organization keeps monitoring project outcomes to ensure the achievement of all benefits expected in the business case |

*Source:* Adapted from Serra, C. E. and M. Kunc. "Benefits Realisation Management and Its Influence on Project Success and on the Execution of Business Strategies." *International Journal of Project Management,* 33, no. 1 (2015). Used with permission.

A fully worked example of the benefits handover form for this case study is provided in *Appendix D,* using the scenario above as a contextual reference.

## 6.6 Chapter Summary: Realizing Benefits

When the project starts to deliver outputs, and then outcomes start to occur, it is necessary to perform a set of previously planned activities to ensure the assimilation of new capabilities by the business. Without the required support, the business cannot realize all the planned benefits. Then, more than part of project scope, organizations should perform all required activities to integrate project outcomes into business routines. Table 6-1 summarizes some key practices (Serra and Kunc 2015) discussed in this chapter to ensure the effectiveness of benefits realization, which are instrumental for effective project governance, and consequently in supporting project success.

The process of realizing benefits includes a set of activities, which were discussed in this chapter. These activities produce a series of outputs that can be also called management products, which are summarized as follows:

- Program- and Project-Level Benefits Realization Management Planning Management Products
- Program Benefits Realization Strategy
- Project Benefits Realization Strategy
- Benefits Risk Log
- Benefits Stakeholder Engagement Plan
- Benefits Control and Handover Management Products
- Benefits Change Log
- Benefits Handover Form

## 6.7 End-of-Chapter Review Questions—Chapter 6

In this section, a set of end-of-chapter review questions are provided to enable a self-assessment of the understanding of Chapter 6. The answers to all questions can be found at the end of the book in *Appendix A*.

1. What is benefit realization?
2. Which are the four different types of plans or strategies that are directly related to benefit realization?
3. What is a benefit change log?
4. List five different types of project closeout.
5. Why is the management of change activities important for the benefit realization process?
6. When does benefit realization start?

# Chapter 7

# Reviewing and Evaluating Benefits

Once benefits begin to be realized, the process of benefit realization has to be monitored, and benefits have to be reviewed and evaluated. Environmental changes and business changes may affect the rationale behind some of the expected benefits, and as a result some benefits may no longer be needed; they may require adjustments to their benefit profiles; or they may require updates to the program and project business cases. In addition, the realization process may not happen as planned; therefore, issues should be identified and treated in a timely manner. In case the changes or deviations affecting some benefits are not identified and treated accordingly, the achievement of the expected targets for benefit realization becomes extremely unlikely, as does the achievement of the strategic objectives related to those benefits.

This chapter discusses the process of benefits review and evaluation to ensure that the benefits realized match the expectations defined during the benefits planning process, or that plans and baselines are updated as required by changes to business strategies or to other circumstances that may affect these plans and baselines.

## 7.1 Introduction: Managing the Ongoing Portfolio of Initiatives

After the organization has begun to execute its portfolio of initiatives, the ongoing initiatives need to be aligned with business strategies. It requires the organization to continually monitoring and controlling these initiatives as well as reviewing their alignment with business strategies.

Similarly, the organization has to ensure effective communication to the relevant stakeholders about the status of the ongoing initiatives. Stakeholders need to be aware of the status of the benefits realization process to know whether the expected benefits will be realized, when they will be realized, whether the benefit realization process will have any impacts that need resolution, and what they can do to contribute to the successful realization of the expected benefits. In the same way, the program and project teams as well as the benefit owners must monitor stakeholders to identify whether their needs are changing or their commitments to the benefits realization process will still be delivered.

The processes required to maintain a cohesive and effective portfolio are presented in this chapter.

## 7.2 Keeping Programs and Projects on Track

Effective monitoring and controlling requires the constant management of the expected benefits from the programs and projects, which can be achieved through the performance of program and project periodic reviews, periodic realignment between the project portfolio and business strategy, postreview reporting, and stakeholder engagement. These key processes are discussed in the following topics.

| Subsection | Subject |
|---|---|
| 7.2.1 | Performing Periodic Program and Project Reviews |
| 7.2.2 | Ensuring Stakeholder Awareness, Alignment, Support, and Engagement |
| 7.2.3 | Reviewing the Alignment between the Portfolio and the Business Strategy |

### 7.2.1 Performing Periodic Program and Project Reviews

Program and project reviews are usually performed routinely to assess performance against the planned baselines. Measures related to performance are appraised using techniques such as the Critical Path Method and the Earned Value Analysis (Levine 2005; PMI® 2013a). However, in addition to the assessment of performance against the schedule, budget, and scope objectives, the performance component related to the program or project ability to enable the creation of the expected value for the business must also be periodically reassessed. Therefore, projects should be periodically evaluated using their selection criteria to identify whether they are still fulfilling these criteria (Levine 2005). The assessment includes criteria relevant to project management performance and also criteria related to the creation of business value.

The business case and the project plan are usually the best references available in terms of formal expectations, providing a sound basis to assess project success. Therefore, the likely or actual achievement of the objectives defined in the business case and in the project plan must be verified (APM 2012) during the periodic review cycles. This assessment evaluates performance against criteria that has been clearly described in the business case and in the project plan. This process monitors the projects against their baselines to verify delivery on time and on budget, changes, and accuracy of estimates (Chittenden and Bon 2006). The outputs are reviewed in order to confirm that they are still meeting the desired objectives (Chittenden and Bon 2006). Consequently, the review report provides enough information to support informed decision making in view of realigning any eventual deviations of performance toward the achievement of the expected objectives.

## 7.2.2 Ensuring Stakeholder Awareness, Alignment, Support, and Engagement

Stakeholder support is critical for success, and the stakeholder communication process is essential to maintaining stakeholder awareness and commitment, managing stakeholder expectations, and delivering relevant information (Chittenden and Bon 2006). Clear and reliable information supported by key success indicators should be provided to project stakeholders (APM 2004).

The reporting process used to disseminate the results of each review to the appropriate audiences must be useful and should support the organization's decision-making processes (APM 2004). To provide such support, the reporting process must be planned at the program or project level and aligned with the portfolio governance processes.

Stakeholder communication should also be planned, clearly defining the objectives, the contents, the periodicity, the channels, the key messages, and the key stakeholders. It should seek the engagement of stakeholders (Bradley 2010). The plan also should contain actions to overcome resistance to change (Bradley 2010; Chittenden and Bon 2006).

Additionally, the stakeholders' engagement process should be carefully carried out in order to ensure clear and effective communication. Messages should be easy to understand, the right messages should be employed, and feedback should be collected from the stakeholders about the messages (Chittenden and Bon 2006).

### 7.2.3 Reviewing the Alignment between the Project Portfolio and the Business Strategy

Since business strategies are always changing, the ongoing portfolio of changes is constantly updated, enabling a meaningful and successful execution of business strategy. Therefore, to support the execution of business strategies, a key process of project portfolio management and project governance is to ensure effective alignment between business strategies and program and project strategies.

One practice that supports effective governance of a project portfolio is to hold regular Portfolio Governance Board meetings in order to enable senior managers to deliberate and make decisions regarding the performance of the strategy execution on the project portfolio level. Before the Portfolio Governance Board meetings, the board members should be prepared to make decisions by evaluating the summary status of active projects, preparing proposed changes, and listening to recommendations from portfolio managers (Kendall and Rollins 2003). The information generated by the regular program and project reviews is a key input to this process of senior-level decision making.

During the portfolio level reviews, Portfolio Governance Boards should manage performance against the plan, but they also need to take into consideration any impact that changes to business strategies may have over the project portfolio. As discussed in previous chapters, in order to be successful in managing long-term business strategies, organizations need to change whenever necessary (Amason 2011; OGC 2011b). This happens because in constantly changing internal and external environments, changes are needed for maintaining and continuously developing competitive advantage, which should be the main goal of any business (Amason 2011; Porter 1998). Further effective strategists should know during the strategy implementation, their plans meet the real world; they will be challenged, and they invariably have to be changed (Amason 2011). Therefore, goals, objectives, targets, and measures are always changing.

Because of the constantly changing characteristics of the global business environment, organizations should be able to rapidly respond to any changes and to make sure that the ongoing portfolio of changes will be maintained effectively and aligned to the current business strategies, despite any changes that those strategies may suffer. An effective way to keep the alignment between business strategies and the strategy execution is by constantly reviewing and evaluating the benefits expected to be enabled by the ongoing portfolio of programs and projects, as well as the benefits being realized by programs, projects, and business operations.

## 7.3 Reviewing and Evaluating Benefits

To keep programs and projects aligned with the business strategies, and to ensure the success of strategy execution, the ability of programs, projects, and operations to deliver expected benefits must be periodically reassessed. Therefore, benefits reviews should be performed regularly (Chittenden and Bon 2006) by updating benefits maps, benefits profiles, and benefits realization plans (OGC 2011b). Benefits reviews are an effective way to maintain the alignment between projects, programs, and business strategies. Even if the benefits realization planning and executing activities are effective, the lack of a benefits review can result in projects delivering outputs that are no longer needed by the organization, leading to project failure from a strategic perspective.

In addition, reviews are important to track the actual realization of any planned benefits and to evaluate the actual success of change initiatives in creating value to the business. As a result, the evaluation of investments after completion is an element that differentiates the most successful companies from the others (Ward and Daniel 2012). Nevertheless, although benefits reviews are important, many organizations do not track their benefits (Bradley 2010; Ward and Daniel 2012). Some professionals even admit they overstate benefits in order to support the approval of business cases, once they know that they will not be evaluated after project closeout (Ward and Daniel 2012). Therefore, reviewing and evaluating benefits is a key—though perhaps still missing in many cases—point of attention to ensure effective benefits realization. To do so, the following set of activities is recommended.

| Subsection | Subject |
|---|---|
| 7.3.1 | Verifying Actual Realization against Plan |
| 7.3.2 | Verifying Consistency with Business Strategy |
| 7.3.3 | Informing Stakeholders about Progress and Deliveries |
| 7.3.4 | Evaluating the Effectiveness of Benefits Realization Management and Identifying Lessons Learned |
| 7.3.5 | Identifying the Potential for Achieving Further Benefits |

### 7.3.1 Verifying Actual Realization against Plan

Since the benefits realization is strongly recommended to be planned at the initial steps of program and project life cycles, the delivery of benefits is expected to happen according to the plan. Therefore, the organizational role that is assigned in the benefits realization plan to track the benefits is responsible for verifying if the benefits realization is happening according to plan (Chittenden and Bon 2006; OGC 2011b). If necessary, the benefits profile and the benefits realization plan have to be updated to reflect any changes.

Since benefits realization is about creating value to the business, it is necessary to verify how much previous deliveries have changed original performance (Chittenden and Bon 2006; OGC 2011b). This measurement should follow the procedures described in the benefits realization plan. The actual performance should be compared against the baselines and the targets in terms of improvement (see Figure 7-1). The achievement of the planned benefits can be then confirmed, and the achievement of any unexpected benefits and disbenefits can also be identified at this point (Ward and Daniel 2012).

If the actual benefits do not match the expectations, it may be due to problems with the solution that was implemented and should have been managed according to the benefits risk management plan (see Figure 7-2), which should be part of the benefits realization strategy.

Alternately, it might be due to benefit hyperestimation—the wrong estimation of the benefits to be achieved. It may be due to using the wrong assumptions, it can be influenced optimistic bias, or it may even be caused by errors in the calculations. When variances happen due to benefit hyperestimation, it is harder—and sometimes unlikely—for the organization to resolve the problem. In this case, a new benefits realization baseline may be saved even if the new figures do not justify the investment made. In case the operations put in place are no longer viable, further investment in changes may be required, or the operations should be discontinued to avoid additional losses.

Another important element of tracking benefits is the awareness regarding benefits decay (Ward and Daniel 2012) (see Figure 7-3). Once benefits begin to be realized in a regular pattern, there is a risk of becoming too confident that the realization is going to continue in a regular pattern. If the organization stops tracking benefits realization, it can lose sight of any variations and even of a natural decrease as the implementation of the business change loses momentum. Many times, actions will be needed to boost or reenergize the process in order to keep the realization at the same desired pace throughout the entire benefits realization life cycle.

## Template

### Benefits Tracking Sheet—Program Level

| | | | |
|---|---|---|---|
| **Organization:** | <Name of the organization and/or division> | | |
| **Program** | <Name of the program> | | |
| **Version:** | <X.X> | **Version Type:** | <Final/Draft> |
| **Issued by:** | <Name, Surname> | **Issue date:** | <DD-MM-YY> |
| **Department:** | <Department> | **Job title:** | <Job title:> |
| **Approved by:** | <Name, Surname> | **Approval date:** | <DD-MM-YY> |
| **Department:** | <Department> | **Job title:** | <Job title:> |

| Basic Information | | | Realization Start Date | | Measurement | | | | Total Benefit Expected | | | |
|---|---|---|---|---|---|---|---|---|---|---|---|---|
| Project Code/ Name | Benefit Code/ Name | Measure | Benefit Realization Start Date (Baseline) | Benefit Realization Start Date (Actual) | Date | Owner | Total Realized this Period | Total Realized to Date | Total Benefit (Baseline) | Total Benefit (Planned) | End Date (Baseline) | End Date (Planned) |
| | | | | | | | | | | | | |
| | | | | | | | | | | | | |
| | | | | | | | | | | | | |
| | | | | | | | | | | | | |
| | | | | | | | | | | | | |

Figure 7-1  Template: Program-Level Benefits Tracking Sheet.

| Template | | | |
|---|---|---|---|
| **Project-Level Benefits Realization Control Sheet** | | | |
| **Organization:** | *<Name of the organization and/or division>* | | |
| **Project:** | *<Name of the project>* | | |
| Version: | *<X.X>* | Version Type: | *<Final/Draft>* |
| **Issued by:** | *<Name, Surname>* | **Issue date:** | *<DD-MM-YY>* |
| **Department:** | *<Department>* | **Job title:** | *<Job title>* |
| **Approved by:** | *<Name, Surname>* | **Approval date:** | *<DD-MM-YY>* |
| **Department:** | *<Department>* | **Job title:** | *<Job title>* |

| I. Benefit Code/Name |
|---|
| *<Add text>* |
| **II. Benefit Measure** |
| *<Add text>* |
| **III. Benefit Owner** |
| *<Add text>* |

**IV. Benefit Realization Lifecycle**

| Benefit realization start date (baseline) | *<DD-MM-YY>* | Benefit realization end date (baseline) | *<DD-MM-YY>* |
|---|---|---|---|
| Benefit realization start date (actual) | *<DD-MM-YY>* | Benefit realization end date (planned) | *<DD-MM-YY>* |

**V.  Planned vs. Actuals**

| Year | YYYY | | | | YYYY | | | |
|---|---|---|---|---|---|---|---|---|
| Quarter | *Q1* | *Q2* | *Q3* | *Q4* | *Q1* | *Q2* | *Q3* | *Q4* |
| Planned | | | | | | | | |
| Cumulative | | | | | | | | |
| Actual | | | | | | | | |
| Cumulative | | | | | | | | |

**VI.  Issues**

| *List of issues* | *Actions to address the issues* |
|---|---|
| *<Add text>* | *<Add text>* |

**VII.  Risks**

| *List of risks* | *Actions in response to the risks* |
|---|---|
| *<Add text>* | *<Add text>* |

**VIII.  Actions**

| *<Add text>* |
|---|

**Figure 7-2**   Template: Project-Level Benefits Realization Control Sheet.

| Template | | | |
|---|---|---|---|
| **Benefits Realization Health Check** | | | |
| **Organization:** | *<Name of the organization and/or division>* | | |
| **Version:** | *<X.X>* | Version Type: | *<Final/Draft>* |
| **Issued by:** | *<Name, Surname>* | **Issue date:** | *<DD-MM-YY>* |
| **Department:** | *<Department>* | **Job title:** | *<Job title>* |
| **Approved by:** | *<Name, Surname>* | **Approval date:** | *<DD-MM-YY>* |
| **Department:** | *<Department>* | **Job title:** | *<Job title>* |

**I. Benefit Code/Name**

*<Add text>*

**II. Benefit Owner**

*<Name, Surname – Department/Job Title>*

**III. Program(s) and/or Project(s) Associated**

*<Add text>*

**IV. Checklist: Prerealization Process**

| | |
|---|---|
| Y/N | Benefit is clearly identified and defined. |
| Y/N | Benefit is measurable. |
| Y/N | Actions are taken to avoid the risk of benefit double counting or benefit hyper estimation. |
| Y/N | Benefit is clearly relevant to the achievement of strategic objectives. |
| Y/N | Benefit is clearly related to a set of change initiatives |
| Y/N | Benefit is decomposed in terms of the percent contribution expected from each initiative. |
| Y/N | Benefit is described in business case(s) approved at the beginning of the program(s)/project(s). |
| Y/N | Benefits ownership is clearly defined as well as the ownership by the benefits enabling initiatives. |
| Y/N | Actions are planned to ensure benefit realization by business operations. |
| Y/N | A benefits realization strategy defines a plan for the entire benefits realization life cycle. |

**V. Checklist: Realization Process**

| | |
|---|---|
| Y/N | Benefit is frequently reviewed and realigned to the current expectations. |

*(Continued on next page)*

*(Template: Benefits Realization Health Check, Continued)*

| | |
|---|---|
| Y/N | Results of benefit reviews are frequently communicated to the stakeholders. |
| Y/N | Benefit stakeholders needs are frequently reassessed. |
| Y/N | Benefit is monitored by the organization during the entire realization lifecycle. |
| Y/N | Benefit realization is frequently assessed against the expectations described in the business case. |
| Y/N | Benefits are periodically reevaluated against the business case. |
| Y/N | The occurrence of emergent disbenefits is monitored. |
| Y/N | The potential for realization of additional benefits is observed and exploited whenever appropriate. |
| Y/N | Actions are performed to ensure benefit realization by the regular business operations. |
| Y/N | Lessons learned are identified, captured, and applied. |
| Y/N | A benefits realization strategy is followed. |

**VI.  Benefit Measure**

<Add text>

**VII.  Sources of Measurement**

<Add text>

**VIII.  Benefits Realization RAG Status**

| G | A | R | Current amount of benefits realized against benefits realization schedule (baseline). |
|---|---|---|---|
| G | A | R | Current benefits forecast against total benefits expected (baseline). |

**IX.  Current Issues**

| List of issues | Actions to address the issues |
|---|---|
| <Add text> | <Add text> |

**X.  Current Risks**

| List of risks | Actions in response to the risks |
|---|---|
| <Add text> | <Add text> |

**XI.  Recovery Actions**

<Add text>

**Figure 7-3**   Template: Benefits Realization Health Check.

### 7.3.2 Verifying Consistency with Business Strategy

Although it is critical to ensure that the plan is still appropriate to ensure the realization of the expected benefits, it is even more important to review the benefits themselves  to ensure that they are still needed and whether they are still achievable. To do so, the current business needs should be frequently reassessed in periodic intervals as defined in the benefits realization plan. Expected benefits must be frequently reviewed to ensure that they remain consistent with the business strategy (Chittenden and Bon 2006; OGC 2011b).

### 7.3.3 Informing Stakeholders about Progress and Deliveries

After the benefits realization plans are reviewed, after business needs are reassessed and after the relevant updates are made to the benefits realization plans, the stakeholders should be informed about the progress and about the intermediate deliveries achieved to date (Chittenden and Bon 2006; OGC 2011b). This process ensures awareness about what is expected to be achieved and what, if anything, has changed from the original plan. It also provides an opportunity to stakeholders to identify relevant information that can be fed back to the benefits realization team. Appropriate communication channels should be provided so the stakeholders can manifest their views or even provide relevant information to ensure the success in the execution of the benefits realization plan. Figure 7-4 presents a generic Benefits Portfolio Dashboard template.

A diverse set of options is available in terms of communication tools, varying from basic standard templates to sophisticated electronic dashboards. Bradley (2010) recommends a measures dashboard as an effective way to report measures to the appropriate people, so that the required level of awareness can be achieved and any necessary actions can be taken. Bradley (2010) also remarks that according to the concept of management by exception, any dashboards should highlight only cases where there are problems to be addressed, so that efforts are not wasted on the analysis of the entire portfolio instead of focusing the attention only on the relevant cases.

### 7.3.4 Evaluating the Effectiveness of Benefits Realization Management and Identifying Lessons Learned

After reassessing the business needs and assessed the actual achievements against the plan, the effectiveness of Benefits Realization Management can be evaluated (Chittenden and Bon 2006; OGC 2011b). Depending on the results of the other activities included in this process, actions can be taken to recover

| Template | | | |
|---|---|---|---|
| **Benefits Portfolio Dashboard** | | | |
| **Organization:** | *<Name of the organization and/or division>* | | |
| Version: | *<X.X>* | Version Type: | *<Final/Draft>* |
| **Issued by:** | *<Name, Surname>* | **Issue date:** | *<DD-MM-YY>* |
| **Department:** | *<Department>* | **Job title:** | *<Job title>* |
| **Approved by:** | *<Name, Surname>* | **Approval date:** | *<DD-MM-YY>* |
| **Department:** | *<Department>* | **Job title:** | *<Job title>* |

| | **Benefit A** | **Benefit B** | **Benefit C** |
|---|---|---|---|
| **Benefit Code/Name** | | | |
| **Benefit Category** | | | |
| **Is the Benefit Measurable?** | | | |
| **Is the Benefit Financially Quantifiable?** | | | |
| **Measure** | | | |
| **Total Financial Amount** | | | |
| **Total Nonfinancial Amount** | | | |
| **Benefit Owner** | | | |
| **Frequency of Measurement** | | | |
| **Last Measurement Date** | | | |
| **Program(s)/Project(s) Code/Name** | | | |
| **Program/Project Budget** | | | |
| **Cost/Benefit Ratio (Baseline)** | | | |
| **Cost/Benefit Ratio** | | | |
| **Realization Start Date (Planned/ Actual)** | | | |
| **Realization End Date (Planned/ Actual)** | | | |
| **Total Benefit Expected (Baseline)** | | | |
| **Total Benefit Expected** | | | |
| **Benefit Realized to Date** | | | |
| **Benefit Realization RAG Status: Realization Schedule** | | | |
| **Benefit Realization RAG Status: Benefit Amount** | | | |

**Figure 7-4**  Template: Benefits Portfolio Dashboard.

from deviations, to avoid future deviations, or even to redefine expectations (Ward and Daniel 2012). It is also important to capture any lessons learned regarding the achievement or nonachievement of any expected benefits (Ward and Daniel 2012).

If expected benefits were not achieved, that may be explained by events associated to the project of program delivery life cycle. Therefore, program and project closeout reviews—which are part of any comprehensive project management methodology—are valuable elements to support the understanding of reasons for the achievement or nonachievement of expected benefits (Ward and Daniel 2012).

### 7.3.5 Identifying Potential for Achieving Further Benefits

At the beginning of any project, it may be difficult to identify all the benefits that are achievable, and some benefits may become evident only after the business change has been implemented (Ward and Daniel 2012). Therefore, reviews performed during and after implementation may reveal benefits that can be achieved with additional work. Those discoveries should be fed back into the processes associated with business performance management and project portfolio management because they may support the business case for new projects or generate actions to exploit the benefits that can be achieved by business operations without needing another project.

## 7.4 Case Study: Enterprise Benefits Review and Evaluation

This section demonstrates the way ProjectEng reviews and evaluates the realization of the benefits required by its business strategy. This process is exemplified by focusing on two projects. The first subsection shows a periodic control of the realization of benefits associated to a strategic project that is not part of a program. The project generates a nonfinancial benefit that prevents the risk of losing business due to a new regulation. Although the project does not generate financial value, it enables the organization to maintain a revenue stream that has been under risk. The second subsection involves a benefits realization health check applied to another nonfinancial benefit, which is the reduction of the learning curve for new starters. Although this benefit does not generate financial value, it can increase cost efficiency in generating new revenue by reducing the nonchargeable time for new employees. Therefore, it supports the achievement of end benefits that are financially measurable. Both examples address situations in which benefits realization is not happening according to plan, and therefore recovery actions are recommended as a result from both analyses. These two examples reinforce the importance of the review and evaluation of benefits to ensure that benefits realization achieves the expectations and generates the value required by the business strategies.

| Subsection | Subject |
|---|---|
| 7.4.1 | Benefits Realization Control |
| 7.4.2 | Performing Benefits Realization Health Checks |

## 7.4.1 Controlling Benefits Realization

Benefits realization must be controlled as benefits start to be realized. It can happen on a project level, a program level, on a portfolio level or even only after program and project closeout by regular business operations. The example below reports the status of the benefit B005 Professional Registration in January 2016. Although it is an end benefit that directly supports the achievement of the strategic objective SO003, professional registration, that benefit is realized at the project level. The following report describes a situation that faces delay in benefits realization due to unplanned circumstances. In summary, a missed constraint affected the project's ability to realize the benefit as previously planned. Therefore, the baseline plan must be reviewed and updated in accordance with the current situation.

A fully worked example of the utilization of a Project Level Benefits Realization Control Sheet is provided in *Appendix C* by using the scenario above as a contextual reference.

## 7.4.2 Performing Benefits Realization Health Checks

Another relevant tool to be applied during the realization of benefits to ensure the effectiveness of the process is the benefits realization health check, which enables the program and project management team and/or the business operations to identify issues or risks that may, currently or in the future, affect the benefits realization. The following example identified a deviation in the realization of the benefit B003-02 reduction of learning curve against the benefit realization plan. It happened because of a lack of control after program and project closeout. Since there was no one monitoring the benefit, the deviation had not been identified until the benefits health check was issued. It was a violation of the terms planned in the benefit realization strategy and formalized in a benefits handover form,

**Table 7.1  Key Benefits Realization Management Practices to Support Project Success: Reviewing and Evaluating**

| Governance Process | Benefits Realization Management Process | Benefits Realization Management Key Practices |
|---|---|---|
| Managing the ongoing portfolio of changes | Reviewing and evaluating benefits | Project outputs and outcomes are frequently reviewed to ensure their alignment with expectations |
| | | Stakeholders are aware of the results of project reviews, and their needs are frequently assessed with a view to making changes |
| | | Actual project outcomes adhere to the expected outcomes planned in the business case |

*Source:* Adapted from Serra, C. E. *Benefits Realisation Management and Its Influence on Project Success, Project Governance, and Execution of Business Strategy: Analysis of Brazil, the United Kingdom, and the United States of America.* Coventry, UK: University of Warwick (2012); and Serra, C. E. and M. Kunc. "Benefits Realisation Management and Its Influence on Project Success and on the Execution of Business Strategies." *International Journal of Project Management* 33(1) 2015. (Used with permission.)

which was signed off at the program closeout stage. As a result of the health check, a list of actions was produced to identify the root causes of the deviations, produce a recovery plan, and monitor benefit realization going forward.

A fully worked example of the utilization of a benefits realization health check is provided in *Appendix C* using this scenario as a contextual reference.

# 7.5 Chapter Summary: Reviewing and Evaluating Benefits

Project benefits must be reviewed during project execution to ensure that they are still meeting expectations and that the business needs have not been changed. If something has been changed, the project scope can be updated in order to realign the project and the business needs. These reviews should involve or communicate to all the relevant stakeholders in order to align expectations, reestablish priorities, and ensure the required support. Table 7-1 summarizes some key practices (Serra and Kunc 2015) discussed in this chapter to ensure the effectiveness of benefits realization, which are instrumental for effective project governance and consequently for the support of project success.

The process of reviewing and evaluating benefits includes a set of activities discussed in this chapter. These activities produce a series of outputs that can be also called management products, which are summarized below.

- Benefits tracking and controlling management products:
- Benefits tracking sheet
- Benefits portfolio dashboard
- Benefits realization control sheet
- Benefits realization health check

## 7.6 End-of-Chapter Review Questions—Chapter 7

In this section, a set of end-of-chapter review questions are provided to enable a self-assessment of the reader's understanding of Chapter 7. The answers to all questions can be found at the end of the book in *Appendix A*.

1. Briefly speaking, how does one keep programs and projects on track (cite three groups of activities)?
2. What are program and project reviews?
3. Why is stakeholder engagement important?
4. How does one keep the alignment between the portfolio of projects and the business strategies?
5. Why are periodic benefit reviews important (cite five reasons)?

# PART III

## Appendices

# Appendix A

# Answers to End-of-Chapter Questions

## Chapter 1

1. *Benefits Realization Management* is a set of a set of practices needed to ensure that programs, projects, portfolios, and day-to-day business operations work together in a meaningful and organized way to realize the benefits required by the business strategies to perform a meaningful and sustainable creation of value (Serra and Kunc 2013).

2. Benefits Realization Management supports project success by ensuring the prioritization of the investments that are required by the business strategy, supporting the effectiveness of the delivery process in ensuring the focus on the creation of strategic value to the business, and then making sure business operations are realizing the expected benefits even after the end of project and program life cycles.

3. No, organizations in general are reporting high rates of project failure.

4. Yes, we can, because business strategies are mostly plans to change the business. Project management is a set of "knowledge, skills, tools, and techniques" (PMI® 2013a) or a "management discipline" (APM 2012) to manage the implementation of these changes.

5. Between 20 and 30 percent of the global economy is project based (PMI® 2009; Turner 2009), varying from country to country.

6. Organizations need to ensure the success of their most relevant projects, and they can do so mainly by performing effective governance.

7. The increasing performance of strategic governance leads organizations to focus on the delivery of planned benefits, since benefits realization is gradually being seen by organizations as the most relevant criterion to evaluate project success. Therefore, by not performing a well-structured process, organizations may be creating, managing, and succeeding with many projects that may not be relevant, while other, more relevant projects may fail or are not even started.

# Chapter 2

1. Management by Objectives (MBO) was introduced by Peter Drucker in 1954 as a process of participative objectives setting and their subsequent control. It can be considered one of the starting points for the development of further performance management and strategy implementation processes, tools, and techniques such as, for example, the Balanced Scorecard (BSC).

2. Total Quality Control (TQC) is a system in which all organizational departments participate in Quality Control, which is an effective way to manage the performance of business process. Hoshin management defines a set of "vital few objectives" that are cascaded and disseminated throughout the organization. It also establishes long- and short-term policies and goals. These techniques provide a practical way to ensure the achievement of organizational objectives and to motivate workforces in the improvement of performance.

3. The BSC is a tool to support organizations on the management of performance and on the execution of their business strategies by establishing a logical link between a set of objectives, which are distributed across four different perspectives. These objectives usually tend toward the achievement of a final financial objective. By providing an operational and realistic way to translate the strategic plan, BSC expands the concept of MBO and provides a model easily understandable by the workforce.

4. Project management is a set of processes, tools, and techniques that can be applied to ensure the efficient and effective delivery of objectives required by the business strategies. By definition, projects are temporary

and undertaken to achieve unique objectives; therefore, they are different from business-as-usual (BAU) or operational work that is continuous and repetitive.

5. Project portfolio management is a set of processes that are designed to support the successful management of the set of projects needed by the organization. It does that by aligning strategies, composing the portfolio of initiatives, concluding initiatives and embedding changes to realize benefits and managing the ongoing portfolio of initiatives.

6. Program management is a set of processes that are designed to support the management of group of projects and related nonproject work in conjunction toward the achievement of strategic objectives aiming to maximize the realization of benefits that might not be achieved if the projects were managed separately.

7. Strategy execution is the actual execution of business strategies in order to achieve the expected business objectives.

8. Business strategy is a long-term and sustainable orientation for organizations, usually working toward the development of competitive advantage. To accomplish this, the business strategy guides the scope of an organization's processes and activities, which very often requires resource changes and affects operational process and decisions. To provide competitive advantage or to yield new opportunities, it may require the organization to stretch resources and organizational competences. However, it is important to note that business strategy will be heavily affected by resource availability and by the values and expectations of the organization's stakeholders. Finally, business strategy defines and exploits the relationship with the environment, although it is also heavily affected by environmental forces.

9. Project strategy is a way to successfully contribute to the organization, while project management strategy is about successfully delivering scope within the agreed-upon schedule and budget.

# Chapter 3

1. Project success is acceptance of having met success criteria defined by key project stakeholders.

2. Project success is usually assessed in two steps usually called appraisal and evaluation. The first measures the relevance of each project and defines expectations, and the second generates inputs to define whether projects were successful.

3. Successful project management performance is determined by how well project results fit into the expected budget, schedule, and output requirements.

4. Success in delivering benefits to the organization is determined by how well the outputs enabled the business to produce its expected outcomes, avoid undesired benefits, realize the expected benefits needed for the achievement of strategic objectives, and then provide the expected return on investment.

5. The complete assessment of strategic success should apply two different but complementary approaches, which are project management performance and creation of value to the business (Serra and Kunc 2013). By combining the two approaches, an organization makes sure that the project is managed in an effective and efficient way at the same time that it delivers strategic value to the business.

6. No. Organizations do not have infinite resources to invest; therefore, they need to be selective and choose the most effective and efficient projects.

7. Organizations need to invest in the creation of values that support the achievement of their long-term goals in alignment with their business strategies

8. The *value gap* is the difference between the current value of the business and the expected (or desired) future value (Serra and Kunc 2015). This gap is normally filled by the creation of value through the realization of benefits.

9. Projects generate outputs that enable business changes. Business changes create desired outcomes. The outcomes prepare operations to realize intermediate benefits. Intermediate benefits in turn realize end benefits. End benefits help to achieve strategic objectives.

# Chapter 4

1. Business strategies, portfolio strategies, program strategies, project strategies, and project management strategies.

2. Projects of any size require governance, since small projects compete together for scarce resources and consume a large total amount of money, and therefore they must be focused on the business vision on the same way as the large ones.

3. Enterprise Benefits Realization Management maturity enhancement strategies, which can be applied to implement such practices from the beginning or can enhance the organizational maturity in the application

of such practices, and an enterprise Benefits Realization Strategy (eBRS), which describes the way benefits realization management will be applied to guide the strategy execution process to ensure the achievement of the organization's objectives.

4. Benefits realization governance roles; program and project management roles; and benefits ownership roles

# Chapter 5

1. Benefits identification is the first step for planning benefits at the organizational level. Benefits required by business strategies are identified by applying top-down and bottom-up approaches.

2. Benefits mapping is a technique to identify relationships between benefits and the business strategic objectives. The benefits map shows the desired business objectives and all end benefits, intermediate benefits, business changes and project outputs or enablers.

3. Benefits are classified to enable further analysis and to support further steps of the benefits realization process. Since benefits can be associated with different types of value to the business, the goal is to help the business to build an appropriately balanced portfolio of investment.

4. A benefit that is not measurable is also not trackable, and then it cannot be verified whether it has been realized.

5. The benefit owner is responsible and accountable for the benefit realization; this person will champion the benefit realization process.

6. The benefit profile describes the benefit and presents information such as its interdependencies, its ownership, and how to measure it.

7. Projects should be undertaken in order to deliver business needs that support the execution of business strategies.

8. Because uncertainty and certainty help identify how complex it will be to achieve benefits that are meaningful to the business. Uncertainty will often add risks to the realization of expected benefits; therefore, it is a relevant input for project selection and prioritization.

9. Strategic initiatives, operational initiatives, compliance initiates, and external projects.

10. The business case is a document developed in order to establish a clear understanding of the investment and its motivations describing the value for business of the expected outcomes. It covers the achievability and affordability of the investment as well as the attractiveness, explaining

174 Benefits Realization Management

whether the investment will result in cashable savings, noncashable efficiency savings or whether it will have strategic impacts.

11. Organizations do not have sufficient funds to execute all projects. Therefore, they need to select the most viable and strategically aligned set of projects.

## Chapter 6

1. Benefit realization is a process of making benefits happen and also of making people fully aware of them throughout the entire process of realization in order to ensure the creation of strategic and measurable value to the business.

2. Program-level benefits realization strategy, project-level benefits realization strategy, benefit stakeholder management plan, and benefit risk management plan.

3. The benefit change log captures all changes associated to a specific benefit. It enables tracking the history of each benefit from its identification to the end of its realization.

4. Normal, premature, perpetual, failed project, and changed priority.

5. The management of change activities is important to ensure that changes will be understood and accepted by the key stakeholders.

6. Benefit realization can start during project execution, since it is the stage of a project life cycle when projects start to deliver outputs and outcomes. Nevertheless, many benefits are realized after project closeout, when all the project outputs have already been delivered.

## Chapter 7

1. Projects and programs are kept on track by performing program and project periodic reviews; by ensuring stakeholders awareness, alignment, support and engagement; and by periodically reviewing the alignment between the project portfolio and the business strategy.

2. Program and project reviews are periodic assessments of performance against the planned baselines. The sources for such baselines include business cases and program and project management plans.

3. Because stakeholder support is critical for project success as well as for the creation of value to the business.

4. By performing periodic reviews of the project portfolio, which includes constantly reviewing and evaluating the benefits that are expected to be enabled by the ongoing portfolio of programs and projects as well as the benefits being realized by programs, projects, and business operations.

5. Periodic benefit reviews are important to confirm the ability of programs, projects, and operations to deliver the expected benefits; to verify whether such benefits are still aligned to business strategies; to inform stakeholders about the current status of the benefits realization process; to evaluate the effectiveness of the benefits realization strategy; and to identify the potential to achieve further benefits.

# Appendix B

# Recommended Further Reading

This Appendix presents some recommended further reading to support a better understanding of the contents discussed in this book.

## Chapter 1

Amason, A. C. *Strategic Management: From Theory to Practice.* London, UK: Routledge, 2011.

Association for Project Management. *Directing Change: A Guide to Governance of Project Management.* High Wycombe, UK: Association for Project Management, 2004.

Breese, R. "Benefits Realisation Management: Panacea or False Dawn?" *International Journal of Project Management* 30, no. 3 (2012): 341–351.

Breese, R., S. Jenner, C. E. M. Serra, and J. Thorp. "Benefits Management: Lost or Found in Translation." *International Journal of Project Management* 33, no. 7 (2015): 1438–1451.

Johnson, G. and K. Scholes. *Exploring Corporate Strategy.* 6th ed. Harlow, UK: Pearson Education Limited, 2002.

Porter, M. E. *Competitive Advantage: Creating and Sustaining Superior Performance: With a New Introduction,* 1st Free Press ed. New York, NY, USA: Free Press, 1998.

## Chapter 2

Association for Project Management. *APM Body of Knowledge*, 5th ed. Buckinghamshire UK: Association for Project Management, 2006.

Artto, K., J. Kujala, P. Dietrich, and M. Martinsuo. "What Is Project Strategy?" *International Journal of Project Management* 26, no. 1 (2008): 4–12.

Gray, C. F. and E. W. Larson. *Project Management: The Managerial Process*, International Edition. New York, NY, USA: McGraw-Hill/Irwin, 2006.

International Project Management Association. *IPMA Competence Baseline*, 3rd ed. Nijkerk, Netherlands: International Project Management Association, 2006.

Kaplan, R. S. and D. P. Norton. "Using the Balanced Scorecard as a Strategic Management System." *Harvard Business Review* 74, no. 1 (1996): 75–85.

Kerzner, H. *Project Management: A Systems Approach to Planning, Scheduling, and Controlling*, 10th ed. Hoboken, NJ, USA: John Wiley & Sons, 2009.

Mintzberg, H., B. Ahlstrand, and J. Lampel. *Strategy Safari*. 2nd ed. Harlow, UK: Pearson Education Limited, 2009.

Patanakul, P. and A. J. Shenhar. "What Project Strategy Really Is: The Fundamental Building Block in Strategic Project Management." *Project Management Journal* 43, no. 1 (February 2012): 4–20.

Project Management Institute. *A Guide to the Project Management Body of Knowledge*. 4th ed. Newtown Square, PA, USA: Project Management Institute, 2013.

Project Management Institute. *The Standard for Portfolio Management*. 2nd ed. Newtown Square, PA, USA: Project Management Institute, 2013.

Turner, J. R. *The Handbook of Project-Based Management—Leading Strategic Change in Organizations*, 3rd ed. London: McGraw-Hill, 2009.

Williams, D. and T. Parr. *Enterprise Programme Management: Delivering Value*. Basingstoke, UK: Palgrave Macmillan, 2004.

## Chapter 3

Camilleri, E. *Project Success: Critical Factors and Behaviours*. Farnham, UK: Gower Publishing Limited, 2011.

Ika, L. A. "Project Success as a Topic in Project Management Journals." *Project Management Journal* 40, no. 4 (2009): 6–19.

Kaplan, R. S. and D. P. Norton. *The Execution Premium: Linking Strategy to Operations for Competitive Advantage*. Boston, MA, USA: Harvard Business School Publishing Corporation, 2008.

Kerzner, H. *Project Management Metrics, KPIs, and Dashboards: A Guide to Measuring and Monitoring Project Performance*. Hoboken, NJ, USA: John Wiley & Sons, Inc., 2011.

Serra, C. E. M. *Benefits Realisation Management and Strategic Project Success—Analysis of UK, USA, and Brazil.* London, UK: Project Management Institute, 2015.

Serra, C. E. M. and M. Kunc. Benefits Realisation Management and Its Influence on Project Success and on the Execution of Business Strategies. *International Journal of Project Management* 33, no. 1 (2015): 53–66.

Shenhar, A. J., D. Milosevic, D. Dvir, and H. Thamhain. *Linking Project Management to Business Strategy.* Newton Square, PA, USA: Project Management Institute, Inc., 2007.

Zwikael, O. and J. Smyrk. *Project Management for the Creation of Organisational Value.* London, UK: Springer-Verlag London Limited, 2011.

## Chapters 4, 5, 6, and 7

Bradley, G. (2010). *Benefit Realisation Management.* 1st ed. Farnham, UK: Gower Publishing.

Office for Government Commerce. *Managing Successful Programmes,* 3rd ed. Norwich, UK: TSO, 2007.

Jenner, S. *Managing Benefits.* Norwich, UK: The Stationery Office, 2012.

Kendall, G. I. and S. C. Rollins. *Advanced Project Portfolio Management and the PMO: Multiplying ROI at Warp Speed.* Boca Raton, FL, USA: J. Ross, 2003.

Levine, H. A. *Project Portfolio Management: A Practical Guide to Selecting Projects, Managing Portfolios, and Maximizing Benefits.* San Francisco, CA, USA: Jossey-Bass, 2005.

Melton, T., P. Iles-Smith, and J. Yates. *Project Benefits Management: Linking Your Project to the Business.* London, UK: Butterworth-Heinemann, 2008.

Ward, J. and E. Daniel, *Benefits Management: Delivering value from IS & IT Investments.* Chichester, UK: John Wiley & Sons, Ltd. 2006.

# Appendix C

# Case Study: Worked Examples

This appendix provides a set of worked examples for the utilization of the templates provided in this book by using the information provided in the ProjectEng case study.

Following is a list of examples provided in this appendix:

| Enterprise Benefits Realization Management: Maturity Enhancement Strategy | | | |
|---|---|---|---|
| **Organization:** | ProjectEng Civil Engineering Services ltd | | |
| **Version:** | *1.0* | **Version Type:** | *Final* |
| **Issued by:** | *John Johnson* | **Issue date:** | *01/20/2016* |
| **Department:** | *Enterprise PMO* | **Job title:** | *Enterprise PMO director* |
| **Approved by:** | *Michael Clark* | **Approval date:** | *01/30/2016* |
| **Department:** | *Finance* | **Job title:** | *Chief Financial Officer* |

## I. Rationale and Background

Since 2007, ProjectEng has been monitoring its project success rates for investment projects, based on measures that are associated to project management performance. Although the success rates had been always above 85 percent, the return on investment has not been appropriately monitored and the strategic management department has repeatedly identified low levels of achievement of strategic objectives. Therefore, although project success rates are high, there is a perception that projects are not effectively aligned to the achievement of strategic objectives or are not generating the expected value to the business.

Reduced margins, due to an increase in competition allied to a shortage of new projects, have been forcing the organization to optimize its operations in order to increase cost efficiency.

The Senior Executive Board identified the need for more robust Benefits Realization Management practices to enhance the efficiency and effectiveness of the strategy execution projects.

## II. Objectives

To enhance the efficiency and effectiveness of the strategy execution within ProjectEng. This overall objective will be achieved by:

Ensuring the application of a suitable set of best practices in strategy execution all across the business and in a standardized fashion. These best practices are specifically associated to:

- Project Governance
- Benefits Realization Management
- Project, Program and Portfolio Management
- Management of Change

Ensuring the alignment between strategy planning, strategy execution, and business performance management all across the business. This alignment should be achieved through the utilization of strategy execution best practices.

(Continued on next page)

*Enterprise Benefits Realization Management:*
*Maturity Enhancement Strategy (Continued)*

| |
|---|
| **III. Approach** |
| **a. Planning** |
| **i. AS-IS Analysis** |
| The AS-IS Analysis will identify the level of maturity of the Benefits Realization Management practices employed across the organization and any associated systems and tools. In addition, it will identify whether practices are applied on an uneven, nonstandardized, and unaligned way across different divisions and departments.<br><br>The complete AS-IS Analysis, detailing the current set of practices and the utilization of each practice, will be attached as an appendix to this document. |
| **ii. TO-BE Analysis** |
| The TO-BE Analysis will produce a business blueprint that will identify the desired new processes as well as define a high-level desired structure for a Benefits Realization Management framework to be applied across the business.<br><br>The complete TO-BE Analysis, detailing of the future desired set of practices and the expected utilization of each practice will be attached as an appendix to this document. |
| **iii. GAP Analysis** |
| The GAP Analysis will identify the new processes to be designed and implemented, the existing processes that require review and improvement, and the existing processes that will be recommended to be retired.<br><br>The complete GAP Analysis, identifying the GAPs between the current and the desired future situations, will be attached as an appendix to this document. |
| **iv. Changes To Be Implemented** |
| Based on the GAP Analysis, a series of changes will be suggested to the AS-IS environment, including changes to associated systems and tools.<br><br>The complete list of changes, identifying the changes required to the implementation of the TO-BE processes will be attached as an appendix to this document. |
| **b. Implementation** |
| **i. Documentation (Processes and Procedures)** |
| All processes directly associated with the Benefits Realization Management will become part of ProjectEng's Enterprise Benefits Realization Management Framework. The framework should include processes and procedures as well as tools and templates. |

*(Continued on next page)*

Any new processes that are proposed to be implemented will become part of the corporate management system, according to the organizational policies.

Any new processes and procedures will be produced by the project and submitted for review, approval, and publication to the department of quality management, according with the current organizational policies regarding this matter

### ii. Training in Systems and Tools

In parallel with the production of new processes and procedures, systems and tools will be developed or enhanced to support the new processes. The implementation of new software is not expected, although the reconfiguration of the existing PMIS is considered to be required for better alignment with any new processes that will be implemented.

### iii. General Communications and Training in Systems and Tools

The stakeholders needing training will be identified based on the analysis of the users of each new process or procedure to be implemented or even each existing process or procedure to be revised. Different training strategies may be applicable to each public identified.

Because of a budgetary constraint and the geographic spread of some of the public, e-learning should be considered as a preferred option in most of the cases.

The complete general training strategy will be attached as an appendix to this document.

### iv. Senior Management Communication and Training

Management training will be delivered to all business managers because of the relevance of the understanding of the new processes associated to strategy execution. The management-level public may be stratified to ensure that a more in-depth training is delivered to managers who are directly associated with the Benefits Realization Management activities (e.g., PMO Managers, Project Delivery Managers, Program and Project Sponsors, Program Managers, Operations Managers, and Business Performance Managers, among others).

The complete management training strategy will be later attached as an appendix to this document.

### v. Go-Live

The Go-Live is expected to happen in a phased fashion. The initial focus will be investment projects, and the next focus will be revenue-generating projects. Therefore, the implementation will start with the internal back-office functions and then the processes will be rolled out to the four front-office regions.

The complete Go-Live plan will be attached as an appendix to this document.

*(Continued on next page)*

*Enterprise Benefits Realization Management:*
*Maturity Enhancement Strategy (Continued)*

| |
|---|
| **c. Stabilization** |
| **i. Process Control** |
| The service levels of the new processes will be controlled by the business performance management department by using the enterprise business performance dashboard. |
| All investment projects will be identified in the Financial System and also in the appropriate Project Management Information Systems. Reports from these systems will identify the correct links between projects, programs, benefits and strategic objectives. |
| A quarterly report generated by the Enterprise PMO will use indicators to evaluate the correct input of benefits measures into the benefits realization tracking sheets and portfolio dashboard. |
| The correct application of the Benefits Realization Management framework will be monitored by Process Quality Assurance Reviews, in which the quality management team will periodically analyze compliance with the appropriate processes and procedures from a sample of programs and projects. |
| **ii. Support** |
| Support will be provided to all users of the new processes by the project team during all the implementation and stabilization stages. The project team will make Project Analysts available to provide local support in the headquarters as well as in all the four service delivery regions. |
| **d. Handover** |
| **i. Formal Handover to Operations** |
| After the one-year stabilization period, the ownership and governance of the Benefits Realization Management processes will be fully transferred from the project team to the Enterprise PMO. |
| The executive level will be held accountable for the correct application of the practices in their areas of the business, in the same way as with any other processes that are part of the organization's management system. |
| **e. Closeout** |
| **i. Development of Final Report** |
| After the formal handover, a closeout report will be produced according with the standard template for investment projects. This report will be circulated according with the project communications plan, which was produced separately and added as an appendix to this plan. |

*(Continued on next page)*

***Enterprise Benefits Realization Management: Maturity Enhancement Strategy*** ***(Continued)***

| |
|---|
| **ii. Analysis of Lessons Learned**<br>The lessons learned will be analyzed following the organizational procedure for gathering lessons learned at the end of each project.<br>**iii. Formal Closeout**<br>The formal closeout of this initiative should include the financial closeout in the financial system, the demobilization of the project team, and the formal communication to all stakeholders according to the communications plan. |
| **IV. Change Management** |
| The implementation of the new processes will be supported by a change management strategy to be developed by the change management department. It will include:<br>Identification of different groups of stakeholders and the way each group is going to be affected by the change<br>Analysis of the environment and identification of forces pro and against change<br>Definition of actions to remove blockers and exploit opportunities with the appropriate assignment of roles and responsibilities<br>Production of communications strategy, including utilization of the most appropriate channels to engage with each target audience |
| **V. RAID Management** |
| Risks, Assumptions, Issues, and Dependencies (RAID) will be managed according to the organizational RAID management procedure. The current version of the RAID log is attached to this document. |

**Figure C-1** ProjectEng's Enterprise Benefits Realization Management: Maturity Enhancement Strategy.

| eBRS: Enterprise Benefits Realization Strategy | | | |
|---|---|---|---|
| **Organization:** | ProjectEng Civil Engineering Services ltd | | |
| **Version:** | 1 | Version Type: | Final |
| **Next review:** | 09/01/2015 | Next full review: | 12/01/2015 |
| **Issued by:** | John Johnson | **Issue date:** | 06/01/2015 |
| **Department:** | Enterprise PMO | **Job title:** | Enterprise PMO Director |
| **Approved by:** | Michael Clark | **Approval date:** | 06/10/2015 |
| **Department:** | Finance | **Job title:** | Chief Financial Officer |

## I. Key Strategic Drivers

### Driver 1: Drop in oil price

Because of a scenario of reduced investment level in the oil and gas market, a number of ProjectEng's long-term contracts were canceled or put on hold. Similarly, the forecast of new projects was significantly reduced. To ensure the financial stability of the business, a series of strategies must be adopted that will fill the gaps created in the expected cash flow for the following years.

### Driver 2: Increase in global competitors

An increase in the number of competitors with global capability for service delivery has significantly increased the number of qualified offers submitted to tenders in the last few years. This pattern has forced the companies working in this sector to reduce margins and increase efficiency in order to be competitive. Although ProjectEng has strong brand positioning, it has faced fierce competition, especially in the Asian market.

### Driver 3: Competition for qualified processionals

The reduced margin has made the organization unable to compete for qualified professionals with other industries on a salary basis. It has brought to the business an increase in employee turnover and reduction in morale. The loss of qualified professionals has also increased the need for training and contributed to a reduction in productivity because of the loss of specialist and business knowledge.

### Driver 4: Lows level of control over strategy execution

Since 2007, ProjectEng has been monitoring its project success rates for investment projects, based on measures that are associated with project management performance. Although the success rates had been always above 85 percent, the return on investment has not been appropriately monitored, and the strategic management department has repeatedly identified low levels of achievement of strategic objectives. Therefore, although project success rates are high, there is a perception that projects are not effectively aligned with the achievement of strategic objectives or are not generating the expected value to the business.

*(Continued on next page)*

*eBRS: Enterprise Benefits Realization Strategy (Continued)*

| Driver 5: New local regulation enforcing professional registration |
| --- |
| A new regulation issued by a country in the Middle East requires all engineers working in its territory to be registered with the country's engineering professional body. Although the regulation body allows a two-year period for companies to comply with the new regulation, the process requires a lot of documentation to be gathered and translated to the local language. Additionally, an enormous backlog of applications is waiting to be reviewed by the regulations body. This suggests a waiting list of about six months for an application to be reviewed and the professional to be invited for a competence assessment interview. ProjectEng currently has more than 100 engineers working on a large contract in that country, the large majority of whom are from other countries and lack the appropriate local registration. |

| II. Strategic Objectives |
| --- |
| • SO001 Market diversification: To generate in two years annual new revenue from the European and American renewables market sector that is equivalent to 5 percent of the total revenue from these two regions in the financial year of 2014<br><br>• SO002 Operational excellence: To achieve in two years an annual reduction in the operating costs of 5 percent of the total costs registered in the financial year of 2014<br><br>• SO003 Professional registration: To ensure that 100 percent of the engineers are registered with the appropriate professional body according to local regulations<br><br>• SO004 Knowledge Management: To achieve a gain of 5 percent to standard levels of average revenue per employee by minimizing negative impacts from employee turnover<br><br>• SO005 Internal training: To ensure 100 percent of the new employees can start doing billable work in an average of no more the one month after their start date |

| III. End Benefits |
| --- |
| • New Revenue: US $330 million new gross revenue per year by the end of 2017 for 5 years<br><br>• Operating Costs Reduction: US $240 million per year by the end of 2017 for two years<br><br>• Professional registration: 100 percent of the engineers registered according to local regulations from the beginning of 2017 for 5 years |

| IV. Changes Required |
| --- |
| • Development of the capability to generate income from the renewables market sector in Europe and Americas |

*(Continued on next page)*

*eBRS: Enterprise Benefits Realization Strategy (Continued)*

- Development of new clients and contracts in the renewables market sector in Europe and Americas
- Optimization of benefits realization from investment projects and revenue-generating projects
- Increase in efficiency of project delivery, including investment projects and revenue-generating projects
- Increase in efficiency of back office operations (e.g., finance, accounting, procurement, human resources management, etc.)
- Standardization of service delivery activities across different geographies, supported by the appropriate documentation and training
- Identification of key skills needed for service delivery and development of self-service eLearning capability
- Development of a new starter's qualification program
- Professional registration of all employees according to local regulations

## V. Ideas

- Mobilization of renewables specialists resource pool in Europe and Americas
- Business development in the European and American renewables markets
- Benefits Realization Management maturity enhancement
- Business process mapping, improvement, and standardization
- Organizational architecture redesign
- IT systems integration
- New ERP
- Development of competence frameworks for the business core competences
- Review of career pathways for service delivery roles
- Global proactive eLearning program
- New starters program
- Professional registration program

## VI. Selection Criteria

The selection of initiatives to be included in the portfolio will take into consideration specific guidelines by category of investment, as follows.

Compliance initiatives have high priority for selection, since these are "must-do" investments that cannot be avoided. These initiatives should have their compliance requirements reviewed and approved by the Global Investment Review Board. Depending on the required deadlines for implementation, these can be postponed to be part of a future annual investment portfolio. Any decision regarding compliance initiatives is made by the Global Investment Review Board.

(Continued on next page)

*eBRS: Enterprise Benefits Realization Strategy (Continued)*

Strategic initiatives should account as 60 percent of the investment portfolio in the current annual budgeting cycle. These initiatives are appraised by the sponsoring department and submitted to the local finance department for review. The appraisal should follow the guidelines and use the template provided in the global framework for investment appraisal. The local investment committee should approve all investment ideas before these are submitted to the Global Investment Review Board for final review and approval.

Operational initiatives should account as 40 percent of the investment portfolio in the current annual budgeting cycle. These initiatives are appraised by the sponsoring department and submitted to the local finance department for review. The appraisal should follow the guidelines and use the template provided in the global framework for investment appraisal. The local investment committee should approve all investment ideas before these are submitted to the Global Investment Review Board for final review and approval.

External projects should be appraised by the local sales department and submitted to the local finance department for review. The appraisal should follow the guidelines and use the template provided in the global framework for client project appraisal. Projects meeting the strategic requirements described in the framework that demonstrate financial metrics within the predefined thresholds are submitted to the Global Operations Review Board for final approval before submission of a proposal to the client.

Note: For compliance initiatives, benefits realization is tracked against the mandatory requirements, if no financial benefits are expected. For strategic initiatives, strategic initiatives and external projects, the results of the project appraisal will constitute the business case for the project and will be the baseline for benefits realization.

## VII.  High-Level Governance Process

This strategy is produced every two years by the Enterprise PMO with support from the strategic management team. It is approved by the Chief Finance Officer after consultations with the senior executive committee. It should be reviewed every quarter by the Enterprise PMO and resubmitted to the Chief Finance Officer for approval.

The execution of this strategy is controlled on a monthly basis by the Enterprise PMO, which consolidates data about the entire portfolio of initiative and produces a benefits portfolio dashboard. The performance of the business in executing the strategy is reported on a quarterly basis according with the communications plan that is attached to this document.

The senior project governance group meets every two weeks to approve business cases and stage gate reviews and also to make decisions regarding the performance of the benefits realization process across the business.

*(Continued on next page)*

*eBRS: Enterprise Benefits Realization Strategy (Continued)*

| VIII. Initiatives Selected for Implementation |
|---|
| All initiatives that are selected for implementation should be listed as an appendix to this document and should have the approved versions of business cases and any further project management plans made available in the central repository of strategy implementation documents according with the organizational document management policies. |
| IX. Benefits Dependency Network |
| A benefits dependency network should be attached to this document. It should start from the business objectives, which will be associated with end benefits. The end benefits may be associated (or not) with intermediate benefits. The benefits are associated with business changes, which are then associated with outputs/enablers. The last are finally associated with the initiatives listed as an appendix to this document. |

**Figure C-2**    ProjectEng's eBRM strategy, Parts 1 and 2.

| Benefit Profile/Benefit Identification Sheet | | | |
|---|---|---|---|
| **Organization:** | ProjectEng Civil Engineering Services ltd | | |
| **Version:** | 1.0 | **Version Type:** | Final |
| **Issued by:** | John Clark | **Issue date:** | 03/15/2015 |
| **Department:** | Global Finance | **Job title:** | Global Head of Finance |
| **Approved by:** | Matthew Spencer | **Approval date:** | 03/25/2015 |
| **Department:** | Senior Executive Board | **Job title:** | Chief Executive Officer |

| Benefit Basic Details | |
|---|---|
| **Benefit Code/Name** | **B002 Operating Costs** |
| **Benefit Definition** | Reduction in Operating Costs because of an increase in cost efficiency |
| **Benefit Category** | Cost Reduction |
| **Type of Benefit** | Operational Improvement |
| **Strategic Objective Associated** | SO002 Operational excellence |

**Benefit Dependency Network Diagram**

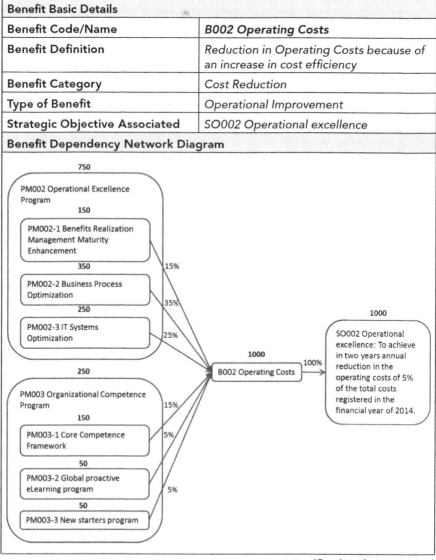

(Continued on next page)

*Benefit Profile/Benefit Identification Sheet (Continued)*

| Benefit Measurement Details | |
|---|---|
| Is the Benefit Measurable? | Yes |
| Is the Benefit Financially Quantifiable? | Yes |
| Measure | Operating Costs (US$) |
| Total Financial Amount | US$240 million per year (cost reduction) |
| Total Nonfinancial Amount | Not Applicable |
| Total Budget | US$100 million (US$25 million in 2015) |
| Cost/Benefit Ratio | 0.21 |
| Frequency of Measurement | At the end of the fiscal year |
| Measure Owner | John Clark, Global Head of Finance |
| Measurement Technique | Sum of all operating cost for the period. |
| Source of Measurements | ERP/End of fiscal year report |
| Disbenefits Associated | Employee turnover<br>Employee satisfaction (reduction) |
| **Benefit Realization and Ownership Details** | |
| Benefit Owner | Hans Braun, Chief Operating Officer |
| Business Areas Responsible for Realizing the Benefit | All areas of the business |
| Realization Start Date (planned/ actual) | 01/01/2017 |
| Realization End Date (planned/ actual) | 12/01/2018 |
| Total Benefit Expected (baseline) | US$480 million |
| Total Benefit Expected | US$480 million |
| **Program(s) and/or Projects Associated** | |
| Program Code/Name | **PM002 Operational Excellence Program** |
| Program Sponsor | Haji Aljaid, Chief Finance Officer |
| Program Manager | Jeff Stuart, Program Manager |
| Project Code/Name | **PM002-1 Benefits Realization Management Maturity Enhancement** |

*(Continued on next page)*

*Benefit Profile/Benefit Identification Sheet (Continued)*

| | |
|---|---|
| **Project Sponsor** | *Jeff Stuart, Program Manager* |
| **Project Manager** | *Sarah Parker, Head of Project Management CoE* |
| **Project Start Date (planned/ actual)** | *04/01/2015* |
| **Project End Date (planned/actual)** | *06/30/2017* |
| **Amount of Benefit Associated** | *15 percent* |
| **Project Code/Name** | ***PM002-2 Business Process Optimization*** |
| **Project Sponsor** | *Jeff Stuart, Program Manager* |
| **Project Manager** | *Xin Zang, Head of Business Services* |
| **Project Start Date (planned/ actual)** | *04/01/2015* |
| **Project End Date (planned/actual)** | *11/30/2016* |
| **Amount of Benefit Associated** | *35 percent* |
| **Project Code/Name** | ***PM002-3 IT Systems Optimization*** |
| **Project Sponsor** | *Jeff Stuart, Program Manager* |
| **Project Manager** | *Amir Khan, Project Manager* |
| **Project Start Date (planned/ actual)** | *09/01/2015* |
| **Project End Date (planned/actual)** | *03/31/2017* |
| **Amount of Benefit Associated** | *25 percent* |
| **Program Code/Name** | ***PM003 Organizational Competence Program*** |
| **Program Sponsor** | *Alice MacDowell, Global HR Director* |
| **Program Manager** | *Carla Duarte, Program Manager* |
| **Project Code/Name** | ***PM003-1 Core Competence Framework*** |
| **Project Sponsor** | *Carla Duarte, Program Manager* |
| **Project Manager** | *Oda Haruki, Project Manager* |
| **Project Start Date (planned/ actual)** | *04/01/2015* |
| **Project End Date (planned/actual)** | *09/30/2016* |
| **Amount of Benefit Associated** | *15 percent* |

*(Continued on next page)*

*Benefit Profile/Benefit Identification Sheet (Continued)*

| Project Code/Name | *PM003-2 Global proactive eLearning program* |
|---|---|
| Project Sponsor | *Carla Duarte, Program Manager* |
| Project Manager | *Afram Okudjeto, Global Head of Learning and Development (L&D)* |
| Project Start Date (planned/actual) | *11/01/2015* |
| Project End Date (planned/actual) | *10/31/2016* |
| Amount of Benefit Associated | *5 percent* |
| Project Code/Name | *PM003-3 New starters program* |
| Project Sponsor | *Carla Duarte, Program Manager* |
| Project Manager | *Amy Watts, Senior Learning and Development Advisor* |
| Project Start Date (planned/actual) | *04/01/2015* |
| Project End Date (planned/actual) | *12/31/2016* |
| Amount of Benefit Associated | *5 percent* |

**Figure C-3**   ProjectEng's Benefit Profile.

| Program Benefits Realization Strategy | | | |
|---|---|---|---|
| **Organization:** | ProjectEng Civil Engineering Services ltd | | |
| **Program:** | Operational Excellence Program | | |
| **Version:** | 1.0 | Version Type: | Final |
| **Issued by:** | Jeff Stuart | Issue date: | 03/31/2015 |
| **Department:** | Operational Excellence Program | Job title: | Program Manager |
| **Approved by:** | Haji Aljaid | Approval date: | 04/15/2015 |
| **Department:** | Finance | Job title: | Chief Finance Officer |

**I.  Initiatives**

PM002-1 Benefits Realization Management Maturity Enhancement

PM002-2 Business Process Optimization

PM002-3 IT Systems Optimization

**II.  Benefits Dependency Network**

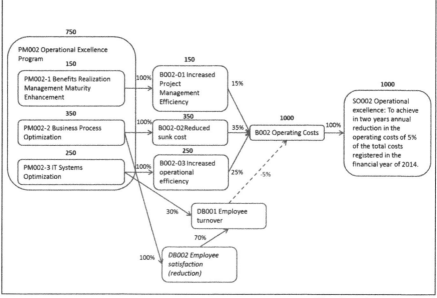

(Continued on next page)

*Program Benefits Realization Strategy (Continued)*

| III.  Benefits to Be Realized |
| :--- |
| B002 Operating cost reduction<br>B002-01 Increased project management efficiency<br>B002-02 Reduced sunk costs<br>B002-03 Increased operational efficiency |
| **IV.  Disbenefits to Be Managed** |
| DB001 Employee turnover<br>DB002 Employee satisfaction (reduction) |
| **V.  Management of Change Strategies** |
| The change management activities will be carried out by the program change management team, which was mobilized and made part of the program organizational structure to provide full time support to the program.<br><br>The organizational change will be supported by a change management plan that is attached as an appendix to this strategy. |
| **VI.  Handover Strategies** |
| For the projects that are part of this program, each project deliverable will be formally accepted by the associated business process owner. All changes enabled by project outputs will be supported by the change management team, in association with the business process owner. The start of the realization of each benefit expected from this program will be identified by the program team in agreement with the benefits owner.<br><br>After the beginning of the realization, the benefit realization will be tracked by the benefit measure owner as specified in the benefit profile. Whenever benefits are realized during the project life cycle, the benefit realization will be reported by the project management team to the program team by using the benefits realization control sheet template. The program team consolidates the information about all program benefits and reports to the Enterprise PMO using the benefits realization tracking sheet template.<br><br>During the program closeout stage, the activities associated with controlling and reporting benefits realization will be fully handed over to benefits owners and measure owners by using the benefits handover form. |

**Figure C-4**  ProjectEng's Program Benefits Realization Strategy.

| Benefits Handover Form | | | |
|---|---|---|---|
| **Organization:** | ProjectEng Civil Engineering Services ltd | | |
| **Version:** | 1 | **Version Type:** | Final |
| **Program Manager:** | Jeff Stuart | **Issue date:** | 06/30/2017 |
| **Department:** | Operational Excellence Program | **Job title:** | Program Manager |
| **Benefit Owner:** | Hans Braun | **Approval date:** | 06/30/2017 |
| **Department:** | Global Operations | **Job title:** | Chief Operating Officer |

**I. Program/Project Manager**

Jeff Stuart, Program Manager

**II. Benefit Owner**

Hans Braun, Chief Operating Officer

**III. Benefit Code/Name**

B002 Operating Costs

**IV. Benefit Measure**

Current annual Operating Costs (US$) – Operating Costs (US$) for the financial year 2014

**V. Measurement Baseline**

Operating Costs (US$) for the financial year 2014 = US$4.8 billion

**VI. Frequency of Measurement**

Yearly (financial year)

**VII. Measure Owner**

John Clark, Global Head of Finance

**VIII. Benefit Reporting Recipients**

Matthew Spencer, Chief Executive Officer
Hans Braun, Chief Operating Officer
Haji Aljaid, Chief Finance Officer
Jeff Stuart, Program Manager

**IX. Expected Benefit (Baseline From Business Case)**

US$480 million

**X. Expected Benefit (Reviewed Baseline)**

US$360 million

**XI. Benefit Realization Timeline**

2 years (from 01/01/2017 to 12/01/2018)

**Figure C-5**    ProjectEng's Benefits Handover Form.

| Project-Level Benefits Realization Control Sheet | | |
|---|---|---|
| **Organization:** | ProjectEng Civil Engineering Services ltd / Global Human Resources Department | |
| **Project:** | Professional Registration project | |
| **Version:** | 1.0 | **Version Type:** | Final |
| **Issued by:** | Jenny Atkins | **Issue date:** | 01/10/2016 |
| **Department:** | Global Human Resources Department | **Job title:** | Senior HR Analyst |
| **Approved by:** | Farah Samara | **Approval date:** | 01/15/2016 |
| **Department:** | Global Human Resources Department | **Job title:** | Global Head of HR |

### I. Benefit Code/Name

B005 Professional Registration

### II. Benefit Measure

Professional Registration Index = (Number of employees subject to professional registration that have already been registered) / (Total number of employees subject to professional registration)

### III. Benefit Owner

Alice MacDowell, Global HR Director

### IV. Benefit Realization Life Cycle

| Benefit realization start date (baseline) | 04/01/2015 | Benefit realization end date (baseline) | 09/30/2016 |
|---|---|---|---|
| Benefit realization start date (actual) | 04/01/2015 | Benefit realization end date (planned) | 11/31/2016 |

### V. Planned vs. Actuals

| Year | 2015 | | | | 2016 | | | |
|---|---|---|---|---|---|---|---|---|
| Quarter | Q1 | Q2 | Q3 | Q4 | Q1 | Q2 | Q3 | Q4 |
| Baseline | 0% | 0% | 10% | 15% | 15% | 30% | 30% | 0% |
| Cumulative | 0% | 0% | 10% | 25% | 40% | 70% | 100% | 100% |
| Actual | 0% | 5% | 18% | 19% | N/A | N/A | N/A | N/A |
| Cumulative | 0% | 5% | 18% | 19% | N/A | N/A | N/A | N/A |
| Planned | 0% | 5% | 18% | 19% | 15% | 30% | 30% | 6% |
| Cumulative | 0% | 5% | 18% | 19% | 34% | 64% | 94% | 100% |

(Continued on next page)

*Project-Level Benefits Realization Control Sheet* (Continued)

| VI.  Issues | |
|---|---|
| **List of issues** | **Actions to treat the issues** |
| *A general election in the main country where the registration has now been required has impacted the work of the registration office in October and November 2015, affecting the schedule of benefits realization.* | *A0011: Liaise with the local government to reduce the backlog in order to not impact the construction of the new refining plan, which is in progress.* |
| **VII.  Risks** | |
| **List of risks** | **Actions to treat the risks** |
| *Subsequent local factors may affect the work of the registration office causing further delays.* | *A0012: Mitigation: Liaise with the local government to identify possible further future bottlenecks and then prepare contingency plans.* |
| **VIII.  Actions** | |
| *A0006 (10/05/2015): Develop a global online database to keep the registration records. Status: Closed.* | |

**Figure C-6**   ProjectEng's Project-Level Benefits Realization Control Sheet.

| Benefits Realization Health Check | | | |
|---|---|---|---|
| **Organization:** | ProjectEng Civil Engineering Services Ltd. / Global Human Resources Department | | |
| **Version:** | 1.0 | **Version Type:** | Final |
| **Issued by:** | Maitreyi Bandopadhyay | **Issue date:** | 06/05/2017 |
| **Department:** | Global Learning and Development | **Job title:** | Senior L&D Advisor |
| **Approved by:** | Afram Okudjeto | **Approval date:** | 06/15/2017 |
| **Department:** | Global Learning and Development | **Job title:** | Global Head of L&D |

| **I. Benefit Code/Name** |
|---|
| B003-02 reduction of learning curve |
| **II. Benefit Owner** |
| Afram Okudjeto, Global Head of L&D |
| **III. Program(s) and/or Project(s) Associated** |
| PM003 Organizational Competence Program |
| **IV. Checklist: Prerealization Process** |

| | |
|---|---|
| Y | Benefit is clearly identified and defined. |
| Y | Benefit is measurable. |
| Y | Actions are taken to avoid the risk of benefit double counting or benefit hyper estimation. |
| Y | Benefit is clearly relevant to the achievement of strategic objectives. |
| Y | Benefit is clearly related to a set of change initiatives |
| Y | Benefit is decomposed in terms of the percent contribution expected from each initiative. |
| Y | Benefit is described in business case(s) approved at the beginning of the program(s)/project(s). |
| Y | Benefits ownership is clearly defined as well as the ownership by the benefits enabling initiatives. |
| Y | Actions are planned to ensure benefit realization by business operations. |
| Y | A benefits realization strategy defines a plan for the entire benefits realization life cycle. |

*(Continued on next page)*

*Benefits Realization Health Check (Continued)*

| V. Checklist: Realization Process | |
|---|---|
| N | Benefit is frequently reviewed and realigned to the current expectations. |
| N | Results of benefit reviews are frequently communicated to the stakeholders. |
| N | Benefit stakeholders needs are frequently reassessed. |
| N | Benefit is monitored by the organization during the entire realization lifecycle. |
| N | Benefit realization is frequently assessed against the expectations described in the business case. |
| N | Benefits are periodically reevaluated against the business case. |
| N | The occurrence of emergent disbenefits is monitored. |
| N | The potential for realization of additional benefits is observed and exploited whenever appropriate. |
| Y | Actions are performed to ensure benefit realization by the regular business operations. |
| Y | Lessons learned are identified, captured, and applied. |
| N | A benefits realization strategy is followed. |

### VI.  Benefit Measure

*Average time before new employee start doing billable work = Sum of (start date of first billable work – employee start date) for all new employees from the beginning of 2017 to end 2020.*

### VII.  Sources of Measurement

*Human Resources Management Systems (HRMS).*

### VIII.  Benefits Realization RAG status

| | | | |
|---|---|---|---|
| | | x | Current amount of benefits realized against benefits realization schedule (baseline) (RED). |
| | | x | Current benefits forecast against total benefits expected (baseline) (RED). |

*(Continued on next page)*

*Benefits Realization Health Check (Continued)*

| IX.  Current Issues | |
|---|---|
| **List of Issues** | **Actions to Treat the Issues** |
| *New employees are starting to do billable work on average 50 days after joining the organization. The deviation against the 30-day target had not been noticed before because the benefit had not been properly monitored after project closeout and beginning of benefit realization.* | *Identify reasons for the deviation and define actions to treat the root causes.*<br><br>*Ensure that the benefit will be monitored and evaluated according with the benefits realization plan.* |
| **X. Current Risks** | |
| **List of Risks** | **Actions to Treat the Risks** |
| *At the end of the benefit realization period, realization of fewer benefits than expected, because of the issue identified above.* | *Investigate the reason for the current deviation and prepare a recovery plan.* |
| **XI.  Recovery Actions** | |
| *Immediate assignment of an HR Coordinator to be responsible for measuring and reporting the benefit realization going forward.* | |

**Figure C-7**   ProjectEng's Benefits Realization Health Check.

# Appendix D

## Enterprise Benefits Realization Management Toolkit: Blank Templates

This appendix contains all blank templates provided in this book.

### Chapter 4

### Chapter 5

### Chapter 6

## Chapter 7

| 1. Enterprise Benefits Realization Management Maturity Enhancement Strategy | | | |
|---|---|---|---|
| Organization: | | | |
| Version: | | Version Type: | |
| Issued by: | | Issue date: | |
| Department: | | Job title: | |
| Approved by: | | Approval date: | |
| Department: | | Job title: | |

**I. Rationale and Background**

**II. Objectives**

**III. Approach**

a. Planning

b. Implementation

c. Stabilization

d. Handover

e. Closeout

**IV. Change Management**

**V. RAID Management**

| 2. Benefits Realization Management Framework | | | |
|---|---|---|---|
| Organization: | | | |
| Version: | | Version Type: | |
| Issued by: | | Issue date: | |
| Department: | | Job title: | |
| Approved by: | | Approval date: | |
| Department: | | Job title: | |

**I. Introduction**

**II. Benefits Realization Management: Theoretical Background**

**III. Benefits Realization Management Life Cycle**

**IV. Benefits Realization Management Processes**

a.  Enterprise Benefits Realization Strategy

b.  Planning Benefits

c.  Realizing Benefits

d.  Reviewing and Evaluating Benefits

**V. Roles and Responsibilities**

# 3. Measures Dictionary

| Organization: | | |
|---|---|---|
| Version: | Version Type: | |
| Issued by: | Issue date: | |
| Department: | Job title: | |
| Approved by: | Approval date: | |
| Department: | Job title: | |

| Measure Name/ Code | Measure Owner | Measure Type | Measure Objective | Associated Business Functions | Associated Business Processes | Associated Tools or IT Systems | Measurement Method | Measurement Periodicity | Benefit Measurer |
|---|---|---|---|---|---|---|---|---|---|
| | | | | | | | | | |
| | | | | | | | | | |
| | | | | | | | | | |
| | | | | | | | | | |
| | | | | | | | | | |
| | | | | | | | | | |

| 4. eBRS: Enterprise Benefits Realization Strategy | | | |
|---|---|---|---|
| Organization: | | | |
| Version: | | Version Type: | |
| Next review: | | Next full review: | |
| Issued by: | | Issue date: | |
| Department: | | Job title: | |
| Approved by: | | Approval date: | |
| Department: | | Job title: | |

**I. Key Strategic Drivers**

**II. Strategic Objectives**

**III. End Benefits**

**IV. Changes Required**

**V. Ideas**

**VI. Selection Criteria**

**VII. High-Level Governance Process**

**VIII. Initiatives Selected for Implementation**

**IX. Benefits Dependency Network**

## 5. Benefits Map/Benefits Dependency Network

| Organization: | | |
|---|---|---|
| Version: | | Version Type: |
| Issued by: | | Issue date: |
| Department: | | Job title: |
| Approved by: | | Approval date: |
| Department: | | Job title: |

| Initiatives | Outputs/Enablers | Business Changes | Intermediate Benefits | End Benefits | Business Objectives |
|---|---|---|---|---|---|
| | | | | | |

| 6. Benefits/Activities Matrix | | | |
|---|---|---|---|
| **Stakeholders** | **Benefits** | | |
| | | | |
| | | | |
| | | | |
| | | | |
| | | | |
| | | | |
| | | | |
| | | | |
| | | | |

| 7. Benefits/Stakeholders Matrix | | | |
|---|---|---|---|
| **Stakeholders** | **Benefits** | | |
| | | | |
| | | | |
| | | | |
| | | | |
| | | | |
| | | | |
| | | | |
| | | | |

| 8. Benefit Profile/Benefit Identification Sheet | | | |
|---|---|---|---|
| Organization: | | | |
| Version: | | Version Type: | |
| Issued by: | | Issue date: | |
| Department: | | Job title: | |
| Approved by: | | Approval date: | |
| Department: | | Job title: | |

| Benefit Basic Details | |
|---|---|
| *Benefit Code/Name* | |
| *Benefit Definition* | |
| *Benefit Category* | |
| *Type of Benefit* | |
| *Strategic Objective Associated* | |

| Benefit Dependency Network Diagram |
|---|
| |

| Benefit Measurement Details | |
|---|---|
| *Is the Benefit Measurable?* | |
| *Is the Benefit Financially Quantifiable?* | |
| *Measure* | |
| *Total Financial Amount* | |
| *Total Nonfinancial Amount* | |
| *Total Budget Associated* | |
| *Cost/Benefit Ratio* | |
| *Frequency of Measurement* | |
| *Measure Owner* | |
| *Measurement Technique* | |

*(Continued on next page)*

*8. Benefit Profile/Benefit Identification Sheet (Continued)*

| | |
|---|---|
| *Source of Measurements* | |
| *Disbenefits Associated* | |
| **Benefit Realization and Ownership Details** | |
| *Benefit Owner* | |
| *Business Areas Responsible for Realizing the Benefit* | |
| *Realization Start Date (Planned/ Actual)* | |
| *Realization End Date (Planned/ Actual)* | |
| *Total Benefit Expected (Baseline)* | |
| *Total Benefit Expected* | |
| **Program(s) and/or Projects Associated** | |
| *Program Code / Name* | |
| *Program Sponsor* | |
| *Program Manager* | |
| *Project Code / Name* | |
| *Project Sponsor* | |
| *Project Manager* | |
| *Project Start Date (Planned/Actual)* | |
| *Project End Date (Planned/Actual)* | |

| 9. Business Case | | | | |
|---|---|---|---|---|
| **Organization:** | | | | |
| Version: | | Version Type: | | |
| **Issued by:** | | **Issue date:** | | |
| **Department:** | | **Job title:** | | |
| **Approved by:** | | **Approval date:** | | |
| **Department:** | | **Job title:** | | |

| **I. Introduction** |
|---|
| |

| **II. Motivation** |
|---|
| |

| **III. Expected Benefits and Success Criteria** |
|---|
| |

| **IV. Options** |
|---|
| *Option A (Doing nothing):* |
| *Option B:* |
| *Option C:* |
| *Option D:* |

| **V. Recommendations** |
|---|
| |

| **VI. Initial Assumptions and Constraints** |
|---|
| |

| **VII. High-Level Cost Estimates** |
|---|
| |

| **VIII. Impact Analysis** |
|---|
| |

| **IX. Risk Analysis** |
|---|
| |

| **X. High-Level Plan** |
|---|
| |

| **XI. Governance and Rules of the Organization** |
|---|
| |

| 10. Program Benefits Realization Strategy | | | |
|---|---|---|---|
| Organization: | | | |
| Program: | | | |
| Program Manager | | Department: | |
| Program Sponsor | | Department: | |
| Version: | | Version Type: | |
| Issued by: | | Issue date: | |
| Department: | | Job title: | |
| Approved by: | | Approval date: | |
| Department: | | Job title: | |

**I. Initiatives**

**II. Benefits Dependency Network**

**III. Benefits to Be Realized**

**IV. Disbenefits to Be Managed**

**V. Management of Change Strategies**

**VI. Handover Strategies**

| 11. Project Benefits Realization Strategy | | | |
|---|---|---|---|
| **Organization:** | | | |
| **Project:** | | | |
| Project Manager | | **Department:** | |
| Program Sponsor | | **Department:** | |
| **Department:** | | **Job title:** | |
| **Approved by:** | | **Approval date:** | |
| **Department:** | | **Job title:** | |

| I. Benefits to Be Realized |
|---|
| |

| II. Disbenefits to Be Managed |
|---|
| |

| III. Management of Change Strategies |
|---|
| |

| IV. Handover Strategies |
|---|
| |

# 12. Benefits Risk Log

| Organization: | |
|---|---|
| Version: | Version Type: |
| Issued by: | Issue date: |
| Department: | Job title: |

## Benefits change log

| Benefit Code/ Name | Description of the Risk | Risk Identifier/ Risk Owner | Probability | Impact | Response Type | Response Strategy | Status |
|---|---|---|---|---|---|---|---|
| | | | | | | | |
| | | | | | | | |
| | | | | | | | |
| | | | | | | | |
| | | | | | | | |
| | | | | | | | |
| | | | | | | | |

# 13. Benefit Stakeholder Engagement Plan

| Organization: | | | | |
|---|---|---|---|---|
| Program or project: | | | | |
| Version: | | Version Type: | | |
| Issued by: | | Issue date: | | |
| Department: | | Job title: | | |
| Approved by: | | Approval date: | | |
| Department: | | Job title: | | |

| Stakeholder | Goals, Motivations, Expectations, and Interests | Influence | Interest | Impact | Level of Involvement | Action Type/ Stakeholder Category | Strategies |
|---|---|---|---|---|---|---|---|
| | | | | | | | |
| | | | | | | | |
| | | | | | | | |
| | | | | | | | |
| | | | | | | | |

# 14. Benefits Change Log

| Organization: | |
|---|---|
| Version: | Benefits changed in this version: |
| Issued by: | Issue date: |
| Department: | Job title: |

## Benefits change log

| Benefit Code/ Name | Description of the Change | Reason for the Change | Originator | Date Received | Date Required | Impact | Stakeholders Notified |
|---|---|---|---|---|---|---|---|
| | | | | | | | |
| | | | | | | | |
| | | | | | | | |
| | | | | | | | |
| | | | | | | | |
| | | | | | | | |
| | | | | | | | |

| 15. Benefits Handover Form | | | |
|---|---|---|---|
| Organization: | | | |
| Version: | | Version Type: | |
| Project Manager: | | Issue date: | |
| Department: | | Job title: | |
| Benefit Owner: | | Approval date: | |
| Department: | | Job title: | |

**I. Program/Project Manager**

**II. Benefit Owner**

**III. Benefit Code/Name**

**IV. Benefit Measure**

**V. Measurement Baseline**

**VI. Frequency of Measurement**

**VII. Measure Owner**

**VIII. Benefit Reporting Recipients**

**IX. Expected Benefit (Baseline from Business Case)**

**X. Expected Benefit (Reviewed Baseline)**

**XI. Benefit Realization Timeline**

## 16. Program-Level Benefits Tracking Sheet

| Organization: | |
|---|---|
| Program | |
| Version: | Version Type: |
| Issued by: | Issue date: |
| Department: | Job title: |
| Approved by: | Approval date: |
| Department: | Job title: |

| Basic Information | | | Realization Start Date | | Measurement | | | | Total Benefit Expected | | | |
|---|---|---|---|---|---|---|---|---|---|---|---|---|
| Project Code/ Name | Benefit Code/ Name | Measure | Benefit Realization Start Date (Baseline) | Benefit Realization Start Date (Actual) | Date | Owner | Total Realized this Period | Total Realized to Date | Total Benefit (Baseline) | Total Benefit (Planned) | End Date (Baseline) | End Date (Planned) |
| | | | | | | | | | | | | |
| | | | | | | | | | | | | |
| | | | | | | | | | | | | |
| | | | | | | | | | | | | |
| | | | | | | | | | | | | |
| | | | | | | | | | | | | |
| | | | | | | | | | | | | |

| 17. Project-Level Benefits Realization Control Sheet | | | | | | | | |
|---|---|---|---|---|---|---|---|---|
| **Organization:** | | | | | | | | |
| **Project:** | | | | | | | | |
| Version: | | | Version Type: | | | | | |
| **Issued by:** | | | **Issue date:** | | | | | |
| **Department:** | | | **Job title:** | | | | | |
| **Approved by:** | | | **Approval date:** | | | | | |
| **Department:** | | | **Job title:** | | | | | |

| I. Benefit Code / Name |
|---|
| |

| II. Benefit Measure |
|---|
| |

| III. Benefit Owner |
|---|
| |

**IV. Benefit Realization Life Cycle**

| Benefit realization start date (baseline) | | Benefit realization end date (baseline) | |
|---|---|---|---|
| Benefit realization start date (actual) | | Benefit realization end date (planned) | |

**V. Planned vs. Actuals**

| Year | | | | | | | | |
|---|---|---|---|---|---|---|---|---|
| Quarter | Q1 | Q2 | Q3 | Q4 | Q1 | Q2 | Q3 | Q4 |
| Planned | | | | | | | | |
| Cumulative | | | | | | | | |
| Actual | | | | | | | | |
| Cumulative | | | | | | | | |

**VI. Issues**

| List of issues | Actions to address the issues |
|---|---|
| | |

*(Continued on next page)*

**17. Project-Level Benefits Realization Control Sheet** *(Continued)*

| VII. Risks | |
|---|---|
| *List of risks* | *Actions in response to the risks* |
| | |
| **VIII. Actions** | |
| | |

| 18. Benefits Realization Health Check | | | |
|---|---|---|---|
| **Organization:** | | | |
| Version: | | Version Type: | |
| **Issued by:** | | **Issue date:** | |
| **Department:** | | **Job title:** | |
| **Approved by:** | | **Approval date:** | |
| **Department:** | | **Job title:** | |

**I. Benefit Code/Name**

**II. Benefit Owner**

**III. Program(s) and/or Project(s) Associated**

**IV. Checklist: Prerealization Process**

| Y/N | Benefit is clearly identified and defined. |
|---|---|
| Y/N | Benefit is measurable. |
| Y/N | Actions are taken to avoid the risk of benefit double counting or benefit hyper estimation. |
| Y/N | Benefit is clearly relevant to the achievement of strategic objectives. |
| Y/N | Benefit is clearly related to a set of change initiatives |
| Y/N | Benefit is decomposed in terms of the percent contribution expected from each initiative. |
| Y/N | Benefit is described in business case(s) approved at the beginning of the program(s)/project(s). |
| Y/N | Benefits ownership is clearly defined as well as the ownership by the benefits enabling initiatives. |
| Y/N | Actions are planned to ensure benefit realization by business operations. |
| Y/N | A benefits realization strategy defines a plan for the entire benefits realization life cycle. |

**V. Checklist: Realization Process**

| Y/N | Benefit is frequently reviewed and realigned to the current expectations. |
|---|---|

(Continued on next page)

*18. Benefits Realization Health Check (Continued)*

| | |
|---|---|
| *Y/N* | Results of benefit reviews are frequently communicated to the stakeholders. |
| *Y/N* | Benefit stakeholders needs are frequently reassessed. |
| *Y/N* | Benefit is monitored by the organization during the entire realization lifecycle. |
| *Y/N* | Benefit realization is frequently assessed against the expectations described in the business case. |
| *Y/N* | Benefits are periodically reevaluated against the business case. |
| *Y/N* | The occurrence of emergent disbenefits is monitored. |
| *Y/N* | The potential for realization of additional benefits is observed and exploited whenever appropriate. |
| *Y/N* | Actions are performed to ensure benefit realization by the regular business operations. |
| *Y/N* | Lessons learned are identified, captured, and applied. |
| *Y/N* | A benefits realization strategy is followed. |

**VI. Benefit Measure**

| |
|---|
| |

**VII. Sources of Measurement**

| |
|---|
| |

**VIII. Benefits Realization RAG Status**

| | | | |
|---|---|---|---|
| G | A | R | Current amount of benefits realized against benefits realization schedule (baseline). |
| G | A | R | Current benefits forecast against total benefits expected (baseline). |

**IX. Current Issues**

| List of issues | Actions to address the issues |
|---|---|
| | |

**X. Current Risks**

| List of risks | Actions in response to the risks |
|---|---|
| | |

**XI. Recovery Actions**

| |
|---|
| |

| 19. Benefits Portfolio Dashboard | | | | | |
|---|---|---|---|---|---|
| **Organization:** | | | | | |
| **Version:** | | **Version Type:** | | | |
| **Issued by:** | | **Issue date:** | | | |
| **Department:** | | **Job title:** | | | |
| **Approved by:** | | **Approval date:** | | | |
| **Department:** | | **Job title:** | | | |

| | **Benefit A** | **Benefit B** | **Benefit C** | **Benefit D** | **Benefit E** |
|---|---|---|---|---|---|
| Benefit Code/Name | | | | | |
| Benefit Category | | | | | |
| Is the Benefit Measurable? | | | | | |
| Is the Benefit Financially Quantifiable? | | | | | |
| Measure | | | | | |
| Total Financial Amount | | | | | |
| Total Nonfinancial Amount | | | | | |
| Benefit Owner | | | | | |
| Frequency of Measurement | | | | | |
| Last Measurement Date | | | | | |
| Program(s)/Project(s) Code/ Name | | | | | |
| Program/Project Budget | | | | | |
| Cost/Benefit Ratio (Baseline) | | | | | |
| Cost/Benefit Ratio | | | | | |

*(Continued on next page)*

| | | | | | |
|---|---|---|---|---|---|
| Realization Start Date (Planned/Actual) | | | | | |
| Realization End Date (Planned/Actual) | | | | | |
| Total Benefit Expected (Baseline) | | | | | |
| Total Benefit Expected | | | | | |
| Benefit Realized to Date | | | | | |
| Benefit Realization RAG Status: Realization Schedule | | | | | |
| Benefit Realization RAG Status: Benefit Amount | | | | | |

# Appendix E

## Enterprise Benefits Realization Management Toolkit: How to Use Guidance

The following pages provide guidance for the utilization of the set of templates that are available all across this book to support readers in the application of Benefits Realization Management practices in their organizations. For each template, a "how to use" guide is provided, which gives generic guidance about its utilization.

It is important to mention that all templates available in this book are generic and applicable to all market sectors and types of organizations. Nevertheless, if needed, the templates can be tailored to address the specific needs of each organization.

Following is a list of templates for which guidance is provided in this appendix:

### Chapter 4

1. Enterprise Benefits Realization Management Maturity Enhancement Strategy
2. Benefits Realization Management Framework
3. Measures Dictionary
4. eBRS: Enterprise Benefits Realization Strategy

**Chapter 5**

**Chapter 6**

**Chapter 7**

# E.1 Enterprise Benefits Realization Management Maturity Enhancement Strategy

## I. Rationale and Background

Add background information about the utilization of Benefits Realization Management across the organization. It can be high-level and/or anecdotal, since more detail analysis will happen during the AS-IS Analysis. Describe the reasons for the change by making it clear to what extent the business performance is below desired levels and what could be improved.

## II. Objectives

Describe the objective of this document. The description clearly identifies the objectives expected to be achieved from the change to the current practices.

If possible, the associated benefits should be identified. For example, they could be improvements in the efficiency in managing business changes, in terms of obtaining better return on investment across the entire program and/or project portfolio. Another example would be a reduction in sunk costs associated with the cancellation of projects or with radical changes in the project scope.

A third example would be an improvement in the organization's consolidated business results—for example, in profit margin, since the company's investments are likely to become more aligned with business strategies, therefore avoiding waste in investments that may not directly support the organization in the achievement of its objectives.

## III. Approach

### a. Planning

#### i. AS-IS Analysis

Describe the way in which the current situation will be analyzed. Identify the business division and or departments to be analyzed. Describe the methods of analysis to be adopted—for example, interviews and observation, business rules analysis, process mapping, and/or any other methods. The identification of problems and opportunities for improvement should be a key outcome of the AS-IS Analysis.

#### ii. TO-BE Analysis

Describe the way in which the desired future situation will be analyzed. Describe the methods of analysis to be adopted, which can be theoretical or empirical—for example, literature review, benchmarking, case studies analysis, and/or any other methods. The TO-BE Analysis must take into consideration the business strategies in terms of changes to business processes and policies, organizational structures, or any other aspects that may influence the organization's benefits realization processes.

#### iii. GAP Analysis

Describe the way the current situation will be compared to the desired future situation by identifying existing gaps. Define the process of review and approval of the final report, as well as the roles and responsibilities.

#### iv. Definition of Changes to Be Implemented

Describe the way changes will be implemented. This section includes the definition of options and the selection of a set of changes to be implemented in order to fill all gaps or some gaps that were identified during the Gap Analysis.

### b. Implementation

#### i. Documentation (Processes and Procedures)

Describe the way changes will be applied to the existing processes and policies. Identify the required steps and the roles and responsibilities involved.

### ii. *Training in Systems and Tools*

Describe the way new processes and procedures will be supported by systems and tools. Identify roles and responsibilities involved.

### iii. *General Communications and Training*

Define preferred ways to deliver training to Benefits Realization Management practitioners. This section can include different communications channels and training strategies depending on the characteristics of each target stakeholder and the objectives to be achieved.

### iv. *Senior Management Communications and Training*

Define preferred ways to deliver training to the senior business management team. This section can include different communications channels and training strategies, depending on the characteristics of each target stakeholder and the objectives to be achieved.

### v. *Go-Live*

Define the preferred approach to the go-live. For large organizations, it can be a phased approach with subsequent waves or tranches of implementation.

## c. Stabilization

### i. *Process Control*

Define the way the process will be controlled after go-live. Audits and performance indicators can be applicable to ensure full control over the utilization of the new processes.

### ii. *Support*

Define the way the new processes will be supported, clearly identifying roles and responsibilities associated to support to practitioners after the go-live.

## d. Handover

### i. *Formal Handover to Operations*

Define the way the new processes will be handed over to operations. Define the ownership of the new processes after the handover.

## e. Closeout

### i. *Development of Final Report*

Define the way a final report will be produced, including the audience and final approval.

### ii. *Analysis of Lessons Learned*

Define the way lessons learned will be gathered, shared, and addressed to ensure the continuous improvement of the organizational processes.

### iii. Formal Closeout

Define the required steps for formal closeout of this initiative including financial closeout and demobilization of project resources.

## IV. Change Management

Describe the change management strategies that will be adopted. Include strategies to the engagement of practitioners and senior managers.

## V. RAID Management

Describe the techniques to be adopted for the management of Risks, Assumptions, Issues, and Dependencies. It is recommended that the risk log, assumption log, issues log, and dependencies log be attached to this document.

# E.2 Benefits Realization Management Framework

## I. Introduction

Describe the objective of this document. If needed, add background information about the utilization of Benefits Realization Management across the organization.

## II. Benefits Realization Management: Theoretical Background

Add theory about Benefits Realization Management, terminology to be adopted, definitions, and rationale.

## III. Benefits Realization Management Life Cycle

This section provides a graphic overview of the processes, activities, and roles involved in Benefits Realization Management across the organization (e.g., benefits realization strategy, benefits planning, benefits realization, benefits review, and evaluation).

## IV. Benefits Realization Management Processes

The next sections describe the processes to be adopted by the organization to manage benefits realization across the business.

**a. Enterprise Benefits Realization Strategy**

Describe the process to develop the Enterprise Benefits Realization Strategy. Explain how to use templates and tools.

**b. Planning Benefits**

Describe the activities involved in planning benefits. Add supporting information, which will be needed for the correct and standardized execution of the activities proposed (e.g., standard components of a benefits map, benefits dictionary or measures dictionary, and categories of benefits to support the assessment of eligibility to be part of the portfolio). Explain how to use templates and tools.

**c. Realizing Benefits**

Describe activities involved in realizing benefits. Present the arrangements to the continuity of the Benefits Realization Management activities after the program or project closeout. Explain how to use templates and tools.

**d. Reviewing and Evaluating Benefits**

Describe activities involved in reviewing and evaluating benefits. Present procedures for assessment of benefit cases during stage-gate reviews and other portfolio-level reviews; activities associated with the utilization of postimplementation reviews; and methods for capturing and utilizing lessons learned to support the enhancement of processes and benefits realization forecasts. Explain how to use templates and tools.

## V. Roles and Responsibilities

List and describe roles and responsibilities associated with Benefits Realization Management in the organization (e.g., Benefits Governance; Benefits Management; PMO; Benefits Measurement).

# E.3 Measures Dictionary

### Measure Name/Code

Enter the organizational code (unique number) associated with the measure and the measure name (a short but meaningful description).

### Measure Owner

Enter the name, surname, department, and job title of the measure owner. The measure owner is likely to be the process owner.

## Measure Type

Identify the measure type. Measures can be:

- Process outputs measures
- Process outcome measures
- In-process measures

## Measure Objective

Identify the objective of the measure. Each measure should have at least one objective regarding the way it supports the management of a specific business process. Apart from supporting the ongoing service levels, the measures also support process improvement initiatives. Therefore, the measures can be classified regarding the way they will be utilized to support beneficial change, such as to support the achievement of:

- Revenue improvement goals
- Cost reduction goals
- Process cycle-time improvement goals
- Customer satisfaction improvement goals

## Associated Business Functions

Identify the business division or function that is associated with the measure (and with the business process); for example:

- Marketing and sales
- Manufacturing
- IS/IT operations
- Project management
- Supply chain management
- Human resources management

## Associated Business Processes

List the high-level business process that are directly associated with the measure; for example, sales process, product XYZ manufacturing process, and the like.

## Associated Tools or IT Systems

Identify the tools associated with the measure. They can be checklists, forms, reports, or any other manual tools to capture and to record measurements.

Alternatively, IT systems or data bases can be listed here, in case the measurement process is automated. A specific report to be generated by an IT system or a database that keeps the information can be also identified in this field.

## Measurement Method

Describe the way the measurement is taken and how it is calculated.

## Measurement Periodicity

Define the periodicity of measurement; for example:

- Daily, at a predetermined hour of the day
- Once a week in a specific weekday
- Once a month in a specific day of the month
- Quarterly, on specific days and months

## Benefit Measurer

Enter the name, surname, department, and job title of the Benefit Measurer (the person responsible for taking readings and reporting the measurements).

# E.4 eBRS: Enterprise Benefits Realization Strategy

## I. Key Strategic Drivers

List and describe the organization's key strategic drivers and their rationales (about 10). The strategic drivers are factors that impact the organization. They can be critical to the organization's success and ability to deliver its mission and, therefore, can be ranked by impact and predictability. Other strategic factors that impact the organization's market sector and other organizations with similar characteristics may be also considered. Some techniques can be employed to identify strategic drivers such as a political, economic, social, technological, legal, and environmental (PESTLE) analysis, a SWOT (strengths, weaknesses, opportunities and threats) analysis and a TOWS* (threats, opportunities, weaknesses and strengths) strategic alternatives matrix.

---

* The TOWS strategic alternatives matrix is a strategic analysis tool that is similar to the SWOT matrix. It supports the identification of strategies to a) use strengths to maximize opportunities; b) use strengths to minimize threats; c) exploit opportunities to minimize weaknesses ; and d) minimize weaknesses and avoid threats in combination.

a. **Driver A**

Describe the strategic driver. Explain what is already known about the driver and what is still unknown or requires more information. Describe the potential impact of the key driver on aspects of the organization by considering the impact of the driver in terms of producing a need or an opportunity to improve existing approaches, to add new things to the business, or to manage internal or external issues or risks.

b. **Driver *N***

Add more strategic drivers as required.

## II. Strategic Objectives

List and describe the strategic objectives associated with the strategic drivers.

a. **Strategic Objective A**

Describe the strategic objective. Each objective should be associated with one or more strategic drivers. Define ownership for the objective, keeping in mind the appropriate level of seniority to be accountable for its achievement.

b. **Strategic Objective *N***

Add more strategic objectives as required.

## III. End Benefits

List and describe the end benefits associated to the achievement of the strategic objectives.

a. **End Benefit A**

Define the benefits and assign ownership to the benefit. Define ways to measure, track, and record benefits, and attribute ownership to these activities.

b. **End Benefit *N***

Add more end benefits as required.

## IV. Changes Required

List and describe the main organizational changes required to realize the expected benefits. The changes are described at an organizational level of detail, since a more detailed description will happen later on program and project levels.

a. **Change Required A**

Describe the change and assign ownership to the change. Each change will enable the realization of all or some benefits, which are expected to support the achievement of the strategic objective. Therefore, the benefits that are expected to be associated with the change should be also identified. For example, changes to the performance of a business process will enable the realization of benefits that are related to the performance measures of the same business process.

### b. Change Required N

Add more changes as required.

## V. Ideas

List and describe the ideas that are available to the enable the changes required to realize the expected benefits.

### a. Idea A

Describe the idea and assign ownership to the idea. An idea will be related to the delivery of outputs and/or outcomes that will enable the realization of the expected benefits. Each idea can support the total or partial achievement of the strategic objective. The ideas, if approved, will often become projects and then may be grouped into programs and to the portfolio.

If possible, provide a high-level cost associated with the idea. In case a single project alone does not enable the realization of benefits, an investment appraisal can be latter applicable at the program level.

### b. Idea N

Add more ideas as required.

## VI. Selection Criteria

Define criteria for the analysis and selection of programs and projects to get into the project portfolio. It will involve traditional project portfolio selection techniques, including previous categorization and the utilization of investment appraisal techniques.

## VII. High-Level Governance Process

Define the process of periodic review and governance of the organizational Benefits Realization Management as the highest level governance of the strategy execution process.

Define the process to govern the execution of the portfolio of changes with the view of realizing the expected end benefits required by the business strategy.

## VIII. Initiatives Selected for Implementation

Define the process of capturing and storing information about the initiatives selected for implementation. List the initiatives and refer to a location where more information can be found about the business cases and implementation plans.

Since such initiatives will be selected after the production of the first version of this strategy, its first version will not have a list attached to it. Nevertheless, the list of initiatives to be implemented should be added as an appendix to this document and periodically updated in order to be complete and up to date at each review cycle of this strategy.

## IX. Benefits Dependency Network

Draw a benefits dependency network that associates all elements of this strategy, from the business objectives to the initiatives that are selected for implementation. Such benefits dependency networks will need periodic updates and can be added as an appendix to this strategy. They can also be produced by using the appropriate specific systems and/or tools.

# E.5 Benefits Map/Benefits Dependency Network

For this form, work from the right to the left to identify dependencies.

## Business Objectives

Identify the strategic business objectives of the organization. Each map can focus on a single objective or on a set of objectives that will have their achievement supported by the same set of end benefits.

## End Benefits

Identify the end benefits directly associated with achieving each strategic objective. Link all the benefits identified to the business objectives that will be achieved based on their realization. The links will be represented by arrows.

## Intermediate Benefits

Identify intermediate benefits, if any, associated with the achievement of the end benefits. Link the intermediate benefits to each other according to the existing logical relationships that may exist between them. The links will be represented by arrows.

## Business Changes

Identify the required business changes to the realization of the expected benefits. Link all identified business changes to the benefits whose realization they will enable. These can be intermediate or end benefits. The links will be represented by arrows.

## Outputs/Enablers

Identify the outputs and/or enablers that will make possible the realization of the expected benefits. Link all identified outputs/enablers to the business changes that will be enabled by them or directly to benefits that will be realized by them. The links will be represented by arrows.

## Initiatives

Identify the initiative that will be carried out to produce outputs and outcomes and/or to implement business changes. These can be projects and/or programs and/or other actions or events. Link all the identified initiatives to the outputs/enablers that will be produced by them. The links will be represented by arrows.

## Additional Step:

Close to each arrow, state the percentage of the achievement of the successor, which is associated to the completion of each predecessor. For each element, the sum of the percentages associated to each incoming arrow should be equal to 100%.

# E.6 Benefit Profile/Benefit Identification Sheet

## Benefit Basic Details

### Benefit Code/Name

Enter the organizational code (unique number) associated to the benefit and the benefit name (short description).

## Benefit Definition

Enter the detailed description of the benefit.

## Benefit Category

Enter the category of the benefit, according to the organization's standard set of benefit categories.

## Type of Benefit

Enter the category of the benefit, according to the organization's standard set of benefit types.

## Strategic Objective Associated

Enter the strategic objective whose achievement will be supported by the realization of the benefit.

## Benefit Dependency Network Diagram

Insert the benefit dependency network diagram.

## *Benefit Measurement Details*

## Is the Benefit Measurable?

Enter YES if the benefit is measurable. Enter NO if the benefit is not measurable.

## Is the Benefit Financially Quantifiable?

Enter YES if the benefit is financially quantifiable. Enter NO if the benefit is not financially quantifiable.

## Measure

Enter the description of the measure.

## Total Financial Amount/Total Nonfinancial Amount

Enter the total financial amount that is expected to be achieved.
Enter the total nonfinancial amount that is expected to be achieved.

## Total Budget Associated

Enter the total budget associated with achieving the benefit (including all relevant business changes).

### Cost/Benefit Ratio

Enter the overall cost benefit ratio associated with the benefit from the business case.

### Frequency of Measurement

Enter the frequency of measurement of the benefit.

### Measure Owner

Enter the name, surname, department, and job title of the measure owner—that is, the person responsible for ensuring that measurements are taken and are reported. The measurement can be performed by another role—the measurer—on behalf of the Measure Owner.

### Measurement Technique

Describe how the measurement is made.

### Source of Measurements

Enter the list of systems and/or organizational processes and/or departments that provide data to calculate the benefit realized to date.

### Disbenefits Associated

Enter the list of disbenefits associated and describe how they are going to be controlled.

## Benefit Realization and Ownership Details

### Benefit Owner

Enter the name, surname, department, and job title of the benefit owner if the benefit owner is different from the measure owner.

### Business Areas Responsible for Realizing the Benefit

Enter the business areas responsible for realizing the benefit.

### Realization Start Date (Planned/Actual)

Enter the planned date to begin benefit realization from the business case and/or project plan. After the actual start of benefits realization, enter the actual date for the beginning of benefit realization.

### Realization End Date (Planned/Actual)

Enter the planned date for the end of benefit realization from the business case and/ or project plan. After the actual conclusion of benefits realization, enter the actual date for the end of benefit realization.

### Total Benefit Expected (Baseline)/Total Benefit Expected

Enter the total amount of benefit expected to be achieved from the business case and/ or project plan (baseline).

Enter the total amount of benefit expected to be achieved from the latest benefit review (current expectation).

## *Program(s) and/or Projects Associated*

### Program Code/Name

Enter the organizational code (unique number) assigned to the program and the program name responsible for the achievement of the expected benefit.

### Program Sponsor

Enter the name, surname, department, and job title of the Program Sponsor.

### Program Manager

Enter the name, surname, department, and job title of the Program Manager.

### Project Code/Name

Enter the organizational code (unique number) associated to the project and the project name of the project responsible for the achievement of the expected benefit.

### Project Sponsor

Enter the name, surname, department, and job title of the Project Sponsor.

### Project Manager

Enter the name, surname, department, and job title of the Project Manager.

### Project Start Date (Planned/Actual)/Project End Date (Planned/Actual)

Enter the project planned start date from the business case and/ or project plan. After the actual start, enter the actual date.

Enter the project planned end date from the business case and/or the project plan. After the actual end, enter the actual date.

## E.7 Business Case

### I. Introduction

Briefly describe the objective (what), the reasons (why), the scope (how), the investment amount (how much), the desired time frames (when and for how long), the locations or geographies involved (where), and the person responsible for carrying out the work and being accountable for the achievement of the results (who).

### II. Motivation

Provide some background in terms of the current context, the business processes involved, and the environment. Describe the reasons for the investment. These should be preferentially linked to the business drivers and strategic objectives.

### III. Expected Benefits and Success Criteria

Describe the expected benefits and the success criteria that will be used to note achievement of the strategic business objectives. These will be later instrumental to the evaluation of the overall success of the initiative.

### IV. Options

Present a list of options to address the business drivers and to support the realization of the expected benefits and the achievement of the associated business objectives. Each option should be presented along with the expected impact of the implementation of the option, in terms of expected benefits and cost as well as any disbenefits (negative impacts).

### V. Recommendations

Recommend the selection, deferral, or rejection of each option, based on a critical analysis.

## VI. Initial Assumptions and Constraints

Present the initial assumptions and constraints for the recommended option.

## VII. High-Level Cost Estimates

Present the high-level cost estimates for the recommended option, based on the initial assumptions and constraints. The high-level costs should be broken down by a set of standard the cost types defined by the financial department of the organization to enable further stratified control (e.g., human resources, materials, third-party suppliers, and indirect costs, among others).

## VIII. Impact Analysis

Analyze the impact of the implementation of the selected option over the current internal and external environment. Identify stakeholders that will be affected by the implementation of the preferred solution.

## IX. Risk Analysis

Identify the uncertainties associated to the selected option and therefore the key risks that may affect the success of the initiative. Suggest plans and owners to treat each identified risks.

## X. High-Level Plan

Provide a high-level plan to implement the recommended option. The plan should include:

- High level required outputs (if known)
- Desired outcomes
- Changes to the existing organizational environment

### Governance and Rules of the Organization

Describe the governance structure for the implementation of the initiative. Identify the benefits owners, initiative sponsor, and main clients, as well as any key stakeholders. Describe the functions the governance group will perform.

Any organizational rules associated to the approval of the investment and to the implementation of the initiative should also be described here.

# E.8 Program Benefits Realization Strategy

## I. Initiatives

List and describe the initiatives that will deliver change. Define the relationship between initiatives (e.g., vision, desired benefits, etc.) and the strategic objectives of the organizations.

Define the key roles and responsibilities for each initiative—for example, project sponsor, users, suppliers, project manager, and key stakeholders.

## II. Benefits Dependency Network

Draw a graphical representation of the benefits dependency network for the program. All initiatives should be linked to enable the achievement of the final objectives of the program.

## III. Benefits to Be Realized

Identify and define benefits that are expected from the program. Identify the strategic objectives associated to each benefit. Assign the business areas responsible for delivering each benefit.

Describe how to perform benefits measurement, tracking, and recording, including frequency of reviews, measurement techniques, and processes employed. Alternatively, this section can also refer to the benefit profile.

## IV. Disbenefits to Be Managed

Describe the way the program will treat disbenefits by managing and trying to avoid them.

## V. Management of Change Strategies

Describe the management of change strategies that will be adopted to ensure the acceptance of the changes, their embedment into the business processes, and the consequent realization of the expected benefits. Describe the ways to establish the needed ownership and commitment to the realization of the benefits.

## VI. Handover Strategies

Describe the way the program will perform the handover of outputs to the business operations in order to ensure the accountability for benefits realization.

It should include when the benefits will be handed over (on project closeout or before) and who will be responsible or its realization after the handover.

# E.9 Project Benefits Realization Strategy

### I. Benefits to be Realized

Identify and define benefits that are expected from the program. Identify the strategic objectives associated with each benefit. Assign the business areas that are responsible for delivering each benefit.

Describe how to perform benefits measurement, tracking, and recording, including frequency of reviews, measurement techniques, and processes employed. Alternately, this section can also refer to the benefit profile.

### II. Disbenefits to be Managed

Describe the way the program will treat disbenefits, manage them, and try to avoid them.

### III. Management of Change Strategies

Describe the management of change strategies that will be adopted to ensure the acceptance of the changes, their embedment into the business routine, and the consequent realization of the expected benefits. Describe the ways to establish the needed ownership and commitment to the realization of the benefits.

### IV. Handover Strategies

Describe the way the program will perform the handover of outputs to the business operations to ensure the accountability for benefits realization.

It should include when the benefits will be handed over (on project closeout or before) and who will be responsible or its realization after the handover.

## E.10 Benefits Risk Log

### Benefit Code/Name

Enter the organizational code (unique number) associated with the benefit and the benefit name (short description).

### Description of the Risk

Describe any risks in terms of this benefit.

### Risk Identifier/Risk Owner

Enter the name, surname, department and job title of the person who identified the risk.

Enter the name, surname, department and job title of the person who owns the risk, and therefore is responsible for managing it.

### Probability

Enter the probability associated with the risk; in other words, identify how likely the risk is to happen and then to become an issue.

### Impact

Enter the impact of the risk in a scale from 1 (low) to 4 (high) regarding how much the risk can affect the benefit value or the benefit realization schedule.

### Response Type

Enter the type of response that will be implemented should the risk occur. The organization can use the same categories employed as part of its existing project risk management procedures. For example, a set of categories to classify risk response types would include: *avoid, transfer, mitigate,* and *accept*; a set of opportunity response types might include *exploit, enhance, share,* or *accept* (PMI® 2013a). It is important to note that a response to an opportunity can lead to realize more benefits than originally expected.

## Response Strategy

Describe the response strategy to respond to the risk. Present the response date, which is the date when the response strategy will be implemented to manage the risk or opportunity.

## Status

Enter the current status of the risk and of the actions that have been implemented to date in an effort to mitigate the risk (or to enhance it if it is an opportunity). This field should be periodically updated.

# E.11 Benefit Stakeholder Engagement Plan

### Stakeholder

Identify the stakeholder, whether it is a person or group of people. Enter the name(s), department(s), and job title(s).

### Goals, Motivations, Expectations, and Interests

Briefly describe the stakeholder's goals, motivations, expectations, and interests related to the benefit.

### Influence

Identify the level of influence on the realization of the benefit, on a scale from 1 (low) to 4 (high).

### Interest

Identify the level of interest in the realization of the benefit, on a scale from 1 (low) to 4 (high).

## Impact

Identify the ability to make changes or influence changes to plan the execution associated with the realization of the benefit on a scale from 1 (low) to 4 (high). Alternatively, this column can also be called importance or power.

## Level of Involvement

Identify the level of involvement on the realization of the benefit, on a scale from 1 (low) to 4 (high).

## Action Type/Stakeholder Category

Identify the type of action that will be taken to engage the stakeholder, in accordance with the appropriate stakeholder group.

## Strategies

Describe the stakeholder's engagement strategies to be applied to each specific stakeholder, including types of communications and periodicity.

# E.12 Benefits Change Log

### Benefit Code/Name

Enter the organizational code (unique number) associated to the benefit and the benefit name (short description).

## Description of the Change

Describe the change to the benefit.

## Reason for the Change

Describe reason for the change to the benefit.

## Originator

Enter the name, surname, department, and job title of the originator (requestor) of the change.

## Date Received

Enter the date when the change request was received.

## Date Required

Enter the date by which the change has to be applied.

## Impact

Enter the impact of the change in terms of benefit value or change to the benefit realization schedule.

## Stakeholders Notified

Enter the name, surname, department, and job title of the stakeholder that will be notified about the change.

# E.13 Benefits Handover Form

### I. Program/Project Manager

Enter the name, surname, department and job title of the program and/or project manager.

### II. Benefit Owner

Enter the name, surname, department, and job title of the benefit owner.

### III. Benefit Code/Name

Enter the organizational code (unique number) assigned to the benefit and the benefit name (short description).

### IV. Benefit Measure

Enter the description of the measure and the associated mathematical formula, if applicable.

### V. Measurement Baseline

Enter the baseline of the measurement of the benefit. Since the benefit is an improvement to a process measure, benefits realization will later be tracked by comparing the future measurements against this baseline measurement.

### VI. Frequency of Measurement

Enter the frequency of measurement of the benefit.

### VII. Measure Owner

Enter the name, surname, department, and job title of the Measure Owner (the person responsible for ensuring that measurements are taken and reported). The measurement can be performed by another role, the measurer, on behalf of the Measure Owner.

### VIII. Benefit Reporting Recipients

Enter the name, surname, department, and job title of the benefit reporting recipients (the people who will receive the benefit reports in accordance with the periodicity planned in the benefits stakeholder engagement plan).

### IX. Expected Benefit (Baseline from Business Case)

Enter the total benefit expected to be achieved from the business case.

### X. Expected Benefit (Reviewed Baseline)

Enter the total benefit expected to be achieved from the latest benefits review. It is recommended that a benefit review be conducted prior to the benefit handover.

### XI. Benefit Realization Timeline

Present the benefit realization timeline according to the current forecast. It can show the expected benefit to be realized by month, quarter, or another periodicity, preferably according to the frequency of the measurement.

## E.14 Program-Level Benefits Realization Tracking Sheet

### Project Code/Name

Enter the organizational code (unique number) for the project and the project name.

### Benefit Code/Name

Enter the organizational code (unique number) for the benefit and the benefit name (short description).

### Measure

Enter the description of the measure.

### Benefit Realization Start Date (Baseline)/Benefit Realization Start Date (Actual)

Enter the planned date to begin benefit realization from the business case and/ or the project plan.

Enter the actual date for the beginning of benefit realization. Leave it blank if has not started.

### Date

Enter the date when the measure was taken.

### Owner

Enter the name, surname, department, and job title of the benefit owner.

### Total Realized This Period

Enter the total amount of benefit realized in the current measurement period.

### Total Realized to Date

Enter the total amount of benefit realized to date.

### Total Benefit (Baseline)

Enter the total amount of benefit expected to be achieved from the business case and/or the project plan (baseline).

### Total Benefit (Planned)

Enter the total amount of benefit expected to be achieved from the latest benefit review (current expectation).

### End Date (Baseline)/End Date (Planned)

Enter the planned date for the end of benefit realization from the business case and/or the project plan.

Enter the current planned date or the actual date for the end of benefit realization.

## E.15 Project-Level Benefits Realization Control Sheet

### I. Benefit Code/Name

Enter the organizational code (unique number) for the benefit and the benefit name (short description).

### II. Benefit Measure

Enter the description of the measure and the associated mathematical formula to calculate it.

### III. Benefit Owner

Enter the name, surname, department and job title of the benefit owner.

### IV. Benefit Realization Life Cycle

Enter the benefit realization start date (baseline), benefit realization start date (actual), benefit realization end date (baseline), and benefit realization end date (planned).

### V. Planned vs. Actuals

Enter the benefit that is expected and the actual benefit realized by measurement period (by quarter in this template).

### VI. Issues

List the key issues that are currently affecting benefit realization. List the actions that are planned to address the issues.

### VII. Risks

List the key risks that the benefit realization is currently subject to. List the actions that are planned in response to the risks.

### VIII. Actions

Describe the recovery actions that are planned or currently in place to recover from any existing deviations (if applicable).

## E.16 Benefits Realization Health Check

### I. Benefit Code/Name

Enter the organizational code (unique number) assigned to the benefit and the benefit name (short description).

### II. Benefit Owner

Enter the name, surname, department, and job title of the benefit owner.

### III. Program(s) and/or Project(s) Associated

List the programs and projects that are relevant to the benefit.

### IV. Checklist: Prerealization Process

The statements provide a simple tool for the assessment of some key aspects of the Benefits Realization Management processes in the first stage of the benefits realization life cycle:

- During the prerealization process, it assesses the effective preparation for benefit realization.

## V. Checklist: Realization Process

The statements provide a simple tool for the assessment of some key aspects of the Benefits Realization Management processes in the second stage of the benefits realization life cycle:

- During the realization process, it assesses the effective management of benefit realization.

## VI. Benefit Measure

Enter the description of the measure and the associated mathematical formula, if applicable.

## VII. Sources of Measurement

Enter the list of systems and/or organizational processes and/or departments that provide data to calculate the benefit realized to date.

## VIII. Benefits Realization RAG Status

- Current amount of benefit realized against benefit realization schedule (baseline): Evaluates the current amount of benefit realized against the expected amount of benefit at the same point in time.
- Current benefit forecast against total benefit expected (baseline): Evaluates the current forecast of the total amount of benefit that will be realized against the expected total amount of benefit (baseline).

The color codes can be used as suggested below:

- *Green*: No deviation or positive deviation.
- *Amber*: Negative deviation that affects the return on investment but does not make the investment nonviable.
- *Red*: Negative deviation that affects the return on investment and does make the investment nonviable.

## IX. Current Issues

List the key issues affecting the benefit realization. List the actions that are planned to address the issues.

## X. Current Risks

List the key risks that may affect benefit realization. List the actions that are planned to mitigate the risks.

## XI. Recovery Actions

Describe the recovery actions that are planned or currently in place to recover from any existing deviations (if applicable).

# E.17 Benefits Portfolio Dashboard

### Benefit Code/Name

Enter the organizational code (unique number) assigned to the benefit and the benefit name (short description).

### Benefit Category

Enter the category of the benefit, according to the organization's standard set of benefit categories.

### Is the Benefit Measurable?

Enter YES if the benefit is measurable. Enter NO if the benefit is not measurable.

### Is the Benefit Financially Quantifiable?

Enter YES if the benefit is financially quantifiable. Enter NO if the benefit is not financially quantifiable.

### Measure

Enter the description of the measure.

### Total Financial Amount

Enter the total financial amount that is expected to be achieved.

## Total Nonfinancial Amount

Enter the total nonfinancial amount that is expected to be achieved.

## Benefit Owner

Enter the name, surname, department, and job title of the benefit owner.

## Frequency of Measurement

Enter the frequency of measurement of the benefit.

## Last Measurement Date

Enter date when the last measurement of the benefit was taken.

## Program(s)/Project(s) Code/Name

Enter the organizational code (unique number) assigned to the program/project and the program/project name for every program and/or project that is directly responsible for the achievement of the expected benefit.

## Program/Project Budget

Enter the total budget required to achieve of the benefit (including all potential business changes).

## Cost/Benefit Ratio (Baseline)/Cost/Benefit Ratio

Enter the overall cost/benefit ratio for the benefit from the business case.

Enter the overall cost/benefit ratio for the benefit based on current cost forecasts and reviewed benefit amounts.

## Realization Start Date (Planned/Actual)

Enter the planned date for the beginning of benefit realization from the business case and/or the project plan. Enter the actual date to begin benefit realization. Leave it blank if not started yet.

## Realization End Date (Planned/Actual)

Enter the planned date for the end of benefit realization from the benefit profile. If the expected benefits have been fully realized, enter the actual date at which benefit realization concluded. Leave it blank if not started yet.

## Total Benefit Expected (Baseline)/Total Benefit Expected/ Benefit Realized to Date

Enter the total amount of benefit expected to be achieved from the business case and/or the project plan (baseline).

Enter the total amount of benefit expected to be achieved from the latest benefit review (current expectation).

Enter the total amount of benefit realized to date.

## Benefit Realization RAG Status: Realization Schedule/ Benefit Amount

- *Realization Schedule*: Evaluate the current amount of benefit realized against the expected amount of benefit at the same point in time.
- *Benefit Amount*: Evaluate the current forecast of the total amount of benefit that will be realized against the expected total amount of benefit (baseline).

The color codes can be used as suggested below:

- *Green*: No deviation or positive deviation.
- *Amber*: Negative deviation that affects the return on investment, but does not make the investment nonviable.
- *Red*: Negative deviation that affects the return on investment and does make the investment nonviable.

## Additional Fields and Guidance:

Other fields can be added to the dashboard as appropriate according to each organization's governance processes. Other suggested fields include: Comments, Measure Owner, and Measurement Source.

# Appendix F

# List of Acronyms

APM     Association for Project Management (British)
AHP     Analytic hierarchy process
BAU     Business as usual
BRM     Benefits Realization Management
BSC     Balanced Scorecard
CEO     Chief Executive Officer
CFO     Chief Finance (Financial) Officer
CIO     Chief Information Officer
CoE     Center of Excellence
COO     Chief Operating Officer
CSF     Critical Success Factor
CWQC     Company-Wide Quality Control
eBRM     Enterprise Benefits Realization Management
eBRMF     Enterprise Benefits Realization Management Framework
eBRS     Enterprise Benefits Realization Strategy
ePMO     Enterprise PMO
EVA     Economic Value Added
HR     Human Resources Management
IPMA     International Project Management Association
IRR     Internal rate of return
IS     Information systems
IT     Information technology
ITIL     Information Technology Infrastructure Library

| | |
|---|---|
| KPI | Key Performance Indicator |
| MBO | Management By Objectives |
| NPV | Net Present Value |
| PDCA | Plan Do Check Act |
| PESTEL | Political, Economic, Social, Technological, Legal, and Environmental Analysis |
| PMI® | Project Management Institute |
| PMO | Project Management Office and/or Program Management Office and/or Portfolio Management Office |
| PSO | Project Support Office and/or Program Support Office and/or Portfolio Support Office |
| QC | Quality Control |
| RAID | Risks, Assumptions, Issues, and Dependencies |
| SWOT | Strengths, Weaknesses, Opportunities, Threats |
| TOWS | Threats, Opportunities, Weaknesses, Strengths |
| TQC | Total Quality Control |
| TQM | Total Quality Management |

# Appendix G

# List of Figures

# Appendix H

## List of Tables

# References

Allport, R., R. Brown, S. Glaister, and T. Travers. "Success and Failure in Urban Transport Infrastructure Projects." Imperial College London (May 1, 2008). Accessed on January 15, 2012, from https://workspace.imperial.ac.uk/rtsc/Public/Success%20 and%20Failure%20in%20Urban%20Transport%20Infrastructure%20Projects. pdf

Alter, A. "The Myth of Frequent Failure." *CIO Insight* 1, no. 69 (2006): 1.

Amason, A. C. *Strategic Management: From Theory to Practice.* London, UK: Routledge, 2011.

Anderson, D. K., and T. Merna. "Project Management Strategy—Project Management Represented as a Process-Based Set of Management Domains and the Consequences for Project Management Strategy." *International Journal of Project Management* 21, no. 6 (2003): 387–393. Accessed from http://www.sciencedirect.com/science/article/ pii/S026378630200087X

Andrews, K. *The Concept of Corporate Strategy.* Homewood, IL, USA: Irwin, 1971.

Artto, K., J. Kujala, P. Dietrich, and M. Martinsuo. "What Is Project Strategy?" *International Journal of Project Management* 26, no. 2 (2008): 4–12. Accessed from http://www. sciencedirect.com/science/article/pii/S0263786307001196%20%C3%A2% E2%82%AC%E2%80%9C%20aff2

Asian Development Bank. "Asian Development Bank—Improving Project Success through Effective Communication and Participation," Asian Development Bank (2011). Accessed on January 15, 2012, from http://www.adb.org/documents/ improving-project-success-through-effective-communication-and-participation

Association for Project Management. *Directing Change: A Guide to Governance of Project Management.* High Wycombe, UK: Association for Project Management, 2004.

Association for Project Management. *APM Body of Knowledge.* Buckinghamshire, UK: Association for Project Management, 2012.

Association for Project Management. "What is Project Management?" APM Website (2015). Accessed on October 31, 2015, from https://www.apm.org.uk/WhatIsPM

Australian Government Information Management Office. *Review of the Australian Government's Use of Information and Communication Technology*. Canberra, Australia: Commonwealth of Australia, 2008.

Bradley, G. *Benefit Realisation Management*. Farnham, UK: Gower Publishing, 2010.

Brazier, J. *Measuring and Valuing Health Benefits for Economic Evaluation*. Oxford, UK: Oxford University Press, 2007.

Breese, R. "Benefits Realisation Management: Panacea or False Dawn?" *International Journal of Project Management* 351, no. 30 (2012): 341.

Bryde, D. "Perceptions of the Impact of Project Sponsorship Practices on Project Success." *International Journal of Project Management* 26 (2006): 800–809.

BSI. *BS EN 12973: 2000 Value Management*. London, UK: British Standards Institution, 2000.

Burnes, B. *Managing Change*, 4th ed. Harlow, UK: Financial Times: Prentice Hall, 2004.

Buttrick, R. *The Project Workout: A Toolkit for Reaping the Rewards from All Your Business Projects*. London, UK: Financial Times Management, 1997.

Camilleri, E. *Project Success: Critical Factors and Behaviours*. Farnham, UK: Gower Publishing Limited, 2011.

Carroll, L. *Alice's Adventures in Wonderland; and Through the Looking Glass; and Phantasmagoria & Other Poems; and the Hunting of the Snark; and a Tangled Tale*. New York, NY, USA: Everyman's Library, 1965.

Chittenden, J., and J. V. Bon. *Programme Management Based on MSP: A Management Guide*. Zaltbommel, Netherlands: Van Haren Pub, 2006.

*Collins English Dictionary*, online ed., s.v. "disbenefit." Accessed on November 1, 2015 from http://www.collinsdictionary.com/dictionary/english/disbenefit

Cooke-Davies, T. "The 'Real' Success Factors on Projects." *International Journal of Project Management* 20, no. 3 (April 2002): 185–190. Accessed from http://www.sciencedirect.com/science/article/pii/S0263786301000679

De Haas, M., and A. Kleingeld. "Multilevel Design of Performance Measurement Systems: Enhancing Strategic Dialogue throughout the Organization." *Management Accounting Research* 10, no. 1 (1999): 233–261.

Drucker, P. *The Practice of Management*. New York, NY, USA: Routledge, 2007.

Dworatschek, S., and A. P. Oekonom. *Present Status of PM in Different Industries*. Ljubljana, Slovenia: International Cost Engineering Council, 2006.

Emam, K. E., and A. G. Koru. "A Replicated Survey of IT Software Project Failures." *IEEE Software* 25, no. 5 (2008): 84–90.

ESI International. *The Challenges to Success for Project/Program Management Offices*. London, UK: ESI International, 2009a.

ESI International. *View from the Ground: The Project Manager Perspective on Project Portfolio Management Effectiveness*. London, UK: ESI International, 2009b.

Eveleens, L., and C. Verhoef. "The Rise and Fall of the Chaos Report Figures." *IEEE Software* 27, no. 1 (2010): 30–36.

First Line Projects LLP. "2010 Project Management Survey Results." Ipswich, UK: First Line Projects LLP, 2010.

Fisher, E. "What Practitioners Consider to Be the Skills and Behaviours of an Effective People Project Manager." *International Journal of Project Management* 29 (2011): 994–1002.

FMI. *FMI 2006 Project Management Survey Report*. Raleigh, NC, USA: FMI Management Consulting, 2006.

Freeman, III, M. A., and J. A. Herriges. *The Measurement of Environmental and Resource Values: Theory and Methods*, 2nd rev. ed. Washington, DC, USA: Taylor & Francis Inc., 2003.

Gardiner, P. D. *Project Management: A Strategic Planning Approach*. New York, NY, USA: Palgrave Macmillan: 2005.

Gartner. "Case Study: High Burden of Proof for New Business-Initiated Projects." (2011a, 09 13). Accessed on January 14, 2012, from http://my.gartner.com/portal/server.pt?open=512&objID=256&mode=2&PageID=2350940&resId=1791215&ref=QuickSearch&sthkw=Benefits+Realization

Gartner. "Executive Summary: Benefits Realization: The Gift That Keeps On Giving." (2011b, September 01). Accessed on October 31, 2015, from https://www.gartner.com/doc/1786314/executive-summary-benefits-realization-gift

German Project Management Association. "Global Project Management Survey." (2010). Accessed on January 12, 2012, from http://www.gpm-ipma.de/know_how/studienergebnisse/global_pm_survey.html

Giaglis, G. M., N. Mylonopoulos, and G. I. Doukidis. "The ISSUE Methodology for Quantifying Benefits from Information Systems." *Logistics Information Management* 12, no. 1/2 (1999): 50–62.

Glass, R. L. "The Standish Report: Does It Really Describe a Software Crisis?" *Communications of the ACM* 49, no. 8 (2006): 15–16.

Glynne, P., and M. Stubbs. Benefits SIG Scottish Conference. (2014, October 12) Accessed from Association for Project Management: http://www.apm.org.uk/news/scottish-conference-14th-march-2012

Gray, C. F., and E. W. Larson. *Project Management: The Managerial Process*, 5th ed. New York, NY, USA: McGraw-Hill, 2010.

Hill, G. M. *The Complete Project Management Office Handbook*. London, UK: Auerbach Publications, 2004.

HM Treasury. *The Green Book*, 2003 ed. London, UK: HM Treasury, 2011.

Hubbard, D. W. *How to Measure Anything: Finding the Value of "Intangibles" in Business*. Hoboken, NJ, USA: John Wiley & Sons, 2007.

Ika, L. A. "Project Success as a Topic in Project Management Journals." *Project Management Journal* 40, no. 4 (2009): 6–19.

International Project Management Association. *IPMA Competence Baseline*, 3rd ed. Nijkerk, Netherlands: International Project Management Association, 2006.

Jenner, S. *Transforming Government and Public Services: Realising Benefits through Project Portfolio Management*. Burlington, VT, USA: Ashgate, 2010.

Jenner, S. *Managing Benefits*. Norwich, UK: The Stationery Office, 2012.

Johnson, G., and K. Scholes. *Exploring Corporate Strategy*, 6th ed. Harlow, UK: Pearson Education Limited, 2002.

Kaplan, R. S., and D. P. Norton. "Using the Balanced Scorecard as a Strategic Management System." *Harvard Business Review* 74, no. 1 (1996): 75–85.

Kaplan, R., and D. Norton. *The Strategy-Focused Organization: How Balanced Scorecard Companies Thrive in the New Business Environment*. Boston, MA, USA: Harvard Business School Press, 2000.

Kaplan, R. S., and D. P. Norton. "The Office of Strategy Management." *Harvard Business Review* (2005, October 1):72–80.

Kaplan, R. S., and D. P. Norton. *The Execution Premium: Linking Strategy to Operations for Competitive Advantage*. Boston, MA, USA: Harvard Business School Publishing Corporation, 2008.

Kay, J. *Foundations of Corporate Success*. Oxford, UK: Oxford University Press, 1993.

Kendall, G. I., and S. C. Rollins. *Advanced Project Portfolio Management and the PMO: Multiplying ROI at Warp Speed*. Boca Raton, FL, USA: J. Ross, 2003.

Kerzner, H. "Strategic Planning for a Project Office." *Project Management Journal* 3, no. 2 (2003): 13–25.

Kerzner, H. *Project Management Metrics, KPIs, and Dashboards: A Guide to Measuring and Monitoring Project Performance*, 2nd ed. Hoboken, NJ, USA: John Wiley & Sons, Inc., 2013a.

Kerzner, H. *Project Management: A Systems Approach to Planning, Scheduling, and Controlling*, 11th ed. Hoboken, NJ, USA: John Wiley & Sons, Inc., 2013b.

KPMG. (2005). Global IT Project Management Survey. Hong Kong: KPMG International.

KPMG. (2008). Adapting to Complexity—Global Major Project Owners Survey 2008. Amestelveen, Netherlands: KPMG International.

KPMG. *KPMG New Zealand Project Management Survey 2010*. Amestelveen, Netherlands: KPMG, 2010a.

KPMG. *PMI-KPMG Study on Drivers for Success in Infrastructure Projects 2010*. Mumbai, India: KPMG International, 2010b.

Levine, H. A. *Project Portfolio Management: A Practical Guide to Selecting Projects, Managing Portfolios, and Maximizing Benefits*. San Francisco, CA, USA: Jossey-Bass, 2005.

Lynch, R. *Corporate Strategy*, 4th ed. Harlow, UK: Pearson Education Limited, 2006.

Maylor, H., T. Brady, T. Cooke-Davies, and D. Hodgson. "From Projectification to Programmification." *International Journal of Project Management* 24, no. 1 (2006): 663–674.

McGrath, R. G. "Failing by Design." *Harvard Business Review* 89, no. 4 (2011): 76–83.

McKinsey Global Institute. "Farewell to Cheap Capital? The Implications of Long-Term Shifts in Global Investment and Saving." McKinsey Global Institute, 2010.

Melton, T. *Project Management Toolkit*, 2nd ed. Oxford, UK: Butterworth-Heinemann, 2007.

Melton, T., P. Iles-Smith, and J. Yates. *Project Benefits Management: Linking Your Project to the Business*. London, UK: Butterworth-Heinemann, 2008.

Meredith, J. R., and S. J. Mantel. *Project Management: A Managerial Approach*, 9th ed. Hoboken, NJ, USA: John Wiley & Sons, Inc., 2014.

*Merriam-Webster Dictionary*, online ed., s.v. "disbenefit." Accessed on November 1, 2015, from http://www.merriam-webster.com/dictionary/disbenefit

Merrow, E. W. *Industrial Megaprojects: Concepts, Strategies, and Practices for Success*. Hoboken, NJ, USA: John Wiley & Sons, Inc., 2011.

Meyer, W. G. *The Psychology of Project Termination*. New Orleans, LA, USA: Project Management Institute, 2013.

Mintzberg, H., B. Ahlstrand, and J. Lampel. *Strategy Safari*, 2nd ed. Harlow, UK: Pearson Education Limited, 2009.

Monden, Y. *Toyota Production System*, 4th ed. Boca Raton, FL, USA: CRC Press, 2012.

Moore, M. H. *Recognizing Public Value*. Cambridge, MA, USA: Harvard University Press, 2013.

Moore, S. *Strategic Project Portfolio Management*. Hoboken, NJ, USA: John Wiley & Sons, Inc., 2010.

Moran, R. T., P. R. Harris, and S. V. Moran. *Managing Cultural Differences: Global Leadership Strategies for Cross-Cultural Business Success*. Oxford, UK: Elsevier, 2011.

Morgan, J. M., and J. K. Liker. *The Toyota Product Development System: Integrating People, Process, and Technology*. New York, NY, USA: Productivity Press, 2006.

Morgan, M., R. E. Levitt, and W. A. Malek. *Executing Your Strategy: How to Break It Down and Get It Done*. Boston, MA, USA: Harvard Business School Press, 2007.

Namaki, M. S. "Does the Thinking of Yesterday's Management Gurus Imperil Today's Companies?" *Ivey Business Journal* 76, no. 2 (2012): 10–13.

OGC: Office for Government Commerce. *Management of Portfolios*. London, UK: TSO, 2011a.

OGC: Office for Government Commerce. *Managing Successful Programmes*, 3rd ed. Norwich, UK: TSO, 2011b.

Patanakul, P., and A. J. Shenhar. "What Project Strategy Really Is: The Fundamental Building Block in Strategic Project Management." *Project Management Journal* 43, no. 1 (2012, February): 4–20.

PIPC. *Global Project Management Survey*. London, UK: PIPC Global Project Solutions, 2005.

Porter, M. E. *Competitive Advantage: Creating and Sustaining Superior Performance: With a New Introduction*, 1st Free Press ed. New York, NY, USA: Free Press, 1998.

PricewaterhouseCoopers. *Insights and Trends: Current Programme and Project Management Practices.* London, UK: PricewaterhouseCoopers, 2007.

PricewaterhouseCoopers. *Insights and Trends: Current Programme and Project Management Practices.* London, UK: PricewaterhouseCoopers, 2012.

Project Management Institute. "The Talent Gap." *PMI Today,* June, no. 1 (2009): 2–3.

Project Management Institute. *A Guide to the Project Management Body of Knowledge,* 5th ed. Newtown Square, PA, USA: Project Management Institute, 2013a.

Project Management Institute. *Project Management Talent Gap Report.* Newtown Square, PA, USA: Project Management Institute, 2013b.

Project Management Institute. *The Standard for Portfolio Management,* 3rd ed. Newtown Square, PA, USA: Project Management Institute, 2013c.

Project Management Institute. *The Standard for Program Management,* 3rd ed. Newtown Square, PA, USA: Project Management Institute, 2013d.

Project Management Institute. *Pulse of the Profession.* Newtown Square, PA, USA: Project Management Institute, 2014.

Project Management Institute. *Pulse of the Profession 2015.* Newtown Square, PA, USA: Project Management Institute, 2015.

Remenyi, D., A. Money, and A. Twite. *Effective Measurement & Management of IT Costs and Benefits,* rev. ed. Oxford, UK: Butterworth-Heinemann, 1995.

Remland, M. S., T. S. Jones, A. Foeman, and D. R. Arévalo. *Intercultural Communication: A Peacebuilding Perspective.* Long Grove, IL, USA: Waveland Press, 2015.

Serra, C. E. *Benefits Realisation Management and Its Influence on Project Success, Project Governance, and Execution of Business Strategy: Analysis of Brazil, the United Kingdom, and the United States of America.* Dissertation submitted in partial fulfillment for the degree of Master of Science in Programme and Project Management. Coventry, UK: University of Warwick, 2012a.

Serra, C. E. Post-Module Assignment for the Module Programme and Project Strategy of the Masters in Programme and Project Management. Coventry, UK: University of Warwick, 2012b.

Serra, C. E. *The Influence of Benefits Realisation Management on the success of projects in Brazil, the United Kingdom and the United States of America,* Association for Project Management (2012c). Accessed on January 1, 2013, from https://www.apm.org.uk/sites/default/files/Carlos_Serra_APM_Postgrad_Student_Award_2012.pdf

Serra, C. E. "Benefits Realisation Management and Strategic Project Success: Analysis of UK, USA, and Brazil." PMI Global Congress EMEA 2015 Proceedings. London, UK: Project Management Institute, 2015.

Serra, C. E., and M. Kunc. *Benefits Realization Management and Its Influence on Project Success, Project Governance, and Execution of Business Strategy: Analysis of Brazil, the United Kingdom, and the United States of America.* Project Management Institute (2013, January 22). Accessed on October 12, 2014, from http://www.pmi.org/Learning/academic-research/~/media/PDF/Surveys/CarlosSerra-Benefits Realization-Summary-EngUS.ashx

Serra, C. E., and M. Kunc. "Benefits Realisation Management and Its Influence on Project Success and on the Execution of Business Strategies." *International Journal of Project Management* 33, no. 1 (2015): 53–66.

Shenhar, A. J., D. Milosevic, D. Dvir, and H. Thamhain. *Linking Project Management to Business Strategy*. Newton Square, PA, USA: Project Management Institute, Inc., 2007.

Shleifer, A., and R. W. Vishny. "A Survey of Corporate Finance." *The Journal of Finance* 52, no. 2 (1997): 737–783.

Smith, R. F. *Business Process Management and the Balanced Scorecard: Using Processes as Strategic Drivers*. Hoboken, NJ, USA: John Wiley & Sons, Inc., 2007.

Sowden, R. *How Do Organizations Benefit from Using the Managing Successful Programmes Framework?* Norwich, UK: The Stationery Office, 2011. Accessed from http://www.best-management-practice.com/gempdf/MSP_Framework_benefits_White_Paper_Dec11.pdf

Teixeira, C. S., and L. L. Pereira. "Pereira Diamond: Benefits Management Framework." *The International Journal of Business and Management* 3, no. 3 (2015): 47–56.

*The Economist* Intelligence Unit. *Closing the Gap: The Link between Project Management Excellence and Long-Term Success*. London, UK: The Economist Intelligence Unit, 2009.

*The New Corporate University Review*. "Drucker's Development of the 'Strategy-Focused' Organization." *The New Corporate University Review* 9, no. 1 (2001): 6–7.

The Standish Group. *CHAOS Report 2015*. (2015). Accessed from www.standishgroup.com

Todnem, R. "Organisational Change Management: A Critical Review." *Journal of Change Management* 5, no. 4 (2005): 369–380.

Turner, J. R. *The Handbook of Project-Based Management: Leading Strategic Change in Organizations*, 3rd ed. London, UK: McGraw-Hill, 2009.

Unger, B. N., A. Kock, H. G. Gemünden, and D. Jonas. "Enforcing Strategic Fit of Project Portfolios by Project Termination: An Empirical Study on Senior Management Involvement." *International Journal of Project Management* 30 (2012): 675–685.

Vohra, N., and K. Mukul. "Relevance of Peter Drucker's Work: Celebrating Drucker's 100th." *Vikalpa: The Journal for Decision Makers* 34, no. 4 (2009): 1–7.

Ward, J., and E. Daniel. *Benefits Management: How to Increase the Business Value of Your IT Projects*, 2nd ed. Chichester, UK: John Wiley & Sons Ltd., 2012.

Wheatley, M. "Making the Cut." *PM Network* 23, no. 6 (2009): 44–48.

Williams, D., and T. Parr. *Enterprise Programme Management: Delivering Value*, 2nd rev. ed. Basingstoke, UK: Palgrave, 2006.

Witcher, B., and R. Butterworth. "Hoshin Kanri: A Preliminary Overview." *Total Quality Management* 8, no. 2–3 (1997): 319–323.

Zwikael, O., and J. Smyrk. *Project Management for the Creation of Organisational Value*. London, UK: Springer-Verlag London Limited, 2011.

# Index